JOHN LYLY

Poems

With an Introduction, Notes, and
Glossary by

JOHN NORTON-SMITH

OXFORD
AT THE CLARENDON PRESS
1966

Oxford University Press, Ely House, London W.1

GLASGOW NEW YORK TORONTO MELBOURNE WELLINGTON
CAPE TOWN SALISBURY IBADAN NAIROBI LUSAKA ADDIS ABABA
BOMBAY CALCUTTA MADRAS KARACHI LAHORE DACCA
KUALA LUMPUR HONG KONG

PRINTED IN GREAT BRITAIN

PREFACE

THE frontispiece portrait of Lydgate is reproduced by courtesy of the Trustees of the British Museum. It now serves as the make-shift frontispiece to MS. Harley 4826 (f. 1a), 'The Life of St. Edmund', the first item in a collection. It was doubtless intended to be prefixed to a presentation copy of the 'Pilgrimage of the Life of Man' which was commissioned by Thomas Montacute, Earl of Salisbury, whilst he was on campaign in France in 1426. The drawing shows the poet presenting his translation of Deguileville's 'Pèlerinage' to his patron. A pilgrim (perhaps personifying the original poem) assists in offering the book.

The editor has much pleasure in acknowledging the help and criticism given by Professor J. A. W. Bennett and Mr. Emrys Jones. Mr. K. B. McFarlane and Professor Rossell Hope Robbins kindly helped him on particular points.

Portington Hall

April 1965

CONTENTS

INTRODUCTION

DURING the years 1413–51 the great English monastic foundations enjoyed an Indian summer of secular influence. The Benedictine Abbey of Bury St. Edmunds fostered a poet who gave official expression to its worldly influence and who was chosen to commemorate the allied political power of royal authority. John Lydgate may be said to have personified the combined political vision of the Crown and the great abbeys. These two temporal powers proved able to nurture and administer individual institutions and systems, but were unable to sustain the medieval ideal of a unified society. If Lydgate's poetic inventiveness lacked comprehensive power, it did possess a grasp of local reality. When Jove's eagle in the *Hous of Fame* directed Chaucer's gaze from the books of Old Authorities towards the road to Canterbury he did not foresee that a lively interest in contemporary things was to receive its strongest answering impulse in the person of Lydgate. Lydgate from the first found his 'right veyn' in a certain realism.

The complex interplay of forces in the *Book of the Duchess* was translated in Lydgate's *A Complaynt of a Loveres Lyfe* from a philosophic dream landscape into an everyday garden of human anxiety. The puzzling *mélange* of humour, philosophy, allegorical and realistic description we find in the *Hous of Fame* was recast in a more transparent *Temple of Glas*. The 'Chaucerian' dream is no longer wonderful, encyclopedic, inquiring. Lydgate's romantic love landscapes and architecture return to the matter-of-factness of the *Roman de la Rose*, and his human situations and psychology similarly revert to the downright realism of Graunson. His moral simplicity recalls the earnestness of Deschamps. Yet his simplifications preserve some of the literary complexity of Chaucer, especially in verse detail and in various elaborations of literary formulae: invocations, expressions of humility, and scientific accounts of nature, the seasons, and astronomy. The underlying complexity of thought characteristic of Chaucer is absent.

The huge bulk of Lydgate's literary output makes a balanced estimate difficult, but a just assessment need not take into account everything he wrote. Most of his work was inspired by social pressures. Nevertheless, certain personal artistic preferences and disinclinations assert themselves. Judged on the basis of the monumental hack-work which he dutifully performed, the poet in Lydgate may be sharply characterized— although not in the language of Ritson ('. . . a most prolix and voluminous poetastor . . . this voluminous, prosaick and driveling monk . . .'). Within the double columns of the *Troy Book* and the *Fall of Princes* a painful pattern of poetics may be traced. Much of Book II of the *Troy Book* is well written, and the first three books of the *Fall of Princes* (before Duke Humphrey's meanness became apparent to the translator) contain good writing. The stories of Canace, Sardanapalus, and Lucrece testify to Lydgate's narrative and dramatic ability.

The unevenness in his writing extends beyond the compilations. For, although the religious lyrics exhibit verbal riches, the aureate surface imperfectly covers an unimaginative centre. Lydgate's imagination was not a powerful shaping force. It is enfeebled by a too mechanical application of rhetorical discipline. There is little in him of Geoffrey of Vinsauf's *archetypus* ('creative intuition'). Too often ornament of language and of thought seems to be treated as a surface which may be added to the narrative. Even in poems where Lydgate has invented new total form (as in the *Life of Our Lady*, the *Temple of Glas*, or the *Life of St. Giles*) the prolix, episodic, deliberate manner obscures the newly created shape.

But Lydgate's place in English literature should not be determined by the good passages which may be detached from the longer works, or by currently fashionable accounts of the linguistic achievements of his religious verse. It is the shorter, occasional, poems treating public and private matters that show Lydgate at his best. The chosen poet of many and various estates of the fifteenth century, Lydgate belongs to the world

of late medieval polite versifying (although the term '̶
requires perhaps some qualification). He never achieve̶
Horatian intimacy, economy, and intelligence of Chau̶
polite verse (the *Envoys* to Scogan and Bukton) yet his artistry
is not much inferior to Chaucer's in, for example, the *Letter to
Gloucester*, the *Departing of Thomas Chaucer*, or the *Balade
Sente to the Shirrefs Dyner*. Here, in the translating of everyday
event into a compact form he is the equal of Deschamps or
Dunbar. It was Lydgate who created the 'mumming' poem—
making literary allegory an essential part of the descriptive
celebratory poem—just as it was Lydgate who invented the
'polysyllabic language' of aureate diction. These are the aesthetic facts that matter, though on a wider view English literature
is indebted to him for the long compilation that made acces-
sible the material of Boccaccio's *De Casibus*. If the *Fall of
Princes* exerted a fascination for Tudor poets and provided
a certain poetic continuity for politics, history, and tragedy,
the *Troy Book* fulfilled a similar function in conveying to the
Elizabethans (not least to Shakespeare) that complex sense of
Troy's perfection which came to symbolize the acme of civilization and its tragic vulnerability.

Of the longer religious works, with the possible exception of
the *Life of Our Lady*, little can be appreciated at this date. The
Pilgrimage of the Life of Man (a verse translation of Deguileville's 'Pèlerinage') is unattractive by the literary standards
of any age. The Saints' Lives have lost their power, as a result
of our more scrupulous attitude to biographical evidence and
testimony.

Stylistically, however, Lydgate deserves close attention.
Four main tendencies in his verse may be noticed: (1) a
Chaucerian style closely modelled on the *Complaint unto Pity*,
Anelida, and the *Book of Troilus*, *inter alia*; (2) a flat explana-
tory style modelled on that of the *Monk's Tale*; (3) a later
cryptic style, abounding in headless lines, trochaic rhythms,
and epigrammatic jerkiness; (4) a larger, Latinate use of
syntax. These periods are accompanied by incessant stylistic
experimentation: (i) the extending of the sense of words,

especially verbs; (ii) importation of scientific terminology into secular verse; (iii) invention of aureate diction, especially for religious verse (cf. Appendix); (iv) extensive use of refrains and moral maxims.

But, in spite of the experimentation, the shaping sensibility usually fails in Lydgate. He surrendered to the general tendency of medieval civilization—an indiscriminating appetite for style. Occasionally, in *A Defence of the Holy Church* or the *Balade in Commendation of Our Lady*, the 'style' justified the enumerative structure; in the case of the *Defence* through the skilful use of Latinate syntax, and in the *Commendation* through an exact reproduction of Latin liturgical vocabulary and images.

Fifteenth- and sixteenth-century poets extolled Lydgate's rhetorical skill by ranking him with Chaucer and Gower. For the modern reader it is likely that the creative Lydgate will emerge in the short occasional poems where he was able to give events a modest, imaginative form. It is probably no accident that a member of a great religious house should have developed a gift for describing and expounding secular rituals and occasions.

BIOGRAPHICAL AND TEXTUAL NOTE

JOHN LYDGATE was born at Lydgate, Suffolk, c. 1370. He was admitted c. 1385 to Bury St. Edmunds Abbey, Suffolk. In 1397 he was ordained priest by John Fordham, Bishop of Ely. As a Benedictine monk he studied at Oxford, probably at Gloucester College. From a letter written by Henry V, when Prince of Wales, to the Abbot of Bury St. Edmunds (1406–8) it would appear that Lydgate studied at the University on two separate occasions; the second period falling after 1406. For most of his life he lived outside the cloister. He probably returned, more or less permanently, to residence at Bury St. Edmunds after 1434. The following dates may give some indication of the shape of his literary career. His poems concerned with romantic love, *A Complaynt of a Loveres Lyfe*, the *Temple of Glas*, and *Reson and Sensuallite* (a translation of *Les Echecs Amoureux*), are usually dated before c. 1412. But this is conjecture. After 1412, which forms a terminus for Lydgate's second period of study at Oxford, there is fuller evidence:

1412–20   The *Troy Book* compiled for Henry V.

?1414   *On the Departing of Thomas Chaucer.*

?1414–17 *Benedic Anima Mea Domino* for (?) Edmund Lacy, Dean of the Chapel Royal at Windsor.

?1420+   *Gloriosa Dicta Sunt De Te* for (?) Edmund Lacy, Bishop of Exeter. *The Siege of Thebes.*

1422–3   *On Gloucester's Approaching Marriage* for Duke Humphrey.

1423   Lydgate became nominally Prior of Hatfield Broad Oak, Essex. On 23 February a quarter share of a lease was made to Lydgate by Sir Ralph Rocheford of the lands of the alien Priory of Longville Gifford or Newenton Longville with the pension of Spalding, formerly appertaining to the Abbey of Angers.

1423+   *The Fifteen Joys of Our Lady* for Isabell, Countess of Warwick.

?1424   *Mumming at Windsor.*

1425+   *Guy of Warwick* for Margaret, Countess of Shrewsbury.

1426   Lydgate was in Paris. *Title and Pedigree of Henry VI* for Richard de Beauchamp, Earl of Warwick, acting Regent of France.

1426–?8   *The Pilgrimage of the Life of Man* for Thomas Montacute, Earl of Salisbury.

?1429+   *Balade Sente to the Shirrefs Dyner* for the Sheriff and Aldermen of London.

1429 or

1437   *Mumming for the Mercers of London* for presentation before William Eastfield, the Lord Mayor.

        Mumming for the Goldsmiths of London for presentation before William Eastfield.

1429–30   *Legend of St. Margaret. Coronation Banquet at Windsor. Roundel for the Coronation of Henry VI.*

?1430   *Mumming at Hertford* at the request of the Controller of the Royal Household, John Brys.

?1430+   *Interpretation and Virtues of the Mass* for Alice, Countess of Suffolk.

c. 1431–9   The *Fall of Princes* for Humphrey, Duke of Gloucester.

1432   *Ordenaunces for the Kyng made in the Cite of London.*

1434   The *Lives of St. Edmund and St. Fremund* presented to Henry VI during his visit to Bury St. Edmunds. On 8 April Lydgate was relieved of the office of Prior of Hatfield Broad Oak at the request of his Abbot, William Curteys, 'propter frugem melioris vitae captandam'.

?1434+   The *Life of Our Lady.*

1439   ? *Letter to Gloucester. The Lyfe of Seint Albon and the Lyfe of Seint Amphabel* for John Whethamstede, Abbot of St. Albans. Lydgate was paid 100 shillings for it. On 22 April Lydgate was

	awarded a life grant of 10 marks per annum from the Customs at Ipswich.
?1446–9	The translation and adaptation of the *Secreta Secretorum* (unfinished).
1449	At Michaelmas Lydgate drew his royal grant for the last time.
1449–50	Death of Lydgate and burial in the Abbey of Bury St. Edmunds.

Most of Lydgate's works have been edited for the Early English Text Society. There is a full discussion of the Lydgate canon in W. F. Schirmer's *John Lydgate* (Appendix III). The MSS. containing his works are numerous, and a list of MSS. authorities for the poems included in this edition is given in the Notes. MSS. have been closely followed and MS. spelling is usually retained, save in the case of John Shirley's MSS. Editorial procedure, serious emendations, and departures from MSS. are recorded in the Notes. Merely scribal devices have been ignored. The punctuation is editorial. Lacunae and emendations are marked by square brackets. Excerpted passages are marked by bracketed line references in the margin.

SELECT BIBLIOGRAPHY

I. GENERAL

W. F. Schirmer, *John Lydgate: A Study in the Culture of the XVth Century*, translated A. E. Keep (1961).

II. LIFE

D. Knowles, *The Religious Orders in England*, vol. ii (1955), pp. 273–5.

A. B. Emden, *A Biographical Register of the University of Oxford to 1500*, vol. ii (1958), pp. 1185–6.

III. CRITICAL

Thomas Gray, 'Some Remarks on the Poems of John Lydgate' reprinted in Everyman's Library, vol. no. 628, pp. 366–82.

C. S. Lewis, *The Allegory of Love* (1936), pp. 232–43.

G. Wickham, *Early English Stages: 1300 to 1660*, vol. i (1959), pp. 191–207.

IV. LANGUAGE

J. Schick, *Temple of Glas*, EETS, Extra Series (1891), lxiii–lxxv.

E. Tilgner, *Die 'Aureate Terms' als Stilelement bei Lydgate* (1936).

V. METRE

J. Schick, *Temple of Glas*, EETS, lvi–lx.

M. Manzalaoui, 'Lydgate and English Prosody', *Cairo Studies in English* (1960), pp. 165 ff.

VI. MISCELLANEOUS

S. Moore, 'Patrons of Letters in Norfolk and Suffolk, *c.* 1450', *PMLA*, xxvii (1912), pp. 188 ff.

E. P. Hammond, 'Poet and Patron in the *Fall of Princes*', *Anglia*, xxxviii (1914), pp. 121 ff.

J. Norton-Smith, 'Lydgate's Changes in the *Temple of Glas*', *Medium Ævum*, xxvii (1958), pp. 166 ff.

A. Renoir, 'Attitudes towards Women in Lydgate's Poetry', *English Studies* (1961), pp. 1 ff.

LETTER TO GLOUCESTER

Riht myghty prynce, and it be your wille,
Condescende leiser for to take
To seen the content of this litil bille,
Which whan I wrot myn hand I felte quake.
Tokne of mornyng, [I] weryd clothys blake   5
Cause my purs was fal in gret rerage,
Lynyng outward, his guttys wer out-shake:
Oonly for lak of plate and of coignage.

I souhte leechys for a restoratiff,
In whom I fond no consolacioun,   10
Appotecaryes for a confortatiff:
Drag nor dia was noon in Bury toun.
Botme of his stomak tournyd vp-so-doun
A laxatif did hym so gret outrage,
Made hym slendre by a consumpcioun: 15
Oonly for lak of plate and of coignage.

Ship was ther noon nor seilis reed of hewe,
The wynd froward to make hem ther to londe.
The flood was passyd and sodeynly of newe
A lowh ground-ebb was faste by the stronde   20
Þat no maryneer durste take on hand
To cast an ankir for streihtnes of passage.
The custom skars (as folk may vndirstonde):
Oonly for lak of plate and of coignage.

Ther was no token sent doun from the Tour,   25
As any gossomer the countirpeys was liht.

A fretyng etyk causyd his langour
By a cotidian whi[c]h heeld hym day and nyht;
Sol and Luna wer clypsyd of ther liht,
Ther was no cros nor preent of no visage,   30
His lynyng dirk, ther wer no platys briht:
Oonly for lak and scarste of coignage.

Hard to lik hony out of a marbil stoon
For ther is nouthir licour nor moisture.
An ernest-grote whan it is dronke and goon,   35
Bargeyn of marchaunts, stant in aventure.
My purs and I be callyd to the lure
Of Indigence, our stuff leyd in morgage.
But ye, my lord, may al our soor recure:
With a receyt of plate and of coignage.   40

Nat sugre-plate maad by th'appotecarye,
Plate of briht metal yevith a mery soun:
In Boklerys-bury is noon such letuary.
Gold is a cordial, gladdest confeccioun
Ageyn etiques of oold consumpcioun: 45
Aurum Potabile for folk ferre ronne in age,
In quynt-essence best restauracioun
With siluer plate enprentyd with coignage.

[*L'envoy*]

O seely bill why art thu nat ashamyd
So malapert to shewe out thy constreynt?   50
But pouert hath so nih thy tonne attamyd
That *nichil habet* is cause of thy compleynt.
A drye tisyk makith oold men ful feynt,
Reediest wey to renew ther corage
Is a fressh dragge, of no spycis meynt,   55
But of briht plate enpreentyd with coignage.

Thu mayst afferme, as for thyn excus,
Thy bareyn s[a]ile is sool and solitarye:

2

Of cros nor pyle ther is no reclus,
Preent nor impressioun in al thy seyntuarye. 60
To conclude breefly and nat [to] tarye:
Ther is no noyse herd in thyn hermitage.
God sende soon a gladder letuarye
With a cleer soun of plate and of coignage.

ON THE DEPARTING OF THOMAS CHAUCER

O þow Lucyna, qwene and empyresse
Of waters alle and of floodes rage,
And cleped art lady and goddesse
Of iorneying and fortunate passage,
Governe and guye by grace þe viage,   5
Þow heuenly qween, sith I of hert[e] prey,
My maystre Chaucer goodly to convey,

Him to expleyte and firþern on his way
With holsom spede, ay in his iournee.
And Neptunus, make eke [þow] no delaye   10
Hym to fauour whan he is on þe see,
Preserving him from al aduersytee,
From al trouble of wynd and eke of wawe:
And lat þy grace so to him adawe

Þat wher to hym may be [þe] moost plesaunce,   15
Þer make him lande, he and his meynee.
And God I prey, þe whyle he is [in] Fraunce,
To sende him helthe and prosparytee,
Hasty repayre hoom to his cuntree
To recomfort þer with [his] presence   20
Folks þat mowrne moost for his absence.

For soþely now þ'agreable sonne
Of housholding and fulsum haboundaunce
Eclipsid is, as men recorden konne
Þat founden þer so ryche souffisaunce,   25
Fredam, bountee with gode governaunce,
Disport, largesse, ioye and al gladnesse,
And passingly good chere with gentylesse.

4

Ceres also, godesse of welfare,
Was ay present, hir chaare with plentee lade:　　30
And Bacus þer ne koude neuer spare
With his lycour hertes for to glade,
Refresshe folks þat were of colour fade.
[Wher] his conduyts moost plentyvous habounde
Þe wellis hed so fulsome ay is founde.　　35

His moost ioy is innly gret repayre
Of gentilmen of heghe and lowe estate,
Þat him thenkeþ, boþe in foule and fayre,
Withouten hem he is but desolate:
And to be loued þe moost fortunate　　40
Þat euer I knew, with othe of soþefastnesse,
Of ryche and pore, for bounteuous largesse.

And gentyl Molyns, myn owen lord so der,
Lytel merveyl þough þow sighe and pleyne:
Now to forgone þin owen pleying-fere,　　45
I wot right wel hit is to þe[e] gret peyne.
But haue good hope soon for to atteyne
Þin hertis blisse agayne, and þat right sone,
Or foure tymes chaunged be þe mone.

Lat be your weping, tendre creature,　　50
By my Sainte Eleyne fer away in Ynde.
How shul ye þe gret[e] woo endure
Of his absence, þat ben so truwe and kynde?
Ha[u]e him amonge enprynted in your mynde,
And seyth for him, shortly in a clause,　　55
Goddes soule to hem þat ben in cause.

Ye gentilmen dwelling envyroun,
His absence eke ye aught to compleyne,
For farwell now, as in conclusyoun,
Your pley, your ioye, yif I shal not feyne:　　60
Farwel huntyng and hawkyng, boþe tweyne,

5

And farwel now cheef cause of your desport,
For he absent, farwel your recomfort.

Lat him not now out of remembraunce
But euer amonge ha[u]e him in memorye.   65
And for his sake, as in your dalyaunce,
Sayth euery day deuotely þis memorye:
'Saint Iulyan, oure ioye and al our glorye,
Come hoom ageyne, lyche as we desyre,
To suppowaylen al þe hole shyre.'   70

And for my part, I sey right as I th[i]nk,
I am pure sory and hevy is myn hert
More þan I express can wryte with ink,
Þe want of him so sore doþ me smert.
But for al þat, hit shal me nought astert   75
Day and night, with hert[e] debonayre,
[To] prey to God þat he soon may repayre.

3

BALADE SENTE TO THE SHIRREFS DYNER

Mighty Flora, goddes of fresshe floures,
Which cloþed haþ þe soyl in lusty grene,
Made buddes springe with hir swote showres
By influence of þe sonne so shene,
To do plesaunce of [hir] entent ful clene   5
Vnto þ'estates which þat now sitt here,
Haþ Ver dovn sent, hir owen doughter dere,

Making þe vertue þat dured in þe roote
(Called of clerks þe vertue vegytable)
For to transcend, most holsom and most swoote,   10
Into the crop, þis saysoun so greable.
Þe bawmy lykour is so comendable
Þat it reioyeþ with þe fressh moysture
Man, beest, and foul and every creature——

Which haþ repressed, swaged, and bore dovne   15
Þe grevous constreint of þe frostes hore,
And caused fouls, for ioy of þis saysoune
To chees þeir makes þan by Natures lore
With al gladnes þeir courage to restore,
Sitting on bowes fresshly now to synge,   20
Ver for to salue at hir hom comynge:

Ful pleinly mening in þeir ermonye
Wynter is goone which did hem gret peyne,
And with þeir swoote, sugre[d] melodye,
Thanking Nature, þeir goddes souereyne,   25
That þey now have no mater to compleyne,
Hem for to proygne every morwenyng
With lusty gladnes at Phebus vprysinge:

7

And to declare þe hye magnifysence
How Ver inbringeþ al felicytee,   30
After wynters mighty vyolence
Avoyding storms of al adversytee;
For she haþ brought al prosperitee
To al þ'estates of þis regyoun
At hir comyng tofor your hye renoun.   35

To mighty prynces, þe palm of þeir victorie
And til knighthode now she doþ presente
Noblesse in armes, lawd, honnour and glorie,
Pees to þe people in al hir best entente,
With grace and mercy fully to consente   40
Þat provydence of hye discressioun
Avoyd descorde and al devysyoun.

Wynter shal pas of hevynes and trouble,
Flowres shal spring of perfit charite,
In hertes þer shal be no mening double,   45
Budds shal [blosme] of trouþ and vnytee,
Pleinly for to exyle duplicytee,
Lords to regne in þeire noble puissance,
Þe people obey with feythful obeyssaunce.

Of al estats þer shal be oon ymage,   50
And princes first shal ocupye þe hede,
And prudent iuges to correct outrage
Shal trespassours constreynen vnder drede,
Þat innosentes in þeir lowlyhede
As truwe comvnes may be þeir socour,   55
Truwly contune in þeir faithful labour:

And by the grace of Oure Lord Ihesu
Þat Holly Chirch may have parseuerance,
Be faythful found in alle hir [vertu].

8

Mayre, provost, shirreff, ech in his substaunce,   60
And aldremen, which haue þe governaunce
Over þe people, by vertu may avayle
Þat non oppression be don to þe pourayle.

Þus as þe people, of prudent pollycye,
Pryncis of þe righte shal governe,   65
Þe Chirche prey, þe Iuges iustefye,
And Knighthod manly, and prudently discerne
Til light of trouþ so cleerly þe lanterne
Þat rightwysnesse thorogh þis regyoune
Repress derkness of al extorcyoune.   70

Þes be þe typings which þat Ver haþ brought,
Troubles exyling of wynters rude derknesse;
Wherfor reioye in hert[e], will and thought,
Somer shall folow to yow of al gladnesse;
And siþen she is ministre of lustynesse,   75
Let hir be welcom to yow at hir comyng,
Siþ she to yow haþ brought so glad typinge.

Þe noble Princesse, of most magnifisence,
Qween of al ioy, of gladde suffisaunce,
May is now come to your Hye Excellence,   80
Presenting yowe prosperous pleasaunce,
Of al welfare most fulsom haboundance,
As she þat haþe vnder hir demayne
Of floures fressh, most holsom and souraine.

L'envoye to alle þ'estates present
Þis Princesse haþ, by favour of Nature,   85
Repared agein þat wynter haþ so fade;
And [smale] foulis lustely recvvre
Þeir lusty notes and þeir ermonye glade,
And vnder braunches, vnder plesant shade
Reioyssing þer with many swote odoures.   90
And Zepherus with many fresshe [sh]oures

9

T[a]pyted fayre with motleys whyte and rede
Al hilles, pleyns and lusty bankes grene
And made hir bawm to flete in every mede
[Whan] firy Tytan shews h[i]s tresses sheene.   95
And vppon busshes and hawthornes kene
Þe nightingale with plesant ermonye
Cold wynter stormes now she doþ defye.

On Parnaso þe lusty Muses nyne,
Citherra with hir sone nowe dwellis,   100
Þis sayson singe and þeir notes twyne
Of poetrye besyd þe cristal wellis;
Calyope þe dytes of hem tellis,
And Orpheus with h[i]s stringes sharpe
Syngeþ a roundell with his temperd herpe.   105

Wherfor to al estates here present,
Þis plesant tyme most of lustynesse,
May is now com tofor yow of entent
To bring yow al to ioye and fresshnesse,
Prosparitee, welfare and al gladnesse: 110
And al þat may Your Hyeness qweme and plese
In any part, or doon your hertes ese.

4

AN EXCLAMACIOUN OF THE DETH OF ALCIBIADES

[*Fall of Princes*, III. 3655–82]

O fatal sustren which span his lyues threde
So short a term: whi did ye determine
To suffre hym brenne among the colis rede?
Ye wer to hasti to breken and vntwyne
His web of knihthod that thoruh the world did shyne   5
And cast of nobless bemys out most clere,
Alas that euer he fill in your daungere.

O out on Styx and out on Attropos,
That han of malis slayn so good a kniht.
Out on you thre that kepe yoursilff so clos,   10
Douhtres icallid of the dirke niht.
And thou Letum, that quenchest eke the liht
Of Alcibiades, merour and lanterne
To speke in knihthod how men hem shold gouerne.

Ye slen the worthi, wrechis ye don spare: 15
Torcites lyuth, Ector is slayn in dede.
Your funeral smoks makþ rewmys now so bare,
To race vp cedris, ther braunches may not sprede,
Ye pall the laurer, ye make the firses sede.
Ful litil thank in kingdams ye disserue   20
Kaitiffs to fostre and do the worthi sterue.

Alcibiades is passed into fate,
Liht of knihthod clipsed in the shade:
The Parchas sustren to soon sett his date
Of hih nobless to make the laurer fade.   25
Lacedemoynes of his deth were glade:
Funeral fyr his bodi hath defied,
For hih prowess his soule stellified.

A TALE OF FROWARD MAYMOND

A froward knave pleynly to descryve
And a sloggard schortly to declare:
A precious knave that cast hym neuer to thryve,
His mouth wel wet, his slevis riht thredbare,
A turnebroche, a boy for Hogge of Ware,   5
With louryng face, noddyng and slombryng,
Of newe crystened and callid Iakke Hare:
Wich of a boll can plukke out the lynyng.

This boy Maymond, ful styborne of his bonys,
Sloggy on morwen his lemes vp to dresse,   10
A gentel harlot chose out for the nonys:
Son and cheef eyr to dame Idylnesse,
Cosyn to Wecok, brother to Reklesnesse,
Wich late at eve and morwe at his rysyng
Ne hath no ioie to do no besynesse,   15
Saue of a tancard to plukke out þe lynyng.

A boy Chekrelyk was his sworen brother
Of euery dyssh a lypet out to take.
And Fafyntycol also was another
Of euery brybe the caryage for to make.   20
He can wel waytyn on an oven cake
And of newe ale been at the clensyng:
And of purpos his thruste for to slake
Kan of a pechur plukke out the lynyng.

This knave be leyser wil don al his massage   25
And holde a tale with euery maner wight:
Ful pale dronk, wel vernysshed of visage
(Whos tonge ay faileth whan it draweth to nyht)

Of o candell he weneth too wer lyght.
As barkyd leder his face ys schynyng,   30
Glasy-eied wol cleyme of dew right
Out of a boll to plukke out the lynyng.

He can abedd an horskambe wel shake
Lyk as he wold coray his masters hors.
And with his on hand his masters doublet take   35
And with the tother preuly kutt hys purs.
Al swech knavis shul haue Cristys curs
Erly on morwe at ther vprysyng.
To fynde a boy I trow ther be non wors
Out of a pot to plukke out the lynyng.   40

He may be sold vpon warantyse
As for a truant that no thyng wil doon:
To sel hors prouendre is his chef marchaundise
And for a chevesaunce can pluk of ther shoon.
And at the dyse pley the mony soon   45
And with hys wynnyngs he maketh his offryng,
At the ale-stakes, sittyng ageyn the moon,
Out of a cup to plukke out the lynyng.

L'envoye

Wassail to Maymond and to his iousy pate,
Vnthryft and he be togedre met.   50
Late at eve he wol onspere the gate
And grope on morwe yif Riggis bak be wet
And yif the bak of Togace be out-het.
Hys heuy noll at mydmorwe vplyfftyng
With onwassh hands, not lased his doublet,   55
Out of a boll to plukke out the lynyng.

6

THE REBUILDING OF TROY

[*Troy Book*, II. 479–710]

The sorwe aswaged and þe syȝes olde   [479–551]
By longe process, (lich as I ȝow tolde)
Þis worþi kyng ycallyd Priamus
Is in his herte now so desyrous
Vpon þe pleyn þat was so waste and wylde,   5
So strong a toun of newe for to bilde:
At his devyse a cite edefye
Þat shal th'assautys outterly defye
Of all enmyes and his mortal foon
With riche tours and wallys of hard stoon.   10
And al about þe contres enviroun
He made seke in euery regioun
For swiche werkmen as wer corious,
Of wyt inventyf, of castyng merveilous,
Or swych as coude crafte of gemetrye,   15
Or wer sotyle in her fantasye;
And for eueryche þat was good devysour,
Mason, hewer, or crafty quareour;
For euery wriȝt and passyng carpenter
Þat may be founde owþer fer or nere;   20
For swych as koude graue, grope or kerue,
Or swich as weren able for to serue
With lym or stoon for to reise a wal
With bataillyng and crestis marcial;
Or swich as had[de] konyng in her hed,   25
Alabastre, owþer white or rede,
Or marbil graye for to pulsche it pleyn
To make it smoþe of veynes and of greyn.
He sent also for euery ymagour
Boþe in entaille and euery purtreyour   30

14

Þat coude drawe or with colour peynt
With hewes fresche þat þe werk nat feynt;
And swich as coude with countenaunces glade
Make an ymage þat wil neuer fade,
To counterfet in metal, tre or stoon   35
Þe sotil werke[s] of Pygmaleoun
Or of Apell[es], þe which as bokis telle
In ymagery all oþer did excelle.
For by his crafty werkyng corious
Þe towmbe he made of Kyng Daryus   40
Which Alysoundre did on hey3t[e] reise
Only for men[ne] schuld his fame preise
In his conquest by Perce whan he went.
And þus Priam for euery maister sent:
For eche keruer and passyng ioignour   45
To make knottis with many corious flour,
To sette on crestis withinne and withoute
Vpon the wal þe cite round aboute;
Or who þat wer excellyng in practik
Of any arte callyd mekanik   50
Or had a name flouryng or famus
Was after sent to come to Priamus.
For he purposeth, þis noble worthi kyng,
To make a cite most royal in byldyng:
Brod, large and wyde, and lest it were assailled,   55
For werre proudly about[en] enbatailled.
And first þe grounde he made to be sou3t
Ful depe and lowe, þat it faille nou3t
To make sure þe fundacioun.
In þe place where þe olde toun   60
Was first ybilt, he þe wallis sette.
And he of lond[e] many mile out mette
Aboute in compas for to make it large,
As þe maisters toke on hem þe charge,
Divysed han þe settyng and þe syt,   65
For holsom eyr to be more of delyt.
And whan þe soil, defouled with ruyne

Of walles old was made pleyn as lyne,
Þe werkmen gan þis cite for to founde
Ful myȝtely with stonys square and rounde   70
Þat in þis world was to it non lyche
Of werkmanschip nor [non] of bilding riche,
Nor of crafte of corious masounry.
And þat it myȝt in prosperite,   [565–72]
In hyȝe honour and felicite   75
From al assaut perpetually contune,
It reysed was in worschip of Neptune
And namyd Troye, as it was toforn
Lych þe first þat was þoruȝ Grekis lorn.
Þe lengthe was, schortly to conclude,   80
Thre day[es] iourne, lych þe latitude.
And, as I rede, þe wallis wern on hiȝte   [578–631]
Two hundrid cubits al of marbil gray,
Maskowed without for sautis and assay.
And it to make more plesaunt of delyt   85
Among þe marbil was alabaster white
Meynt in the walles round þe toun aboute
To make it schewe withinne and withoute
So fresche, so riche and so delitable
Þat it alone was incomperable   90
Of alle cites þat any mortal man
Sawe euer ȝit sith [that] the world began.
And at the corner of euery wal was set
A crowne of golde with riche stonys fret
Þat schone ful briȝt ageyn þe sonne schene.   95
And euery tour bretexed was so clene
Of chose stoon (þat wer nat fer asondre)
Þat to behold it was a verray wonder.
Þerto þis cite compassed enviroun
Had sexe gatis to entre into toun: 100
Þe first of al and strengest eke withal,
Largest also and most principal,
Of myȝty bildyng allone peer[e]les,
Was by þe kyng callyd Dardanydes.

16

And in story (lyche as it is founde)   105
Tymbria was named þe secounde;
And þe þridde callyd Helyas;
Þe fourte gate hiȝt also Cethas,
Þe fyfte Troiana, þe syxte Athonydes,
Strong and myȝty boþe in werre and pes   110
With square toures set on euery side.
At whos corners, of verray pompe and pride
Þe werkmen han, with sterne and fel visages
Of riche entaille set vp gret ymages
Wrouȝt out of ston, þat neuer ar like to fayle,   115
Ful coriously enarmed for batayle.
And poruȝ þe wal, her fomen for to lette,
At euery tourn wer grete gunnys sette
For assaut and sodeyn aventurys.
And on touretts wer reysed vp figurys   120
Of wylde bests, as beris and lyouns,
Of tigers, bores, of serpents and dragouns
And hertis eke with her brode hornes,
Olyfauntes and large vnicornes,
Buglis, bols and many grete grifoun   125
Forged of brasse, of copur and latoun:
Þat cruelly by signes of her facys
Vpon her foon made fel manacys.
Barbykans and bolewerkys huge
Afore þe toun made for hiȝe refuge   130
Ȝif nede were, erly and eke late.
And portecolys stronge at euery gate
Þat hem þar noon assailyng charge;
And þe lowkis þikke, brode and large,
Of þe gatys al of ȝoten bras.   135 [638–41]
And euery hous þat was bilt withinne,
Euery paleys and euery mancioun
Of marbil werne poruȝ[out] al þe toun,
Of crafty bildyng and werkyng most roial.   [651–67]
And if I schulde rehersen by and by   140
Þe korve knottes by crafte of masounry,

Þe fresche enbowyng with vergis riȝt as linys
And þe vowsing ful of babewynes,
Þe riche copurnyng, þe lusty tablementis,
Vynnettis rennynge in þe casementis—   145
Þouȝ þe terms in English wolde ryme
To rekne hem alle I haue as now no time:
Ne no langage pyked for þe nonys
Þe sotil ioynyng to tellen of þe stonys,
Nor how þei putten in stede of morter   150
In þe ioynturys copur-gilt ful clere,
To make hem ioyne by leuel and by lyne,
Among þe marbil freschly for to schyne
Agein þe sonne whan his schene lyȝt
Smote in þe gold þat was bornyd briȝt   155
To make þe werke gletere on euery syde.
And þoruȝ þe toun by crafty purviaunce,   [681–92]
By gret avys and discret ordynaunce,
By compas cast and squared out by squires,
Of pulsched marbil vpon strong pilleris   160
Deuised wern, long[e], large and wyde,
In þe frontel of euery stretis syde,
Fresche alures with lusty hiȝe pynacles,
And moustryng outward riche tabernacles
Vowted aboue like reclinatories   165
Þat called werne deambulatories,
Men to walk togydre tweine and tweyne,
To kepe hem drie whan it did reyne.
And euery hous cured was with led   [695–710]
And many gargoyl and many hidious hed   170
With spoutis þoruȝ and pipes as þei ouȝt
From þe ston-werke to þe canel rauȝt
Voyding filþes low into þe grounde
Þoruȝ gratis percid of yren percid rounde.
Þe stretis paued boþe in lengþe and brede   175
In cheker wyse with stonys white and rede.
And euery craft þat any maner man
In any lond deuise or rekene can,

Kyng Priamus of hiȝe discrecioun
Ordeyned hath to dwellyn in þe toun: 180
And in stretis, seueryd her and ȝonder,
Eueryche from oþer to be sette asonder,
Þat þei myȝt for more comodite,
Eche for hym silfe werke at liberte.

7

AS A MYDSOMER ROSE

Lat no man booste of konnyng nor vertu,
Of tresour, richesse, nor of sapience,
Of wor[ld]ly support—al comyth of Ihesu:
Counsayl, confort, discresioun, prudence,
Prouisioun, forsight, and providence,   5
Like as the Lord of grace list dispoose:
Som hath wisdam, som hath elloquence,
Al stant on chaung like a mydsomyr roose.

Holsom in smellyng be the soote flourys,
Ful delitable outward to the sight,   10
The thorn is sharp curyd with fressh colourys.
Al is nat gold that outward shewith bright.
A stokfyssh boon in dirknesse yevith a light,
Twen fair and foul[e], as God list dispoose,
A difference atwix[en] day and night: 15
Al stant on chaung like a mydsomyr roose.

Floures open vpon euery grene,
Whan the larke, messager of day,
Salueth þ'uprist of the sonne shene
Moost amerously in Apryl and in May;   20
And Aurora ageyn the morwe gray
Causith the daysye hir crown to vncloose:
Worldly gladnes is medlyd with affray,
Al stant on chaung like a mydsomyr roose.

Atwen the cokkow and the nightyngale   25
Ther is a maner straunge difference.
On fressh braunchys syngith the woode-wale.
Iayes in mysyk haue smal experyence.
Chateryng pyes whan they come in presence
Moost malapert ther verdite to purpoose: 30
Al thyng hath favour, breffly in sentence,
Of soffte or sharp like a mydsomyr roose.

The roial lioun lette calle a parlement,
Alle beests abowt hym enviroun,
The wolff of malys, beyng ther present,   35
Vpon the lamb compleyned, ageyn resoun,
Said he maad his watir vnholsom,
His tend[re] stomak to hyndre and vndespoose:
Raveynours reign, the innocent is bore doun,
Al stant on chaung lyk a mydsomer roose.   40

Al wor[ld]ly thyng[es] braydeth vpon tyme:
The sonne chaungith, so doth the pale moone,
The aureat noumbre in kalends set for prime.
Fortune is double, doth favour for no boone,
And who that hath with that queen to doone   45
Contrariously she wyl his chaunce dispoose:
Who sittith hihest moost like to fall soone.
Al stant on chaung like a mydsomyr roose.

The golden chaar of Phebus in the ayr
Chasith mysts blak that þay dar not appeere,   50
At whos vprist mounteyns be made so fayr
As they were newly gilt with his beemys cleere;

The nyht doth folwe, appallith al his cheere
Whan western wawes his streemys ouer-close.
Rekne al bewte, al fresshness that is heere: 55
Al stant on chaung lyke a mydsomyr roose.

Constreynt of coold[e] makith flour[e]s dare
With wyntir froosts that they dar nat appeere.
Al clad in russet the soyl of greene is bare.
Tellus and I[oue] be dullyd of ther cheere   60
By revolucioun and turnyng of the yeere:
As gery March his stoundys doth disclose:
Now reyn, now storm, now Phebus bright and cleere.
Al stant on chaung like a mydsomyr roose.

Wher is now Dauid, moost worthy kyng   65
Of [al] Iuda, moost famous and notable?
Wher is Salomon most soureyn of konnyng,
Richest of bildyng, of tresour incomparable?
Face of Absolon, moost fair, moost amyable?
Rekne vp echon, of trouthe make no gloose,   70
Rekne vp Ionathas, of frenship immutable,
Al stant on chaung lyke a mydsomyr roose.

Wher is Iulius, proudest in his empyre
With his tryumphes moost imperyal?
Wher is Pirrus that was lord and sire   75
Of [al] Ynde in his estat roial?
And wher is Alisaunder that conqueryd al,
Failed leiser his testament to dispoose?
Nabugodonosor or Sardanapal?
Al stant on chaung like a mydsomyr roose.   80

Wher is Tullius with his sugryd tonge?
Or Crisistomus with his golden mouth?
The aureat ditees that be red and songe
Of Omerus in Grece both north and south?
The tragedyes diuers and vnkouth   85
Of moral Senek, the mysteryis to vncloose?
By many example this matere is ful kouth:
Al stant on chaung like a mydsomyr roose.

Wher been of Fraunce al the dozepeers
Which [þat] in Gawle had the governaunce?   90
Vowes of the Pecok with al ther proude cheers?
The worthy nyne with al ther hih bobbaunce?
Troian knyhtis, grettest of alliaunce?
The flees of gold, conqueryd in Colchoos?
Rome and Cartage, moost souereyn of puissaunce? 95
Al stant on chaung like a mydsomyr roos.

Put in a som al marcial policye,
Compleet in Affryk and boundys of Cartage,
The Theban legioun, example of cheualrye,
At Roda[n]us Ryuer was expert ther corage: 100
Ten thousand knyhtes born of hih parage
Ther martirdam, rad in metre and proose,
Ther golden crownys maad in heuenly stage,
Fressher than lilies or ony somyr roose.

The remembraunce of euery famous knyht,   105
Ground considerid, is bilt on rihtwisnesse.
Race out ech quarel that is not bilt on riht,
Withoute trouth what vaileth hih noblesse?

23

[Þ]'aw[ti]ers of martirs foundid on hoolynesse:
Whit was maad red ther tryumphes to discloose: 110
The whit[e] lillye was ther chaast clennesse,
Ther bloody suffraunce was no somyr roose.

It was the Roose of the bloody feeld,
Roose of Iericho that greuh in Beedlem:
The five Roosys portrayed in the sheeld, 115
Splayed in the baneer at Ierusalem.
The sonne was clips and dirk in euery rem
Whan Christ Ihesu five wellys lyst vncloose
Toward Paradys, callyd the rede strem,
Of whos five woundys prent in your hert a roos. 120

8

A BALADE IN COMMENDATION OF OUR LADY

A thowsand storiis kowde I m[o] reherse
Off olde poets touchyng this matere:
How that Cupide the hertis gan to perse
Off his seruauntis, settyng tham affere:
'Lo here [the fin of] th'errour and the weere,   5
Lo here of loue the guerdoun and greuaunce
That euyr with woo his seruaunts doth avaunce.'

Wherfore I wil now pleynly my stile redresse,
Of on to speke, at nede that will not faile.
Allas, for dool I [ne] can nor may expresse   10
Hir passand pris, and that is no mervaile.
O wynd of grace, now blowe into my saile,
O auriat lycour of Clyo, for to wryte
Mi penne enspire of that I wold endyte.

Allas, vnworthi I am and [al] unable   15
To lo[u]e suche on, all women surmountyng
[To be benigne to me and] mercyable,
That is of pite the welle and the spryng.
Wherefore of hir, in laude and in preysyng,
So as I can, supported by hir grace,   20
Right thus I say, knelyng toforn hir face:

O sterne of sternys with thi stremys clere,
Sterne of the see, to shipman lyght and gyde,
O lusty leem[yng], most plesaunt to appere,
Whos bright bemys the clowdis may not hide,   25
O way of lyfe to hem þat goo or ride,
Haven aftyr tempest surrest [up] to ryve,
On me haue mercy for thi ioyes fyve.

O rightest rewl, O rote of holynesse,
And lightsom lyne of pite [for] to pleyne,   30
Origynal gynnyng of grace and al goodnesse,
And clennest condite of vertu souerayne,
Modyr of mercy, oure troubyl to restreyne,
Chambyr and closet clennest of chastyte,
And namyd herberwe of þe deyte,   35

O closid gardeyn, al void of weedes wicke,
Cristallyn welle, of clennesse cler consigned,
Fructif olyve, of foilys faire and thicke,
And redolent cedyr, most derworthly ydynged,
Remembyr of pecchouris [unto thee] assigned,   40
Or þe wyckid fend his wrath upon us wreche,
Lantyrn of light, be þu oure lyfis leche.

Paradys of plesaunce, gladsom to all good,
Benygne braunchelet of the pigment-tre,
Vinarye envermailyd, refrescher of oure food,   45
Lycour aȝens langour that pallid may not be,
Blisful bawm-blossum, b[y]dyng in bounte,
Thi mantel of [mercy] on oure myschef spred,
Or woo awak us, wrappe us undyr thi weed.

Red[e] rose, flouryng withowtyn spyne,   50
Fonteyn of fulnesse, as beryl corrent clere,
Some drope of thi graceful dewe to us propyne;
þu light without nebule, shynyng in thi spere,
Medicyne to myscheu[e]s, pucelle withoute pere,
Flawme down to doolful, lyght of thyn influence,   55
Remembryng thi servant for thi magnificence.

Of alle Cristen protectrix and tutele,
Retour of exilid, put in proscrypcyoun,
To hem þat erryn, the path of her sequele,
To wery wandrid, the tente, pavil[i]oun,   60
[The feynte to fresshe, and the pawsacioun,]
Vnto deiecte rest and remedye,
Feythfull unto all þat in the affye.

To hem that rennyth þu art itinerarie,
O blisful bravie to knyghtis of thi werre,   65
To wery workmen þu art dyorne denarye,
Mede to mareyners þat haue sailed ferre,
Lauriat corown, stremand as a sterre
To hem þat put hem in pal[e]styr for thi sake,
Cours of her conquest, þu, white as ony lake.   70

Thow myrthe of martyrs, swetter than cytolle,
Of confessouris richest donatyff,
Unto virginis th'eterne aureolle,
Aforne all women hauyng prerogatyff,
Maiden and modyr, both wedow and wyff,   75
In all this world nys noon but þu allone,
Now s[i]n þu may, be su[cou]r to my mone.

O tresti turtyl, trowest of all trewe,
O curteys columbe, replet of all mekenesse,
O nyghtyngale with thi notys newe,   80
O popynjay, plumed in clennesse,
O larke of lo[u]e, syngynge in swetnesse,
Phebus awaitynge, till in thi brest he lyght,
Undyr thi w[i]nge at domysday vs dyght.

O ruby rubifyed in the passyoun   85
All of thi sone, among haue vs in mynde,
O stedfast dyamaunt of duracyoun,
That fewe feris þat tyme myght þu fynde,
For noon to hym was founde half so kynde.
O h[a]rdy herte, O louynge creature,   90
What was it but lo[u]e þat made þe so t'endure?

Semely safyr, dep lowp, and blew ewage
(Stable as the lowpe, ay ewage to pite),
This is to sayn, O frescheste of visage,
Thu louyst hem unchaungid þat serue the,   95
Or ȝif offence or writhyng in hem be
Þu art ay redy upon her woo to rewe,
And hem resyuyst [with b]eemis of thyn ewe.

27

O goodly gladid, when þat Gabriell
With joie the grette þat may not be noumbrid,   100
Of halfe the joie, who cowde wryte or telle,
When the Holy Goost to the was obvmbrid
Wherthorgh þat fends were utterly encombrid?
O wemles mayden, enbelysshed with his byrthe,
That man and aungell þeroff had[den] myrthe.   105

Loo here the blossum and bud of all oure glorye
Off whech þat prophets spak so long aforn.
Loo here the same þat was in memorye
Of Ysaie [so] long or she was born.
Loo here [of] Dauid the delicyows corn,   110
Lo here the ground that list [him] to onbelde,
Becomyn[g] man, [our] raunsoun for to ȝelde.

O glorious viole, O vitre inviolate,
O[f] f[i]ry Tytan percyd with the lemys,
Whos vertuous bryghtnesse was in thi brest vibrate   115
That all this world enbelisshed with his [b]emys,
Conseruatrix of kyngdamys and remys,
O Isaye[s] seed, O swete Sunamyte,
Mesure my mo[u]rnynge, myn owne margarite.

O soueraynest, sowht out of Syon,   120
O punycall pome agens all pestilence,
And auryat vrne, in whom was book and bo[u]n
The agnelet that fought for oure offence
Aȝens the serpent with so high defence
That like a lyoun in victory he was founde,   125
To Him commende vs, of mercy moost habounde.

O precyous [perle] withoutyn ony pere,
Cockyl with gold dew from aboue Ireyned,
Þu busshe vnbrent, ferle[s] set affere,
Flawmyng in feruence, not with hete peyned,   130
Duryng days[y]e with no weder steyned,
Fles[e] vndefoulyd of gentyl Gedeon,
[Þe fructefyng yerde, þowe, of Aron,]

28

The my[ȝ]ti arke, probatyk piscyne,
Lawghynge Auror[a], and of pees olyve,   135
Columpne and base up-beryng from abyme,
Why ner[e] I connyng the forto discrive?
Chesen for Iosep[h], whan he took to wyve,
Unknowyng hym, chyldyng be mirakyll,
And of our ma[nly] figure tabyrnakyll.   140

9

A DEFENCE OF HOLY CHURCH

[M]ost worthi prince, of whome the noble fame
In vertue floureth and in hih prudence,
Laude and honoure be vnto thi name
And to thi worthi roial excellence,
The which hast been protectour and diffence   5
Thoruh thy manhode ageyn thy mortall foon
Off Cristis spouse, douhtir of Syoun,

That was oppressid almost in thy rewme
Even at the poynt of hir destruccioun
Amyd hir citee of Ierusalem,   10
Al bysett with enmyes envyroun:
Tamade a new transmygracioun
When she, allas, disconsolat, allone
Ne kneuh to whome for to make hir moone,

But on the floodis of fell Babiloun,   15
Al solitair and trist in compleynyng,
Sat with hir children aboute hir euerichoun,
Almost fordrownyd with teerys in weepyng.
And wher as she was won[t]e to play and syng
In pr[a]ys and honour of hir eternall lorde,   20
On instruments of musik in accorde,

Constreyned was, and almost at the prikk
Talefft hir song of holy notis trewe,
And on the salwys olde, foule and thikk
To hang hir orgnes þat were entvned newe,   25
O Goddis knyht, till þu list to rewe
Upon hir pitouse lamentable woo:
Off reuth and mercy to deliuer hir froo

The mortall honds that wrouhte hir al þis soore,
Hir to have put in captyuytee   30
Off the tyraunte Nabugdonosor,
Ferr frome the boundis, allas, of hir citee;
Till thou of grace grauntest libertee
Zorobabell and also Neemye
Ierusalem ageyn to edyfye,   35

And kepe the Temple hoole and sounde bi grace
That stoode in way of perdicioun,
Thorough hem þat gan to threten and menace
The libertees of Cristys mansioun,
And for to pynch att her fundacioun   40
In pre[judic]e of the olde and newe lawe,
The patrymony of Petir to withdrawe;

That ther was noon her malis to withstonde,
Cristys quarell manly to susteen,
Til thow were chose for to lay to honde,   45
Only by grace hir champioun to been,
For to delyuer out of woo and teen
Noees shipp, bysett with many [a] wawe,
Tyl thow the watres madist to withdrawe,

That Karibdis myht it nat devoure,   50
Nor fierce Silla with hir bittyr rage,
For noon but thow myht [yt] tho socour
To make the floodis fully to aswage,
Thoruh the straytis to holden the passage,
Thi silff of goodnesse the rother list to guye   55
Til on the hyllys hy of Armonye

The shipp gan rest out of all dawngeere,
Maugre the rokkis of vengeaunce mercilesse,
And that the skies wex[e] faire and clere;
And thoruh thyn helpe that the dowe chese   60
For to repaire with a braunch of pes,
When as the raven hath a careyn take,
Oute of the shipp, upon his praye to wake,

With coverte tresoun falsely to lachche
(When he seeth tyme) his desired praye: 65
Liche a bosarde vnwarly for to cachche
Smale briddys that thynke on noon affraye.
Wherfor I rede, both nyght and day,
To Goddys knyght, so goode wachch to make
Off Philistees the [Arke] be nat take,   70

All Israel to bryngen in distresse
Whos ioy and helth lith in thi persoone,
The welfaire eke and holly þe gladnesse
In every thyng of what thai ha to doone;
Wherfor beware of chaungyng of the moone,   75
Eclipse of falsehed betrassh nat the liht
Off thi goodnesse that shyneth yitt so briht.

Thynke, how to Dauid full innocente
Saul was fals for all his othis sworne,
Nad God by grace makid resistence   80
His chose knyght[e] had[de] be forlorne.
Wherfor I rede þe, greyn and purid corne
Thow cherrish wel, and lay the chaff aside
That trouth han voided, for to been her gide.

And thynke how Dauid ageyn Iebusee   85
When that he fouht, in *Regum* as I fynde,
How he made voide from Syon his Citee
Unweldy, crokid, both[e] lame and blynde:
By which example alway have in mynde
To voide echon, and for to do the same   90
Oute of thi siht, that in the faith be lame.

For who is blynde or haltith in þe faith
For any doctryne of these sectys newe
And Cristes techyng therfor aside laith,
Unto thy corone may he nat be trewe.   95
He may dissymule with a feynyd hewe—
But take good heede, what way þat he faire,
Thy swerde of knyhthoode, that no swich ne spaire,

And Cristis cause alway fyrst preferre
And althirnexte thi knyhtly state preserue,   100
And lat this lawe be thi loode-sterre;
Than grace shall thyn honour ay conserve.
And Goddys foon manly make to sterue:
For any fals feynyd repentaunce,
Of right lat rigour holden the ballaunce.   105

Thynke how Saule from his kyngly place
And frome th'onour of his royall see,
Whilome was abiect for he did[e] grace
To Amalech ageyne the voluntee
Of Goddys precepte, of feynyd fals pitee   110
To spare his swerde rihtfully to bite,
When as God bad that he shulde smyte,

Wher Samuel, the perfite hooly man,
Chosen of God to execute trouth,
With a swerde the rihtfull doome he gan   115
And slouh Agag, withouten any routh
In Galgalis wher Saule for his slouth
Forsaken was, and hoolly al the lyne
That cam of hym in myscheff did[e] fyne.

Slouh nat Helye in all his holinesse   120
The fals prophetis longyng vnto Baal?
O noble prynce, exaumple of rightwisnesse,
Off God preservid to be the myhty wall
Of Hooly Churche in thyn estate royall,
Distroye hem tho, that falsely now werrey   125
Her own modir, to whome thai shulde obeye.

And namely hem that of presumpcyoun
Dispraven hir, and hir ornamentes,
And therwithall, of indignacioun
Withdrawe wolde hir rich[e] paramenteȝ.   130
O prudent prynce, thynke what her entent is,
Who falsely the Hooly Churche accuse,
For thay hemsilff the riches wolden use.

Remembre also, for swich transgressioun
What was the fyne of kyng Antiochus   135
That proudely tooke by extorsioun
The sacred iewels from Goddis hooly hous:
Was he nat slawe, this tiraunt trecherous,
With smale worms hym fretyng manyfolde
Whan [that] he fill down from his chare of golde? 140

What myht availe his pompe or all his pride,
Or all the gliteryng of his riche chare
In which that he so proudely did ride?
The surquedye also of Baltasar
Was it nat abatid or that he was war,   145
In Babiloun, with a soden fall,
Whan that the honde wrote upon the wall?

10

LIFE OF OUR LADY

[ii. 519–903]

And whanne þe angelle from her parted was
And she aloon in hir tabernacle,
Right as the sonne persheth thorugh the glas,
Thorugh the cristall, byrell or spectacle
Withoutyn harme, right so by miracle   5
Into hir closet the Faders sapience
Entrede is withoutyn violence

Or any wemme vnto hir maydenhede
On any side, in party or in all.
For Godes sonne, takyng our manheed,   10
In hir hathe bilte his paleys prynci[p]all,
And vndir-pight this mansion rial
With seven pilers, as made is memorye,
And therin sette his reclynatorye:

Wheche is performed al of [pured] golde   15
Only to vs forto signyfye
That he all holy maked hath his holde
Withinne this mayde that callet is Marye.
And seven pillours that shulde this mayden gye
Been seven spirites (so as I can decerne)   20
Of God above, this mayde to gouerne.

For all the tresoure of his sapience
And all the wisdome of hevyn and erthe therto,
And all the richesse of spirituall science
In hir were sette and closyde eke also.   25
For she is the tour, withoutyn wordes moo,
And hous of yvour in wheche Salamon
Shette all the tresoure in his possession.

She was the castell of the cristall wall
That neuer man myght yet vnclose   30
Whiche the kyng that made and causyth all,
His dwellyng chefe by grace gan dispose.
And like as dewe descendeth on the rose
With siluer dropes, vpon the leves fayre
The fresche be[aute] ne may not apayre,   35

[Ne] as the rayne in Apryll or in May
Causying the vertu to renne oute of the rote,
The grete fayrenesse nought apayre may
On violeteȝ and on erbes soote:
Right so this grace, of al our grev[is] bote,   40
The grace of God, amydde the lyly white
The beaute causith, to be of more delyte.

And as the cocle, with hevyn[s] dew so clene
Of kynde engendreth white perles ronde,
And hathe no cheryshyng but the sonne shene   45
To his fostryng (as it is playnely founde):
Right so this mayde, of grace most habounde,
A perle hath [closed] within hir brest[e] white
That from the dethe myght al our raunsom quyte.

She was eke the gates with the lokeȝ br[i]ght   50
Sette in the northe of high deuocion,
Of wheche sumtyme the prophete had a sight:
Ezechiel in his avision:
Wheche stoode ay clos; in conclusion,
That neuer man entre shall ne pace   55
But God hymselfe to make his dwellyng place.

And right in sothe (as I reherse can)
So as the flees of Gedeon was wette
(Toforn he fawte [with] hem of Madian)
With hevynly dewe environ all bysette,   60
In signe onely he shall spede the bette.
Right so hathe Godde in hir his grace shewed,
Withe the Holy Goste when she was al bydewed;

In token playnly she sholde socour be
Vnto mankynde, manly forto fyght   65
Agayne the devill that hath in his powste
Al Madyan with his fel[le] myght.
But thorough the helpe of the mayden bryght
And thorughe the dwe of hir hevynly grace,
We shall this serpent from our bo[u]ndes chase.   70

She was of golde also the riche ourne
Kepyng the manna of our saluacion,
That all our wo may to ioy[e] tourne
With holsome foode of full perfection.
And eke she was, in sygnyficacion,   75
The yerde of Aron with frute and leves lade,
Of vertu moste to comfort vs and glade.

She was the auter of cedre, gold and stone,
Stedefast and trwe thorugh perfecion;
And as the cedre, conservyng ay in oon   80
Hir body clene from all corruppcion.
And for to make a full oblacion
Of euery vertu, to God in chastite
She shone as golde by perfyte charite.

And on this auter she made hir sacrifice   85
With fyre of love brynnyng also bryght
To God and man in euery manere wyse.
As done the sterres in the frosty nyght,
Hir frankensense gaffe so clere a light
Thorugh good ensample þat the perfite levyn   90
Of hir l[o]ving raught vnto hevyn.

She was the trone where that Salamon
For worthynesse sette his rial see
With golde and yvory, that so bright shone,
That al aboute the beaute men may se.   95
The golde was loue, the yvory chastyte,
And twelf leouns so huge, grete and large,
That of this werke baren vp the charge,

37

Of the olde lawe werne the propheteʒ twelffe,
That longe aforne gan beholde and see   10(
That Salamon (Goddys sonne hymself)
Shulde in þis maide bild his rial see.
So that, in sothe, hir clene virginyte
To be a mothir sholde no thyng lette,
Amydde hir breste he his trone sette.   10ʒ

She was also the woman that saint John
Sawe in the hevyn so richely apere,
Clad in a sonne [þe] whiche brighter shon
Than Phebus dothe in his large spere.
And twelf sterres that passyngly were clere   11(
(So as to hym playnely dyd seme)
Were sette above in hir diademe.

And, as hym thought, at hir feet there stode
A large mone, bryght and nothyng pale:
In fygure onely þat, she that is so goode   11ʒ
To swage the bitter of our [olde] bale,
The sonne of [rightwisnesse] made to avale
Downe to the erthe to gouerne vs and gye.
And eke the moone [to] us doth signifie

All Holy Chirche, large to beholde,   12(
Whiche in this mayde had his orygynall,
Whanne that finally, with hise rightis olde
The Synagoog of Iues had a fall.
For in this mayde the first faythefull wall
Of Holy Chirche God gan first to bilde   12ʒ
Whan with his sonne he made hir goo with chylde.

And to reforme the rudeness vtterly
Of blynde folkes that ko[u]th not perceyve
How that Marye myght [so] kyndely
A mayde be and a chylde conceyve.   13(
And, if h[e]m l[i]st reason to receyve,
They may ensamples right inowe fynde
Of this matier, accordyng vnto kynde:

38

O blynde man thorough thyne inyquyte
Why hast thou lost thy reason and thy sight,   135
That thou of malise list not for to see
How Criste Ihesu thorough his gret might
To his disciples helde the waye right
Thoroughe the gates shette by gret defence,
Withoutyn brekyng or any violence?   140

Why myght he not, of his magnificence,
Within a mayde make his mansion
And she yet stonde in the excellence
Of maydynhede, from all corrupcion?
Ye be to blynde in your discrecion,   145
That l[i]st nat se also howe he rose
Frome dethe to lyfe [in] his sepulcre close.

And herewithal thou maiste also aduerte
How he in sothe, of his myghty grace,
Made Petre oute of prison sterte,   150
And where hym l[i]st frely [for] to pace;
And yet the dores were shette of the place.
What wondre than though, God by myracle
Within a mayde made his habitacle:

She beyng close and perfytely shette   155
With all the bonde₃ of virginyte,
For, sothefastely, hir clennesse was not lette
In no kynnes kynde nor her chastite,
But encreseth and fayrere for to see
That Goddes son liste to light adowne,   160
With this mayde to make his mansion.

Eke Hildefons tellyth of a tree
In stede of frute that beryth byrde₃ smalle
Fro yere to yere by kynde (as men may see)
Withoutyn meddelyng of femall or of male,   165
This is verrey sothe, playnely and not tale.
Than wondir nat though Crist were bore betwene
The chaste syde₃ of a maydyn clene.

39

[Eke certyn] briddes called vultures
Withoutyn medelyng conceyved by nature,   170
As bokes sayen withoute any lees,
And of her lyfe an hundreth yere endure.
Than [siþ] the lorde of euery creature
Causeth all, no wondre þat I sayde
Þat she w[as] conceyved of a [clene] mayde.   175

Eke Pl[y]nius in *Bokes Naturell*
Wryteʒ of a roche, grete and large also,
That will remove with a fyngre small,
But if a man do all his might therto
It will not stirre, nethir to ne froo.   180
Right so this mayde, that th[u]s of vertu moste
With a fyngre of the Holy Goste

And with a touche of his myghty grace
Conceyvede hath sothefast God and man,
That neuer myght remove from hir place   185
Of thilke avowe: that she first began
To be a mayde, as ferforthe as she can,
In hert and will, as any roche stable
That frome his grownde is not removable.

This clerke also, this wyse Pl[y]nius,   190
Saythe in Tawrygge ther is an erthe fovnde
That of nature is so vertuouse
That [it] will cure euery maner wovnde.
Right so Marye was the erthe ifounde
That God oute-chees by eleccion   195
To bere the frute of our redempcion:

That shulde be helpe and eke medycyne
To all our woundeʒ when thay ake or smerte,
And all our greves and our hertys fyne,
Fro the dethe to make vs to asterte,   200
With holsome bavme pershyng to the hert
That shall to [helþe] sodenly restore
Our festrede sores that thay shall ake no more.

And ferthermore, this auctor can eke telle
Withinne his boke (whoso loke aright):   205
To Iubiter sacrede is a welle
That whan [it] hath quenched brondeȝ bright
Eft ayen it [yeveth] hem newe light:
Whoso l[i]st asaye, sothe as he shal fynde.
What wondre than though, the God of Kynde   210

Amyddes this well, fro fylthe of synne colde,
Full of vertu, with fayre stremys clere
His loogyng toke and his myghty holde;
And thorough his grace set it new a-fyre
With the Holy Goste, that, withoutyn werre,   215
Thow she were colde from euery flesshlihede
She brent in love hatter than the glede.

And in Falisco (as hym liste to wryte)
Is a well that causithe eke of newe
Whan [that] thay drynke oxen to be white   220
And sodenly forto chaunge her hewe.
What merveile than though, the well trwe,
The well of helthe and of lyfe eterne,
The Lorde of all (so as I can discerne)

His stremes shede into this mayde fre   225
To make hir whitest, as in holynesse,
That bothe shulde mayde and modir be,
And euere in one, kepyng hir clennesse
Withoutyn chaunge: so that hir whitnesse
Ne fadith never, in beaute ne in colour,   230
Of maydenhede to bere bothe lefe and flowre.

And who that will dispute in this matier
I holde hym madde or ellys oute of mynde,
For if he haue his eene hole and clere
He shall mow see (preef I nowe by kynde):   235
For he that made bothe leef and lynde,
And with oo worde this waste worlde wilde,
Might make a mayde for to goo with chylde.

41

And he that made the high[e], cristall hevyn,
The firmament and also euery spere,   240
The golden axeltre and the sterres seven,
Cithera so lustly for to apere,
And reed Mars with his sterne chere,
Myght he nat eke, onely for our sake,
Withinne a mayde, of man the kynde take?   245

And he that causith foulez in the eyre
In hir kynde to waxe and multiplie,
And fisshes eke with fynnes syluer fayre
In depe wawes to gouerne hem and gye,
And dothe oon lyve and another dye,   250
And giffith bestes her foode vpon the grovnde
And in her kynde dothe hem to abounde,

Sythen he is Lorde and causith all thyng
To haue beyng (if I shall not feyne)
And is the Prince and the worthy Kyng   255
That all enbraseth in his myghty cheyne,
Why myght he nat, by power souereygne,
At his free cho[i]se that all may save and lese,
To his mothir a clene mayden chese?

Who causith frute oute of the harde tree   260
By vertu onely that spryngeth from the rote
To growe and wexe, lyche as men may see,
With levys grene and newe blosmes sote?
[Hit is oure Lorde] that for our alþer bote
Wolde of a mayde (as I reherse can)   265
Mekely be borne withoute touche of man.

For he that dothe the tendre branches spryng
And fresshe floures in the grene mede
That werne in wyntir dede and eke droupyng,
Of bawme voyde and of all lustyhede,   270
Myght he nat make his greyne to growe and sprede
Withinne hir brest that was bothe mayde and wyfe,
Wherof is made the sothefaste brede of lyfe?

42

And he that graved of his grete myght
Withoutyn poyntell in the hard[e] stone   275
And in the tables, with lettres fayre and bryght,
His ten precepte3 and byddynges eueryche one,
The same Lorde, of his power aloon,
Hath made this mayde here on erthe lowe
A chylde conceyve and no man to knawe.   280

And he that made [þe] busche to apere
All on flame with ferfull sparkelle3 shene
When Moyses beganne to aproche nere,
And yet no harme came to the bowes grene,
The same Lorde hath concerved clene   285
His habitacle and hir erbor swete
In this mayde from all flesshely hete.

And he that made the yerde of Moyses
Of a serpent to take the lykenesse
In the hall amonge all the prees   290
Where Pharao his people did oppresse,
And in deserte (the Byble beryth witnesse)
The ryver made to rynne oute of a stoon
The thurste to staunche of his people anoon,

And ouere this, for to verefye   295
His grete myght, Sampson the stronge man
(As *Iudicum* dothe playnely specyfye)
Dranke the water that from the kanell ranne;
And he that made the flode3 of Iordan
To turne agayne for love of Iosue   300
That al his peple myght[e] clerly see:

And how the wawes gan asondre breke
And like an hyll stande high alofte;
And he that made the asse for to speke
To Balaham, for he rode vn-soffte,   305
Why myght he not (by power previd ofte)
Sithe he the yrne made on the water hove,
Be of a mayde borne for man[ne]s love?

And he that made an angell for to take
Abacuk by his lytyll here   310
And sodenly brought hym to the lake
In Babylone whiche was so far;
And to visite, lygyng in his feer,
Danyell amonge the bestes rage,
Till he to hym brought[e] the potage   315

(The dores shet of the stronge pr[i]sovne)
For to asswage of hungre al his payne,
And in a moment to his mansion
Full sodenly restored hym agayne:
Why myght he not (as wel in certeyne),   320
The same Lorde, of a mayde than
Take flesshe and blod and become man?

And he that made the sonne at Gabaon
To stonde and [s]chyne vpon the bryght shelde
Of Iosue and taward Achalon   325
The mone also, as all the host behelde,
The long[e] day while thay faught in the felde
Agayne the kynges of myghty Ammorie
That his people clerly myght[e] see,

And he that made the shade to retourne   330
In the orlage of kyng Eȝechye
By ten degrees, only to performe
The heest[e] made to Hym of Isaye,
Why myght He not, þis Lorde that all doth gye,
Of a mayde, by the same skylle,   335
Frely be borne at his owne wille?

And he that fedde with fyve loveȝ small
Fyve thousand in solitarie place,
Fer in desert sittyng in a valle,
Thorough the foyson and plente of his grace: 340
The same Lorde, why myght he not purchase
Withinne a mayde, duryng hir maydenhede,
Whan that hym l[i]ste to take his manhede?

For as the be dothe wax and hony shede
At the evyn (who taketh hede therto), 345
Right so Marye, flouryng in maydenhede,
Bare in hir wombe God and man also,
And yet in sothe she was bothe too
(I dar afferme) in oo person ifer:
A mayde clene and Cristis mothir dere. 350

For as the beem shynyng from aferre
Shedyng his light (as men may well aspye)
Withoutyn harme or hyndryng to the sterre,
And so as manna fel doun fro the sky,
Right so this floure that callet is Marye, 355
With wombe halowed into chastyte,
Conceyved hath in hir virgynyte.

And as the barnacle in the harde tre
Of kynde bredith, and the vyne floure
Causyth the wyne, [in] floures for to be 360
Thorough Bachus myght, [of] grapes gouernour,
Right so, in sothe, mankynde3 Savyour
As the bernacle, or floure oute of the vyne,
Spronge of Marye, she beyng a virgyne.

And as a worme vndre the harde stone 365
Of erthe comyth withoutyn engendrure,
And as the Fenyx (of which ther is but one)
To asshes brent renuyth by nature,
Right so this Lorde that all hathe in cure,
Our kynde, agayne, fro synne to renewe 370
Toke flesshe and blode in this maydyn trewe.

And as the snawe fro Iubiter dothe falle
Thorough the force of [Sagitarrius] bowe,
And Zepherus dothe the flores calle,
On white blosmes when [that] he dothe blowe, 375
Right so in sothe, the grace alight lowe
Of the Holy Goste, like a wynde cherschyng,
Amydde this mayde to make his dwellyng,

And to the floure ne ded noo duresse,
But perfitely concervyde hir beaute   380
From euery storme of flesshely lustynesse,
Euere ylike of fayrnesse fresche to see:
As by ensamples moo than two or three
H[e]r to serve, as thay haue herde devyse,
Whiche, as me semyth, [ought] inow suffice.   385

A COMPLAYNT OF A LOVERES LYFE

In May when Flora, the fressh[e] lusty quene,
The soyle hath clad in grene, rede and white,
And Phebus gan to shede his stremes shene
Amyd the Bole wyth al the bemes bryght,
And Lucifer to chace awey the nyght   5
Ayen the morow our orysont hath take
To byd[de lovers] out of her slepe awake:

And hertys heuy for to recomforte
From dreryhed of heuy nyghtis sorowe,
Nature bad hem ryse[n] and disporte   10
Ageyn the goodly, glad[e], grey[e] morowe.
And Hope also, with Seint Iohn to borowe,
Bad in dispite of Daunger and Dispeyre
For to take the holsom lusty eyre.

And wyth a sygh [I] gan for to abreyde   15
Out of my slombre and sodenly [vp]-stert
As he, alas, that nygh for sorow deyde,
My sekenes sat ay so nygh myn hert.
But for to fynde socour of my smert,
Or attelest sum relesse of [my] peyn   20
That me so sore halt in euery veyn,

I rose anon and thoght I wol[de] goon
Vnto the wode to her the briddes sing
When that the mysty vapour was agoon
And clere and feyre was the morw[e]nyng.   25
The dewe also lyk syluer in shynyng
Vpon the leves as eny bavme suete
Til firy Tytan with hys persaunt hete

47

Had dried vp the lusty lycour nyw
Vpon the herbes in [the] grene mede,   30
And that the floures of mony dyuers hywe
Vpon [her] stalkes gunne for to sprede
And for to splay[en] out her leves on brede
Ageyn the sun golde-borned in hys spere
That dovn to hem cast hys bemes clere.   35

And by a ryuer forth I gan costey
Of water clere as berel or cristal
Til at the last I founde a lytil wey
Tovarde a parke enclosed with a wal
In compas round; and by a gate smal   40
[W]hoso that wolde frely myght[e] goon
Into this parke walled with grene stoon.

And in I went to her the briddes songe
Which on the braunches bothe in pleyn [and] vale
So loude song that al the wo[de] ronge   45
Lyke as hyt shold sheuer in pesis smale.
And, as me thoght[e], that the nyghtyngale
With so grete myght her voys gan out wrest
Ryght as her hert for love wolde brest.

The soyle was pleyn, smothe and wonder softe,   50
Al ouersprad wyth tapites that Nature
Had made herselfe, celured eke alofte
With bowys grene the flo[u]res for to cure
That in her beaute they may long endure
Fro al assaute of Phebus feruent fere   55
Which in his spere so hote shone and clere.

The eyre atempre and the smothe wynde
Of Ʒepherus among the blosmes whyte
So holsom was and norysshing be kynde
That smale buddes and round blomes lyte   60
In maner gan of her brethe delyte
To yif vs hope [that] their frute shal take
Ayens autumpne redy for to shake.

I saw ther Daphene closed vnder rynde,
Grene laurer and the holsom pyne,   65
The myrre also that wepeth euer of kynde,
The cedre high, vpryght as a lyne,
The philbert eke that lowe doth enclyne
Her bowes grene to the erthe dovne
Vnto her knyght icalled Demophovne.   70

Ther saw I eke [the] fressh[e] haw[e]thorne
In white motele that so soote doth smelle,
Asshe, firre and oke with mony a yonge acorne,
And mony a tre mo than I can telle.
And me beforne I saw a litel welle   75
That had his course (as I gan beholde)
Vnder an hille with quyke stremes colde.

The grauel gold, the water pure as glas,
The bankys round, the welle environyng,
And softe as veluet the yonge gras   80
That thervpon lustely [cam spryngyng].
The sute of trees about[e] compassyng
Her shadow cast, closyng the wel[le] rounde
And al th[e] erbes grovyng on the grounde.

The water so holsom and so vertuous   85
Throgh myght of erbes grovyng [ther] beside:
[Nat] lyche the welle wher as Narci[s]us
Islayn was thro vengeaunce of Cupide,
Wher so covertly he did[e] hide
The greyn of deth vpon ech[e] brynk   90
That deth mot folow, who that euer drynk.

Ne lyche the pitte of the Pega[c]e
Vnder Parnaso wher poetys slept,
Nor lyke the welle of [pure] chastite
Which as Dyane with her nymphes kept   95
When she naked into the water lept,
That slow Atteon with his ho[u]ndes felle
Oonly for he cam so nygh the welle.

But this welle that I her reherse
So holsom was that hyt wolde aswage 100
Bollyn hertis and the venym per[se]
Of pensifhed with al the cruel rage
And euermore refressh[e] the visage
Of hem that were in eny werynesse
Of gret labour or fallen in distresse. 105

And I that [had] throgh Daunger and Disdeyn
So drye a thrust, thogh[t] I wolde assay
To tast a draght[e] of this welle, or tweyn,
My bitter languor yf hyt myght alay;
And on the banke anon dovne I lay 110
And with myn hede into the welle araght
And of the watir dranke a [gode] draght.

Wherof me thoght I was refressed wel
Of the brynnyng that sate so nygh my[n] hert
That verely anon I gan to fele 115
An huge part relesed of my smert
And therwithalle anon vp I stert
And thoght I wolde walke[n] and se more
Forth in the parke and in the holtys hore.

And thorgh a launde as I yede apace 120
And gan about[e] fast[e] to beholde
I fonde anon a delytable place
That was beset with trees yong and olde,
Whos names her for me shal not be tolde,
Amyde of which stode an erber grene 125
That benched was with [clourys] nyw and clene.

This erber was ful of floures [ynde]
Into the whiche as I beholde gan
Betwex an hulfere and a wodebynde,
As I was war, I saw [w]her lay a man 130
In blake and white, colour pale and wan,
And wonder dedely also of his hiwe,
Of hurtes grene and fressh[e] woundes nyw.

And ouermore destreyned with sekenesse
Besyde (as thus he was) [ful] greuosly,   135
For vpon him he had a[n] hote accesse
That day be day him shoke ful petously;
So that for constreyn[t] of hys malady
And hertly wo, thus ly[i]nge al alone,
Hyt was a deth for to [her] him grone.   140

Wherof astonied, my fote I gan withdrawe,
Gretly wondring what hit myght[e] be
That he so lay and had[de] no fel[a]we,
Ne that I coude no wyght with him se.
Wherof I had routhe and eke pite   145
And gan anon so softly as I coude
Among the busshes priuely me shroude,

If that I myght in eny wise espye
What was the cause of his dedely woo,
Or why that he so pitously gan crie   150
On hys fortune and on his eure also,
With al my myght I leyde an ere to
Euery word to marke what he sayde
Out of his swogh among as he abreyde.

But first yf I shal make mencyon   155
Of his persone and pleynly him discrive,
He was, in soth, without excepcion,
To speke of manhod oon the best o[n] lyve.
Ther may no man ayein[es] trouthe stryve,
For of his time and of his age also   160
He proued was there men shuld haue ado.

For oon the best[e] ther of brede and lengthe
So wel ymade by good proporcion
Yf he had be in his delyuer strengthe.
But thoght and sekenes wer occasion   165
That he thus lay in lamentacion,
Gruffe on the grounde in place desolate,
Sole, by himself, awaped and amate.

51

And for me semeth that hit ys syttyng
His wordes al to put in remembraunce,   170
To me that herde al his compleynyng
And al the grounde of his woful chaunce,
Yf therwithal I may yow do plesaunce,
I wol to yow (so as I can) anone
Lych as he seyde reherse[n] euerychone.   175

But who shal helpe me now to compleyn?
Or who shal now my stile guy or lede?
O Nyobe, let now thi teres reyn
Into my pen; and eke helpe in this nede,
Thou woful Myrre that felist my[n] hert blede   180
Of pitous wo, eke my[n] honde quake
When that I write for this mannys sake.

For vnto wo accordeth compleynyng
And delful chere vnto heuynesse:
To sorow also, sighing and wepyng   185
And pitous mo[u]rnyng vnto drerynesse;
And who[so] that shal write[n] o[f] distresse
In party nedeth to know felyngly
Cause and rote of al such malady.

But I, alas, that am of wit but dulle   190
And no knowyng haue of such mater
For to discryve and write[n] at the fulle
The wofull compleynt which that ye shul here,
But euen like as doth a skryuener
That can no more what that he shal write   195
But as his maister beside doth endyte:

Ryght so fare I, that of no sentement
Sey ryght noght, as in conclusion,
But as I herde when I was present
This man compleyn[e] wyth a pytous son.   200
For euenlych wythout addissyon
Or disencrese, outhir mor or lesse,
For to reherse anon I wol me dresse.

And yf that eny now be in this place
That fele in love brennyng or fervence 205
Or hyndred were to his lady grace
With false tonges that with pestilence
Sle tr[e]we men that neuer did offence
In word ne dede, ne in their entent,—
If eny such be here now present 210

Let hym of routhe ley to audyence
With deleful chere and sobre contenaunce
To here this man, by ful high sentence,
His mortal wo and his [grete] perturbaunce:
Compleynyng, now lying in a traunce 215
With loke[s] vp-cast and [with] ruful chere
Th'effect of which[e] was as ye shal here:

'The thoght oppressed with inward sighes sore,
The peynful lyve, the body langwysshing,
The woful gost, the hert[e] rent and tore, 220
The pitous chere pale in compleynyng,
The dedely face lyke asshes in shynyng,
The salt[e] teres that fro myn yen falle:
Parcel declare [þe] grounde of peynes alle:

'Whos hert ys ground to blede [i]n heuynesse, 225
The thoght resseyt of woo and of compleynt,
The brest is chest of dule and drerynesse,
The body eke so feble and so feynt;
With hote and cold my[n] acces ys so meynt
That now I shyuer for defaute of hete 230
And hote as glede now sodenly I suete.

'Now hote as fire, now colde as asshes dede,
Now hote for cold, [now cold] for hete ageyn,
Now colde as ise, now as coles rede
For hete I bren; and thus betwex[e] tweyn 235
I possed am and al forcast in peyn;
So that my[n] [hete], pleynly as I fele,
Of greuous colde ys cause euerydele.

'This ys the colde of ynward high dysdeyn,
Colde of dyspite and colde of cruel hate.   240
This is the cold that euer doth besy peyn
Ayen[e]s trouth to fight[en] and debate.
This ys the cold that wolde the fire abate
Of trwe menyng (alas the harde while):
This ys the colde that will me begile.   245

'For euere the better that in trouth I ment
With al my myght[e] feythfully to serue,
With hert and al[le] to be diligent
The lesse thanke, alas, I can deserue.
Thus for my trouthe Daunger doth me sterue,   250
For oon that shuld my deth of mercie let
Hath made Dispite now his suerd to whet

'Ayen[e]s me and his arwes to file
To take vengeaunce of wilful cruelte
And tonges fals[e] throgh her sleghtly wile   255
Han gonne a werre that wol not stynted be.
And fals Envye [and] Wrathe and Enmyte
Haue conspired ayens al ryght and lawe
Of her malis that Trouthe shal be slawe.

'And Male-bouche gan first the tale telle   260
To sclaundre Trouthe of Indignacion,
And Fals-Report so loude rong the belle
That Mysbeleve and Fals-Suspecion
Haue Trouthe brought to hys damnacion:
So that, alas, wrongfully he dyeth   265
And Falsnes now his place occupieth

'And entred ys into Trouthes londe
And hath therof the ful possessyon.
O ryghtful God, that first the trouthe fonde,
How may thou suffre such oppressyon,   270
That Falshed shuld have iurysdixion
In Trouthes ryght, to sle him gilt[e]les?
In his fraunchise he may not lyve in pes.

'Falsly accused and of his foon for-iuged,
Without [a]nswer while he was absent   275
He damned was, and may not ben excused:
For Cruelte satte in iugement
Of hastynes without avisement
And bad Disdeyn do[n] execute anon
His iugement in presence of hys fon.   280

'Atturney non ne may admytted ben
To excuse Trouthe, ne a word to speke.
To feyth or othe the iuge list not sen:
Ther ys no geyn but [þat] he wil be wreke.
O Lorde of Trouth to the I call and c[reke]:   285
How may thou se thus in thy presence
Without mercy, mordred Innocence?

'Now God that art of Trouth[e] souereyn,
And seest how I lye for trouthe bounde,
So sore knytte in Loves firy cheyn,   290
Euen at the deth, thro-girt with mony a wounde
That lykly ar neuer for to sounde,
And for my trouthe am damned to the dethe
And noght abide but drawe along the brethe:

'Consider and se in thyn eternal sight   295
How that myn hert professed whilom was
For to be trwe with al my ful[le] myght
Oonly to oon; the which[e] now, alas,
Of volunte, withoute more trepas,
Myn accussours hath taken vnto grace   300
And cherissheth hem my deth forto purchace.

'What menth this, what ys this wonder vre
Of purveance, yf I shal hit calle,
Of God of Love that fals hem so assure,
And trewe, alas, dovn of the whele be falle? 305
And yet in soth, this is the worst of alle:
That Falshed wrongfully of Trouth hath the name
And Trouth, ayenward, of Falshed bereth the blame.

'This blynde chaunce, this stormy aventure
In love hath most[e] his experience: 310
For who that doth with Trouth[e] most his cure
Shal for his mede fynde most offence
That serueth Love with al his diligence.
For who can feyne vnder loulyhede
Ne fayleth not to fynde grace and spede.   315

'For I loved oon ful longe syth agoon
With al my[n] hert[e], body and ful myght,
And to be ded my[n] hert[e] can not goon
From his hest but hold that he hath hight.
Thogh I be banysshed out of her syght   320
And by her mouthe damned that I shal deye,
Vnto my hest yet I wil euer obeye.

'For euer sithe that the world began,
Whoso lyste loke and in storie rede,
He shal ay fynde that the tr[e]we man   325
Was put abake, wheras the falshede
Ifurthered was: for Love taketh non hede
To sle the trwe and hath of hem no charge,
Wheras the fals goth frely at her large.

'I take recorde of Palamides   330
The tr[e]we man, the noble worthy knyght,
That euer loved and neuerh] ad] relese.
Notwithstondyng his manhode and myght
Love vnto him did ful grete vnright:
For ay the bette he did in cheualrye   335
The more he was hindred by envye.

'And ay the bette he dyd in euery place
Throgh his knyghthode and [his] besy peyn
Ther ferther was he fro his lady grace:
For to her mercie myght he neuer atteyn,   340
And to his deth he coud hyt not refreyn
For no daunger but ay [ob]ey and serue
As best he coude, pleynly til he sterue.

56

ERRATA

Text, p. 56, l. 332: neuerh]ad] = [neuer had]
Notes, p. 120, note 12: refinne = retinue
Notes, p. 185, note 436: Libide = Libido

'What was the fyne also of Ercules
For al his conquest and his wor[t]hynesse   345
That was of strengthe alone pereles?
For lyke as bokes of him list expresse
He set[te] p[ilers] thro his high provesse
Away at Gades for to signifie
That no man myght him passe in cheualrie.   350

'The whiche Pilers ben fer b[e]yonde Ynde
[I]set of golde for a remembraunce.
And for al that was he set behynde
With hem that Love list febly avaunce:
For [he] him set[te] last vpon a daunce   355
Ayen[e]s whom helpe may no strife.
For al his trouth[e] [ʒit] he lost his lyfe.

'Phebus also for a[l] his persaunt lyght
When that he went her in erthe lowe
Vnto the hert with [fresshe] Venus sight   360
Ywounded was th[o]ro[w] Cupides bowe:
And yet his lady list him not to knowe
Thogh for her love his hert[e] did[e] blede.
She lat him go and toke of him non hede.

'What shal I say of yong[e] Piramus?   365
Of trwe Tristram for al his high renovne?
Or Achilles or of Antony[u]s?
Of Arcite, or of him, Palamovne?
What was the ende of her passion
But after sorow, deth and then her grave.   370
Lo, her the guerdon that [thes] louers haue.

'But false Iasoun with his doublenesse
That was vntrwe at Colkos to Mede[e],
And Tereus, rote of vnkyndenesse,
And with these two eke the fals Ene[e]:   375
Lo, thus the fals ay in oon degre
Had in love her lust and al her wille;
And save falshed ther was non other skille.

'Of Thebes eke, [lo], the fals Arcite
And Demophon eke for his [foule] slouthe,   380
They had her lust and al that myght delyte
For al her falshede and [her] grete untrouthe.
Thus euer Love (alas and that is routhe)
His fals[e] legys furthereth what he may
And sleeth the trwe vngoo[d]ly, day be day.   385

'For trwe Adon was slayn with the bore
Amyd the forest in the grene shade:
For Venus love he felt[e] al the sore.
But Vulcanus with her no mercy made,
The foule cherle [ha]d many nightis glade: 390
Wher Mars her [worthy] knyght, her [trewe] man,
To fynde mercy comfort noon he can.

'Also the yonge fresh Ipomenes
So fre [and] lusty as of his corage
That for to serue with al his hert [he] ches   395
Athalan[t], so feire of her visage.
But Love, alas, quyt him so his wage
With cruel daunger pleynly at the last,
That with the dethe guerdonles he past.

'Lo, her the fyne of lover[e]s seruise.   400
Lo, how that Love can his seruantis quyte.
Lo, how he can his feythful men dispise
To sle the trwe men and [þe] fals respite.
Lo, how he doth the swerde of sorow byte
In hertis such as must his lust obey   405
To save the fals and do the tr[e]we dey.

'For feyth nor othe, word ne assuraunce,
Trwe menyng, awayte or besynesse,
Stil[le] port, ne feythful attendaunce,
Manhod, ne myght in armes, worthinesse,   410
Pursute of wurschip nor [no] high provesse
In straunge londe ryding ne trauayle:
Ful lyte, or noght in love doth avayle.

'Peril of dethe, nother in se ne londe,
Hungre ne thrust, sorow ne sekenesse,   415
Ne grete emprises for to take on honde,
Shedyng of blode, ne manful hardynesse,
Nor oft woundynge at sawtes by distresse,
Nor [iu]partyng of lyfe, nor dethe also,
Al ys for noght, Love taketh non hede therto.   420

'But Lesynges with her fals flaterye,
Thro her falshed and with her doublenesse,
With tales new and mony feyned lye,
By fals-semblaunt and countrefet humblesse,
Vnder colour depeynt with stidfastnesse,   425
With fraude cured vnder a pitous face,
Accept ben now rathest vnto grace:

'And can hemself now best[e] magnifie
With feyned port[e] and presumpsion.
They haunce her cause with fals surquedrie   430
Vnder menyng of double-entencion
To thenken on in her opynyon
And sey another to set h[em]selfe alofte
And hynder Tro[u]th, as hit ys seyn ful ofte.

'The whiche thyng I bye now al to dere,   435
Thanked be Venus and the god Cupide,
As hit is seen by myn oppressed chere
And by his arowes that stiken in my side:
That, safe the dethe, I no thing abide
Fro day to day; (alas the harde while)   440
When euer that hys dart hym list to fyle,

'My woful hert[e] for to ryve atwo
For faute or mercye and lake of pite
Of her that causeth al my peyn and woo
And list not ones of grace for to see   445
Vnto my trouthe throgh her cruelte:
And most of al[le] [ʒit] I me compleyn
That she hath ioy to laughen at my peyn

'And wifully hath my deth [y]sworne
Al gilt[e]les and wote no cause why,   450
Safe for the trouth that I have had aforne
To her allone to serue feythfully.
O God of Loue vnto to the I crie
And to thy bl[i]nde double deyte
Of this grete wrong [thus] I compleyn me,   455

'And to thy stormy wilful variaunce
Imeynt with chaunge and gret vnstable[n]esse:
Now vp, now down, so rennyng is thy chaunce
That the to trust may be no sikernesse,
I wite hit no thing but thi doublenesse.   460
And who that is an archer and ys blynde
Marketh no thing but sheteth by wenynge.

'And for that he hath no discrecion
Withoute avise he let his arow goo,
For lak of syght and also of resoun,   465
In his shetyng hit happeth oft[e] soo
To hurt his frende rathir than his foo.
So doth this god with [al] his sharpe flon
The trwe sleeth and leteth the fals[e] gon.

'And of his woundyng this is the worst of alle,   470
When he hurteth he doth so cruel wreche
And maketh the seke for to crie and calle
[V]nto his foo for to ben his leche—
And h[a]rd hit ys [than] for a man to seche
Vpon the poynt of dethe in [iu]pardie   475
Vnto his foo to fynde remedye.

'Thus fareth hit now euen[ly] by me
That to my foo that yaf my[n] hert a wounde
Mot axe grace, mercy and pite,
And namely ther wher noon may be founde,   480
For now my sore my leche wol confounde;
And God of kynde so hath set myn vre
My lyves foo to haue my wounde in cure.

'Alas the while now that I was borne
Or that I euer saugh the bright[e] sonne,   485
For now I se that ful longe aforne
Or I was born my destanye was sponne
By Parcas sustren to sle me if they conne:
For they my dethe shopen or my shert,
Oonly for trouth I may hit not astert.   490

'The myghty goddes also of Nature
That vnder God hath the gouernaunce
Of worldy things commytted to her cure,
Disposed hath thro her wyse purveaunce
To yive my lady so moch suffisaunce   495
Of al vertues and therwithal purvyde
To mordre trouth hath take Daunger to guyde.

'For bounte, beaute, shape and semelyhed,
Prudence, wit[t]e, passyngly fairenesse,
Benigne port, glad chere with loulyhed,   500
Of womanhed ryght plentevous largesse,
Nature in her fully did empresse
Whan she her wroght—and altherlast Dysdeyne
To hinder Trouth she made her chambreleyne,

'When Mystryst also and Fals-Suspecion   505
With Mysbeleve she made for to be
Chefe of counseyle, to this conclusion,
For to exile Routhe and eke Pite:
Out of her court to make Mercie fle
So that Dispite now haldeth forth her reyn   510
Thro hasty beleve of tales that men feyn.

'And thus I am for my trouth, alas,
Mordred and slayn with wordis sharp and kene,
Gilt[e]les, God wote, of al trespas,
And lye and blede vpon this colde grene.   515
Now mercie, suete, mercye my lyves quene:
And to your grace of mercie yet I prey,
In your seruise that your man may dey.

'But [if] so be that I shal deye algate
And that I shal non other mercye haue,   520
Yet of my dethe let this be the date
That by your wil I was broght to my graue.
[O]r, hastely, yf that y[ow] list me saue,
My sharpe woundes that ake so and blede,
Of mercie charme, and als of womanhede: 525

'For other charme pleynly ys ther noon,
But only mercie to helpe[n] in this case.
For thogh my wounde[s] blede euer in oon,
My lyve, my deth, ston[deth] in your grace.
And thogh my gilt[e] be nothing, alace,   530
I axe mercie in al my best entent
Redy to dye yf that ye assent.

'For ther ayen[e]s shal I neuer strive
In word ne werke, pleynly I ne may,
For leuer I haue then to be alyve   535
To dye sothly and hit be her to pay,
Ye, thogh hit be this ech[e] same day,
Or when that euer hit l[i]st[e] to deuyse,
Sufficeth me to deye in your seruise.

'And God that knowest the thoght of euery wyght   540
Ryght a[s] hit is, in [al] thing thou maist se,
Yet er I dye, with al my ful[le] myght
Louly I prey, to grante[n] vnto me
That ye, goodly, feir[e], fressh and fre,
Which sle me oonly for defaut of routhe,   545
Er then I die, [ye] may know my trouthe.

'For that in soth suffic[et]h [vnto] me,
And she hit knowe in euery circumstaunce,
And after I am wel [a]payed that she,
Yf that she lyst, of deth to do vengeaunce   550
Vnto me that am vnder her legeaunce;
Hit sit me not her doom to dysobey
But at her lust[e] wilfully to dey.

'Without[e] gruching or rebellion
In wil or worde holy I assent   555
Or eny maner contradixion
Fully to be at her commaundement.
And if I dye, in my testament
My hert I send and my spirit also
Whatsoeuer she list with hem to do.   560

'And alderlast[e] to her womanhede
And to her mercy me I recommaunde
That lye now here betixt[e] hope and drede
Abyding pleynly what she list commaunde;
For vtterly (this nys no demaunde)   565
Welcome to me while [that] me lasteth brethe,
Ryght at her cho[i]se, wher hit be lyf or dethe.

'In this mater more what myght I seyn,
Sith in her hond and her wil ys alle:
Both lyf and deth, my ioy and al my peyn.   570
And fynally my hest[e] holde I shall
Til [my] spirit be destanye fa[ta]l
When that her list[e] fro my body w[e]nde.
Haue her my trouth, and thus I make an [e]nde.'

And with that worde he gan sike as sore   575
Lyke as his hert[e] ryve wolde atweyne
And h[e]ld his pese and spak [no] worde more.
But for to se his woo and mortal peyn,
The teres gan[ne] fro myn eyen reyn
Ful pit[o]usly, for [v]erry inward routhe   580
That I hym saw so langwysshing for trouthe.

And al this w[h]ile myself I kep[te] close
Among the bowes and myself gan hide.
Til at the last the woful man arose
And to a logge went[e] ther besyde   585
Wher al the May his custom was t'abide,
Sole to compleyn of his peynes kene,
Fro yer to yer vnder the bowes grene.

And for because that hit drow to the nyght
And that the sunne his ark divrnall   590
Ipassed was so that his persaunt lyght,
His bryght[e] bemes and his stremes all
W[e]re in the wawes of the water fall,
Vnder the bordure of our occean
His chare of gold his course so swyftly ran,   595

And while the twilyght and the rowes rede
Of Phebus lyght wer deaurat a lyte,
A penne I toke and gan me fast[e] spede
The woful pleynt[e] of this man to write,
Worde by worde as he dyd endyte: 600
Lyke as I herde and coud him tho reporte
I haue here set, youre hertis to dysporte.

If oght be mys, leyth the wite on me
For I am worthy for to bere the blame
Yf eny thing[e] mys-reported be   605
To make this dite for to seme lame
Thro myn vnk[o]nnyng. But for to s[ey] the same,
Lyke as this man his compleynt did expresse,
I axe mercie and foryeuenesse.

And as I wrote me thoght I sawe aferre   610
Fer in the west lustely appere
Esperus, the goodly bryght[e] sterre,
So glad, so feire, so persaunt eke of chere:
I mene Venus with her bemys clere
That heuy hertis oonly to releve   615
Is wont of custom for to shew at eve.

And as I fast[e] fel dovn on my kne
And euen thus to her I gan to preie:
'O lady Venus, so fe[i]re vpon to se,
Let not this man for his trouthe dey,   620
For that ioy thou haddest when thou ley
With Mars thi knyght wh[en] Vulcanus [yow] founde
And with a cheyne vnvisible yow bounde

64

'Togedre both tweyne in the same while
That al the court above celestial   625
At your shame gan[ne] laughe and smyle.
O feire lady, wel-willy founde at al,
Comfort to carefull, O goddesse immortal,
Be helpyng now and do thy diligence
To let the stremes of thin influence   630

'Descende dovn in furthryng of the trouthe,
Namely of hem that [lye] in sorow bounde;
Shew now thy myght and on her wo haue routhe
Er fals Daunger sle hem and confounde.
And specialy let thy myght be founde   635
For to socour (what so that thou may)
The trew[e] man that in the erber lay.

'And al[le] trew[e] further for his sake,
O glad[e] sterre, O lady Venus myn,
And [cause] his lady him to grace take,   640
Hert of stele to mercy so enclyne,
Er that thy bemes go vp to declyne
And er that thou now go fro vs adoune
For that love thou haddest to Adon.'

And when [that] she was goon [vn]to her rest   645
I rose anon and home to bed[de] went
For [v]erry wery, me thoght hit for the best.
Preying thus in al my best entent
That al[le] trew that be with Daunger shent
With mercie may, in reles of her peyn,   650
Recured be er May come eft a[g]e[y]n.

And for that I ne may noo lenger wake,
Farewel ye louers al[le] that be trewe,
Praying to God, and thus my leve I take,
That er the sun tomorow be ryse[n] newe   655
And er he haue ayen his rosen hewe,
That eche of yow may haue such a grace
His ovn lady in armes to embrace.

I mene thus, that in al honeste,
Withoute more, ȝe may togedre speke   66•
Whatso y[e] list[e] at good liberte,
That eche may to other her hert breke,
On Ielosie oonly to be wreke
That hath so longe of malice and envie
Werred Trouthe with his tiranye.   66•

L'envoye

Princes, pleseth hit your benignite
This litil dite [for] to haue in mynde,
Of womanhede also for to se,
[That] your trew man may sum mercie fynde,
And Pite eke that long hath be [be]hynde   67•
Let [hym] ayein be prouoked to grace.
For by my trouth, hit is ayen[e]s kynde
Fals Daunger for to occupie his place.

L'envoye de quare

Go litel quayre, go vnto my lyves quene,
And my verry hertis souereigne,   67•
And be ryght glad for [that] she shal the sene,
Such is thi grace, but I, alas, in peyne
Am left behinde and not to whom to pleyn,
For Mercie, Routhe, Grace and eke Pite
Exiled be that I may not ateyne   68•
Recure to fynde of [m]yn adversite.

THE TEMPLE OF GLAS

For thou3t, constreint and greuous heuines,
For pensifhede, and for hei3 distres,
To bed I went nov þis oþir ny3t
Whan þat Lucina wiþ hir pale li3t
Was ioyned last wiþ Phebus in Aquarie,   5
Amyd Decembre, when of Ianuarie
Ther be kalendes of þe nwe yere,
And derk Diane, ihorned, noþing clere,
Had hir bemys vndir a mysty cloude:
Wiþin my bed for sore I gan me shroude,   10
Al desolate for constreint of my wo,
The long[e] ny3t waloing to and fro,
Til at[te] last, er I gan taken kepe,
Me did oppresse a sodein dedeli slepe,
Wiþin þe which me þou3t[e] þat I was   15
Rauysshid in spirit in [a] temple of glas—
I nyst[e] how, ful fer in wildirnes—
That foundid was, as bi lik[ly]nesse,
Not opon stele, but on a craggy roche,
Like ise ifrore. And as I did approche,   20
Again þe sonne that shone, me þou3t, so clere
As eny cristal, and euer nere and nere
As I gan neigh this grisli dredful place,
I wex astonyed: the li3t so in my face
Bigan to smyte, so persing euer in one   25
On euere part, where þat I gan gone,
That I ne my3t noþing, as I would,
Abouten me considre and bihold '
The wondre hestres, for bri3tnes of þe sonne;
Til at[te] last certein skyes donne,   30

Wiþ wind ichaced, haue her cours iwent
Tofore þe stremes of Titan and iblent,
So þat I myȝt, wiþin and withoute,
Whereso I walk, biholden me aboute,
Forto report the fasoun and manere   35
Of al þis place, þat was circulere
In compaswise, round b'entaile wrouȝt.
And when þat I hade long gone and souȝt,
I fond a wiket, and entrid in as fast
Into þe temple, and myn eiȝen cast   40
On euere side, now lowe and eft aloft.
And riȝt anone, as I gan walken soft,
If I þe soth ariȝt report[e] shal,
I sauȝe depeynt opon euere wal,
From est to west, ful many a faire image   45
Of sondri louers, lich as þei were of age
Isette in ordre, aftir þei were trwe,
Wiþ lifli colours wondir fressh of hwe.
And, as me þouȝt, I sauȝe somme sit and stonde,
And some kneling wiþ billis in hir honde,   50
And some with compleint, woful and pitous,
Wiþ doleful chere to putten to Venus,
So as she sate fleting in þe se,
Vpon hire wo forto haue pite.
And first of al I saugh þere of Car[ta]ge   55
Dido þe quene, so goodli of visage,
That gan complein hir aduenture and caas,
Hov she deceyued was of Eneas,
For al his hestis and his oþis sworne,
And said: 'alas, þat euer she was borne,'   60
Whan þat she saugh þat ded she most[e] be.
And next I saugh the compleint of Medee,
Ho[u] þat she was falsed of Iason.
And nygh bi Venus saugh I sit Addoun,
And al þe maner hov þe bore him slough,   65
For whom she wepte and hade pein inouȝe.
There saugh I also hov Penalope,

68

For she so long hir lord ne my3t[e] se,
Ful oft[e] wex of colour pale and grene.
And aldernext was þe fressh[e] quene,   70
I mene Alceste, the noble trw[e] wyfe,
And for Admete hou sh[e] lost hir life,
And for hir trouth, if I shal not lie,
Hou she was turnyd to a dai[e]sie.
There was [also] Grisildis innocence,   75
And al hir mekenes and hir pacience.
There was eke Isaude—and meni anoþir mo—
And al þe turment and al þe cruel wo,
That she hade for Tristram al hir liue.
And hou þat Tesbie her hert[e] did[e] rife   80
Wiþ þilk[e] swerd of him Piramus;
And al þe maner hou þat Theseus
The Minatawre slow amyd þe hous
That was for-wrynk[l]ed bi craft of Dedalus,
When þat he was in prison shette in Crete.   85
And hou þat Phillis felt of loues hete
The grete fire of Demophon, alas,
And for his falshed and [for] his trepas
Vpon þe walles depeint men my3t[e] se
Hov she was honged vpon a filbert tre.   90
And mani a stori, mo þen I rekin can,
Were in þe tempil, and hov þat Paris wan
The faire Heleyne, þe lusti fressh[e] quene,
And hov Achilles was for Policene
Islain vnwarli within Troi[e] toune: 95
Al þis sawe I [walkynge vp and doun.
Ther saw I] writen eke þe hole tale,
Hov Philomene into a ny3tyngale
Iturned was, and Progne vnto a swalow;
And hov þe Sabyns in hir maner halowe   100
The fest of Lucresse 3it in Rome tovne.
There saugh I also þe sorov of Palamoun,
That he in prison felt, and al þe smert,
And hov þat he, þurugh vnto his hert,

Was hurt vnwarli þurugh casting of an eyȝe 105
Of faire fressh, þe ȝung[e] Emelie,
And al þe strife bitwene him and his broþir,
And hou þat one fauȝt eke with þat oþir
Wiþin þe groue, til þei bi Theseus
Acordid were, as Chaucer telliþ us. 110
And forþirmore, as I gan bihold,
I sawȝ hov Phebus with an [arow] of gold
Iwoundid was, þuruȝoute in his side,
Onli bi envie of þe god Cupide,
And hou þat [Dane] vnto a laurer tre 115
Iturned was, when [that] she did fle.
And hou þat Ioue gan to chaunge his cope
Oonli for loue of þe faire Europe,
And into [a] bole, when he did hir sue,
List of his godhode his fourme to transmwe; 120
And hou þat he bi transmutacioun
The shap gan take of Amphitrioun
For his Almen, so passi[n]g of beaute;
So was he hurt, for al his deite,
Wiþ loues dart, and myȝt it not ascape. 125
There sauȝ I also hou þat Mars was take
Of Vulcanus, and wiþ Venus found,
And wiþ þe cheynes invisible bound.
Ther was also al þe poes[i]e
Of him, Mercurie, and Phil[o]log[y]e, 130
And hou þat she, for hir sapience,
Iweddit was to god of eloquence,
And hou þe Musis lowli did obeie,
High into heuen þis ladi to conuei,
And with hir song hov she was magnified 135
With Iubiter to bein istellified.
And vppermore depeint men myȝt[e] se,
Hov with hir ring, goodli Canace
Of euere foule þe ledne and þe song
Coud vndirstond, as she welk hem among; 140
And hou hir broþir so oft holpen was

In his myschefe bi þe stede of bras.
And forþermore in þe tempil were
Ful mani a þousand of louers, here and þere,
In sondri wise redi to complein   145
Vnto þe goddes, of hir wo and pein,
Hou þei were hindred, some for envie,
And hou þe serpent of fals Ielousie
Ful many a louer haþ iput obak
And caus[e]les on hem ilaid a lak.   150
And some þer were þat pleyned on absence
That werin exiled and put oute of presence
Thuruȝ wikkid tungis and fals suspecioun
[Withoute mercy nor remyssyoun.]
And oþer eke her seruise spent in vain   155
Thuruȝ cruel Daunger and also bi Disdain.
And some also þat loued, soþ to sein,
And of her ladi were not louyd again.
And oþir eke, þat for pouerte
Durst [i]n no wise hir grete aduersite   160
Discure ne open lest þai were refusid.
And some for wanting also werin accusid,
And oþir eke þat loued secreli
And of her ladi durst aske no merci
Lest þat she would of hem haue despite.   165
And some also þat putten ful grete wite
On double louers þat loue þingis nwe,
Thurgh whos falsnes hindred be þe trwe.
And some þer were, as it is oft[e] found,
That for her ladi meny a blodi wounde   170
Endurid haþ in mani [a] regioun
Whiles þat anoþer haþ poscessioun
Al of his ladi and beriþ awai þe fruyte
Of his labur and of al his suyte.
And oþer eke compleyned on Riches: 175
Hou he with Tresour doþ his besines
To wynnen al, againes kynd and ryȝt,
Wher trw louers haue noon force ne myȝt.

And some þer were, as maydens ȝung of age,
That pleined sore with peping and with rage   180
That þei were coupled, againes al nature,
Wiþ croked elde þat mai not long endure
Forto perfourme þe lust of loues plai:
For it ne sit not vnto fressh[e] May
Forto be coupled to oold Ianuari.   185
Thei ben so diuers þat þei most[e] varie,
For eld is grucching and malencolious,
Ay ful of ire and suspecious,
And iouth entendeþ to ioy and lustines,
To myrth and plai and to al gladnes.   190
Allas þat euer þat it shuld[e] fal,
[S]o su[o]te sugre icoupled be with gal.
These yong[e] folk criden oft[e] siþe
And praied Venus hir pouer forto kiþe
Vpon þis myschef and shape remedie.   195
And riȝt anon I herd oþir crie
With sobbing teris and with ful pitous soune,
Tofore þe goddes, bi lamentacioun,
That conseiles in hir tender youþe
And in childhode (as it is oft[e] couþe)   200
Yrendred were into religioun
Or þei hade yeris of discresioun,
That al her life cannot but complein,
In wide copis perfeccion to feine:
Ful couertli to curen al hir smert   205
And shew þe contrarie outward of her hert.
Thus saugh I wepen many a faire maide,
Tha[t] on hir freendis al þe wite þei leide.
And oþer next I saugh þere in gret rage
That þei were maried in her tendir age   210
Wiþoute fredom of eleccioun,
Wher loue haþ seld domynacioun,
For loue, at laarge and [at] liberte,
Would freli chese and not with such trete.
And oþer saugh I ful oft wepe and wring   215

[That they in men founde swych variynge,]
To loue a seisoun, while þat beaute floureþ,
And bi disdein so vngoodli loureþ
On hir þat whilom he callid his ladi dere,
That was to him so plesaunt and entere.   220
But lust with fairnes is so overgone
That in her hert trouþ abideþ none.
And som also I sauȝ in teris reyne
And pitousli on God and Kynd[e] pleyne,
That euer þei would on eny creature   225
So mych beaute, passing bi mesure,
Set on a woman, to yeue occasioun
A man to loue to his confusioun:
And nameli þere where he shal haue no grace,
For wiþ a loke, forthbi as he doþ pace,   230
Ful oft falleþ, þuruȝ casting of an yȝe
A man is woundid þat he most nedis deye
That neuer efter, perauenture, shal hir se.
Whi wil God don so gret a cruelte
To eny man or to his creature   235
To maken him so mych wo endure
For hir purcaas whom he shal in no wise
Reioise neuer, but so forþ in iewise
Ledin his life til þat he be graue?
For he ne durst of hir no merci craue   240
And eke, perauenture, þouȝ he durst and would,
He can not wit where he hir find[e] shuld.
I saugh þere eke, and þerof had I rouþe,
That som were hindred for couetise and slouth,
And some also for her hastines,   245
And oþer eke for hir reklesnes.
   But alderlast as I walk and biheld,
Beside Pallas wiþ hir cristal sheld,
Tofore þe statue of Venus set on height
Hov þat þer knelid a ladi in my siȝt   250
Tofore þe goddes, which riȝt as þe sonne
Passeþ þe sterres and doþ hir stremes donne;

And Lucifer to voide þe nyȝtes sorow
In clerenes passeþ erli bi þe morow;
And so as Mai haþ þe souereinte   255
Of euere moneþ of fairnes and beaute;
And as þe rose in swetnes and odoure
Surmounteþ floures and bawme of al licour
Haueþ þe pris; and as þe rubie briȝt
Of al stones in beaute and in siȝt   260
(As it is know) haþ þe regalie:
Riȝt so þis ladi wiþ hir goodli eiȝe
And with þe stremes of hir loke so briȝt
Surmounteþ al þurugh beaute in my siȝte.
Forto tel hir gret semelines,   265
Hir womanhed, hir port, and hir fairnes,
It was a meruaile hou euer þat Nature
Coude in hir werkis make a creature
So aungellike, so goodli on to se,
So femynyn or passing of beaute,   270
Whos sonnyssh here briȝter þan gold were,
Lich Phebus bemys shynyng in his spere,
The goodlihed eke of hir fresshli face,
So replenysshid of beaute and of grace,
So wel ennuyd bi Nature and depeint   275
That rose and lileis togedir were so meint,
So egalli bi good proporcioun,
That, as me þouȝt, in myn inspeccioun
I gan meruaile hou God or werk of Kynd
Miȝten of beaute such a tresour find   280
To yeven hir so passing excellence.
For in good faiþ, þuruȝ hir heiȝ presence
The tempil was enlumynd enviroun.
And forto speke of condicioun
She was þe best þat myȝt[e] ben on lyve: 285
For þer was noon þat wiþ hir myȝt[e] striue,
To speke of bounte [o]r of gentilles,
Of womanhed or of lowlynes,
Of curtesie or of goodlihed,

74

Of spech, of chere or of semlyhed,   290
Of port benygne and of daliaunce
The best[e] tauȝt, and þerto of plesaunce
She was þe wel, and eke of oneste
An exemplarie, and mirrour eke was she
Of secrenes, of trouth, of faythfulnes,   295
And to al oþer ladi and maistres,
To sue vertu, whoso list to lere.
And so þis ladi, benigne and humble of chere,
Kneling I saugh al clad in grene and white
Tofore Venus, goddes of al delite,   300
Enbrouded al with stones and perre
So richeli þat ioi it was to se,
Wiþ sondri rolles on hir garnement
Forto expoune þe trouth of hir entent,
And shew fulli, þat for hir humbilles,   305
And for hir vertu and hir stabilnes,
That she was rote of womanli plesaunce.
Therfore hir woord wiþoute variaunce
Enbrouded was (as men myȝt[e] se):
DE MIEULX EN MIEULX with stones and perre.   310
This to sein þat she, þis benigne,
From bettir to bettir hir hert[e] doþ resigne
And al hir wil to Venus þe goddes,
Whan þat hir list hir harmes to redresse.
For, as me þouȝt, sumwhat bi hir chere,   315
Forto compleyne she hade gret desire:
For in hir hond she held a litel bil
Forto declare þe somme of al hir wil
And to þe goddes hir quarel forto shewe,
[Th'effect of which was this in wordys fewe:]   320

I

'O ladi Venus, modir of Cupide,
That al þis wor[l]d hast in gouernaunce,
And hertes high þat [hauteyn ben] of pride
Enclynyst mekeli to þin obeissaunce,

Causer of ioie, relese of penaunce,   325
And with þi stremes canst eueri þing discerne
Thuru3 heuenli fire of loue þat is eterne,

2

'O blisful sterre, persant and ful of li3t,
Of bemys gladsome, devoider of derknes,
Cheif recounford after þe blak ny3t,   330
To voide woful oute of her heuynes,
Take nov good hede, ladi and goddesse,
So þat my bil 3our grace may atteyne,
Redresse to finde of þat I me compleyne.

3

'For I am bounde to þing þat I nold: 335
Freli to chese þere lak I liberte,
And so I want of þat myn hert[e] would,
The bodi knyt, alþou3e my þou3t be fre;
So þat I most, of necessite,
Myn hertis lust outward contrarie—   340
Thogh we be on, þe dede most varie.

4

'Mi worship sauf, I faile eleccioun:
Again al ri3t, boþe of God and Kynd,
There to be knit vndir subieccion:
Fro whens ferre [a]r boþ witte and mynde,   345
Mi þou3t goþe forþe, mi bodi is behind,
For I am here and yonde my remembraunce;
Atwixen two so hang I in balaunce.

5

'Deuoide of ioie, of wo I haue plente:
What I desire, þat mai I not possede: 350
For þat I nold is redi aye to me,
And þat I loue, forto swe I drede:
To my desire contrarie is my mede.

And þus I stond, departid euen on tweyn,
Of wille and dede ilaced in a chaine.   355

6

'For þou3 I brenne with feruence and with hete,
Wiþin myn hert I mot complein of cold;
And þuru3 myn axcesse tho3e I sweltre and swete,
Me to complein (God wot) I am not boold
Vnto no wi3t—nor a woord vnfold   360
Of al my peyne (allas þe hard[e] stond)
That hatter brenne þat closid is my wounde.

7

'For he þat hath myn hert[e] feiþfulli
And hole my luf in al honesti
Withoute chaunge, al be it secreli,   365
I haue no space wiþ him forto be.
O ladi Venus, consider nov and se
Vnto þe effecte and compleint of my bil,
Siþ life and deþ I put al in þi wil.'

8

And þo me þou3t þe goddes did enclyne   370
Mekeli hir hede, and softli gan expresse
That in short tyme hir turment shuld[e] fyne,
And hou of him, for whom al hir distresse
Contynued had and al hir heuynes,
She [sh]ould haue ioy, and of hir purgatorie   375
Be holpen sone and so forþ-lyue in glorie,

9

And seid[e]: 'Dou3ter, for þe sad[de] trouþe,
The feiþful menyng and þe innocence
That planted bene withouten eny slouþe
In 3our persone, deuoide of al defence,   380
So haue atteyned to oure audience
That þuru3 oure grace 3e shul be wel releuyd,
I 3ov bihote of al þat haþ 3ov greued.

'And for þat ȝe euer be of oon entent
Withoute chaunge or mutabilite,   385
Haue in ȝour peynes ben so pacient
To take louli ȝoure aduersite
(And þat so long þuruȝ þe cruelte
Of old Saturne, my fadur vnfortuned,)
Your wo shal nov no lenger be contuned.   390

'And þinkiþ þis: within a litel while
It shal asswage and ouerpassen sone.
For men bi laiser passen meny a myle,
And oft also, aftir a dropping mone,
The weddir clereþ, and whan þe storme is done   395
The sonne shineþ in his spere briȝt,
And ioy awakiþ whan wo is put to fliȝt.

'Remembreþ eke, hou neuer ȝit no wiȝt
Ne came to wirship withoute some debate,
And folk also reiossh[e] more of liȝt   400
That þei wiþ derknes were waped and amate.
Non manis chaunce is alwai fortunate,
Ne no wiȝt preiseþ of sugre þe swetnes
But þei afore haue tasted bitternes.

'Grisild[e] was assaied at[te] ful   405
That turned aftir to hir encrese of ioye.
Penalope gan eke for sorowis dul
For þat [her] lord abode so long at Troie.
Also þe turment þere coude no man akoye
Of Dorigene, flour of al Britayne: 410
Thus euer ioy is ende and fine of paine.

'And trusteþ þus, for conclusioun,
The end of sorow is ioi ivoide of drede.
For holi saintis þuruȝ her passioun
Haue heuen iwonne for her souerain mede;   415
And plenti gladli foloiþ after nede:
And so, my douȝter, after ȝour greuauns
I ȝov bihote ȝe shul haue ful plesaunce.

15

'For euer of Loue þe maner and þe guyse
Is forto hurt his seruant and to wounde.   420
And when þat he haþ tauȝte hem his emprise
He can in ioi make hem to abounde.
And siþ þat ȝe haue in my lase be bound
Wiþoute grucching or rebellion,
Ye most of riȝt haue consolacioun.   425

16

'This is to sein (douteþ neuer a dele)
That ȝe shal haue ful poss[ess]ion
Of him þat ȝe cherissh nov so wel
In honest maner wiþoute offencioun,
Bicause I cnowe your entencion   430
Is truli set, in parti and in al,
To loue him best and most in special.

17

'For he þat ȝe haue chosen ȝow to serue
Shal be to ȝow such as ȝe desire,
Wiþoute chaunge, fulli, til he sterue.   435
So with my brond I haue him set afire,
And with my grace I shal him so enspire,
That he in hert shal be ryȝt at ȝour will,
Wheþir ȝe list to saue him or to spill.

18

'For vnto ȝow his hert I shal so lowe,   440
Wiþoute spot of eny doubelnes,
That he ne shal escape fro þe bowe
(Thouȝ þat him list þuruȝ vnstidfastnes)
I mene of Cupide þat shal him so distres
Vnto your hond[e] wiþ þe arow of gold,   445
That he ne shal escapen þouȝ he would.

19

'And siþe ȝe list of pite and of grace,
In vertu oonli his ȝouþe to cherice,
I shal, b'aspectes of my benygne face,
Make him t'eschwe euere synne and vice,   450
So þat he shal haue no maner spice
In his corage to loue þingis nwe:
He shal to ȝou so plain be found and trwe.'

20

And whan þis goodli, faire, fressh of hwe,
Humble and benygne, of trouth crop and rote   455
Conceyued ha[d] hov Venus gan to rwe,
On hir praier plainli to do bote,
To chaunge hir bitter atones into soote,
She fel on kneis of heiȝ deuocion
And in þis wise bigan hir orisoun: 460

21

'Heiȝest of high, quene and emperice,
Goddes of Loue, of goode ȝit þe best,
Þat þuruȝ ȝour [beaute] withouten eny vice
Whilom conquered þe appel at þe fest
That Iubiter þurugh [his hygh request]   465
To al þe goddesse aboue celestial
Made in his paleis most imperial:

22

'To ȝov my ladi, vpholder of my life,
Mekeli I þanke, so as I mai suffice,
That ȝe list nov with hert ententif   470
So graciousli for me to deuyse,
That while I liue, with humble sacrifise,
Vpon ȝour auters, ȝour fest ȝere bi ȝere,
I shal encense casten in þe fire.

23

'For of ȝoure grace I am ful reconsiled   475
From euere trouble vnto ioy and ease,
That sorois al from me ben exiled,
[S]iþ [y]e, my ladi, list nov to [appese]
Mi peynes old and fulli my disease
Vnto gladnes so sodeinli to turne,   480
Hauyng no cause from hennesforþ to mourne.

24

'For siþin ȝe so mekeli list to daunte
To my seruyce him þat loueþ me best,
And of ȝour bounte so graciousli to graunte
That he ne shal varie, þouȝe him list,   485
Wherof myn hert is fulli brouȝ[t] to rest:
For nov and euer, o ladi myn benygne,
That hert and wil to ȝow hole I resigne.

25

'Thanking yow with al my ful[le] h[e]rt,
Þat, of ȝoure grace and visitacioun,   490
So humb[e]li list him to conuert
Fulli to bene at my subieccioun
Withoute chaunge or transmutacioun
Vnto his l[a]st: [now] laude and reuerence
Be to youre name and [to] your excellence.   495

'This al and some and chefe of my request
And hool substaunce of myn hole entent,
Yow þankyng euer of ȝour graunt and hest,
Boþ nou and euer, þat ȝe me grace haue sent
To conquere him þat neuer shal repent   50c
Me forto serue and humb[e]li to please
As final tresur [of] myn hertis ease.'

And þan anon Venus cast adoune
Into hir lap braunchis white and grene
Of haw[e]thorn þat wenten enviroun   505
Aboute hir hed, þat ioi it was to sene,
And bade hir kepe hem honestli and clene:
Which shul not fade ne nevir wexin old
If she hir bidding kepe as she haþ told:

'And as þese bowȝis be boþ faire and swete,   51c
Followiþ þ'effect þat þei do specifie:
This is to sein, boþe in cold and hete,
Beþ of oon hert and of o fantasie,
As ar þese leues þe which mai not die
Þuruȝ no dures of stormes þat be kene,   515
Nomore in winter þen in somer grene.

'Riȝt so b'ensaumple, for wele or for wo,
For ioy, turment, or [for] aduersite,
Wherso þat fortune fauour or be foo,
For pouert, riches, or prosperite,   52c
That ȝe youre hert kepe in oo degre
To loue him best, for noþing þat ȝe feine,
Whom I haue bound so lowe vndir ȝoure cheine.'

And with þat worde þe goddes shoke hir hede
And was in peas and spake as þo nomore.   525
And þerwithal, ful femynyne of drede,
Me þouȝte þis ladi sighen gan ful sore
And said again: 'Ladi þat maist restore
Hertes in ioy from her aduersite,
To do ȝoure will *de mieulx en mieulx magre.'*   530

Explicit prima pars ¶ Icy commence le secund parti de la songe.

Thus euer sleping and dremyng as I lay,
Within þe tempil me þouȝt[e] þat I sey
Gret pres of folk with murmur wondirful
To bronte and sho[v]e (the tempil was so ful),
Euerich ful bise in his owne cause,   535
That I ne may, shortli in a clause,
Descriuen al þe rithes and þe gise,
And eke I want kunnyng to deuyse
Hou som þer were with blood, encense and mylk,
And som with floures sote and soft as silk,   540
An[d] som with sparovis and dovues faire and white,
That forto offerin gan hem to delite
Vnto þe goddes, wiþ sigh and with praier
Hem to relese of þat þai most desire.
That for þe prese, shortli to conclude,   545
I went my wai for þe multitude
Me to refressh oute of the prese allone.
And be myself me þouȝt, as I gan gone
Wiþin þe estres and gan awhile tarie,
I saugh a man þat welke al solitarie,   550
That as me semed for heuines and dole
Him to complein, þat he walk so sole
Wiþoute espiing of eni oþir wiȝt.
And if I shal descryuen him ariȝt,
Nere þat he hade ben in heuynes   555
Me þouȝt he was—to speke of semelynes,

Of shappe, of fourme and also of stature—
The most passing þat euir ȝit Nature
Made in hir werkis, and like to ben a man.
And þerwithal, as I reherse can,   560
Of face and chere þe most gracious
To be biloued, happi and ewrous.
But as it semed outward in his chere
That he compleyned for lak of his desire.
For, by [h]ymself, as he walk vp and doune,   565
I herd him make a lamentacioun,
And seid: 'Allas, what þing mai þis be?
That nou am bound þat whilom was so fre
And went at laarge at myn eleccioun,
Nou am I cauȝt vnder subieccioun   570
Forto bicome a verre homagere
To god o[f] Loue, where þat, er I come here
Felt in myn hert riȝt nouȝt of loues peine:
But nov of nwe within his fire cheyne
I am enbraced, so þat I mai not striue,   575
To loue and serue whiles þat I am on lyue
The goodli fressh in þe tempil yonder
I saugh riȝt nov—þat I hade wonder
Hou euer God, forto reken all,
Myȝt make a þing so celestial,   580
So avngellike on erþe to appere.
For wiþ þe stremes of hir eyen clere
I am iwoundid euen to þe hert,
Þat fro þe deþ (I trow) I mai not stert.
And most I mervaile þat so sodenli   585
I was iȝolde to bene at hir merci
Wherso hi[r] list, to do me lyue or deie.
Wiþoute more I most hir lust obeie
And take mekeli my sodein auentur.
For siþ my life, my deþ, and eke my cure   590
Is in hir hond it would[e] not auaile
To gruch agein: for of þis bataile
The palme is hires, and pleinli þe victorie.

84

If I rebelled, honour non ne glorie
I my3t[e] not in no wise acheue. 595
Siþ I am yold, hou shuld I þan preue
To gif a werre (I wot it wil not be)
Thou3 I be loos, at laarge I mai not fle.
O god of Loue, hov sharp is nov þin arowe,
Hou maist þou nov so cruelli and narowe 600
Withoute cause hurt[e] me and wound,
And ta[k]e non hede my soris forto sound?
But lich a brid þat fleith at hir desire
Til sodeinli within þe pantire
She is icau3t, þou3 she were late at laarge, 605
A nwe tempest for-casteþ now my baarge,
Now vp nov dovne with wind it is so blowe,
So am I p[o]ssid and almost ouerþrowe,
Fordriue in dirknes with many a sondri wawe.
Alas, when shal þis tempest ouerdrawe 610
To clere þe skies of myn aduersite;
The lode-ster [I wot] I may not se,
It is so hid with cloudes þat ben blake.
Alas, when wil þis turment ouershake
I can not wit, for who is hurt of nwe 615
And blediþ inward til he wex pale of hwe
And haþ his wound vnwarli fressh and grene,
[He] is not kouþe vnto þe harmes kene
Of my3ti Cupide þat can so hertis davnte
That noman may in your werre him vaunte 620
To get a pris but oonli bi mekenes.
For þere ne vaileþ strif ne sturdines,
So mai I sain, þat with a loke am yold
And haue no power to stryue þou3e I would.
Thus stand I euen bitwix life and deþ 625
To loue and serue while þat I haue breþ
In such a place where I dar not pleyn,
Lich him þat is in turment and in pein
And knoweþ not to whom forto discure.
For þere þat I haue hoolly set my cure 630

85

I dar not wele, for drede and for daunger
And for vnknowe, tellen hou þe fire
Of louis brond is kindled in my brest.
Thus am I murdrid and slain at þe lest
So preueli within my[n owne] þouȝt.   635
O ladi Venus, whom þat I haue souȝt,
So wisse me now what me is best to do
Þat am distrauȝt within myself[en] so
That I ne wot what way for [to] turne,
Sauf be myself solein forto mourne   640
Hanging in balaunce bitwix hope and drede
Withoute comfort, remedie or rede.
For Hope biddiþ pursue and assay,
And Drede againward answeriþ and saiþ nai.
And now wiþ Hope I am iset on loft,   645
But Drede and Daunger, hard and noþing softe,
Haue ouerþrowe my trust and put adoune.
Nou at my laarge, nou feterid in prisone,
Nov in turment, nov in souerein glorie,
Nou in paradise and nov in purgatorie,   650
As man dispeired in a double were,
Born vp wiþ Hope—and þan anon Daunger
Me drawiþ abak and seith it shal not be.
For where as I, of myn aduersite,
Am [b]old somwhile merci to requere,   655
Þan comeþ Dispeire and ginneþ me to lere
A nwe lessoun, to hope ful contrar[i]e
(Thei be so diuers [þat] would do me varie).
And þus I stond dismaied in a traunce:
For whan þat Hope were likli me t'auaunce   660
For drede I tremble and dar a woord not speke.
And if it so be þat I not oute breke
To tel þe harmes þat greuen me so sore
But in mys[elf] encrese hem more and more
And to be slain fulli me delite,   665
Þen of my deþ sh[e] is noþing to wite.
For but if she my constreint pleinli knwe

Hou shuld she euer opon my paynis rwe.
Thus oft[e] tyme with Hope I am imevid
To tel hir al of þat I am so greued,   670
And to ben hardi, on me forto take
To axe merci; but Drede þan doþ awake
And þo[r]uȝ wanhope answeriþ me again
Þat bettir were, þen she haue disdeyne,
To deie at onys, vnknow of eny wiȝt.   675
And þerewith[al] bitt Hope anon riȝt
Me to be bold, to prayen hir of grace:
For siþ al vertues be portreid in hir face
It were not sitting þat merci were bihind.
And riȝt anone within myself I finde   680
A nwe ple brouȝt on me with Drede
Þat me so maseþ þat I se no spede,
Bicause he seith, þat stonieþ al my bloode,
I am so symple and she is so goode.
Thus Hope and Drede in me wil not ceasse   685
To plete and stryue myn harmes to encrese.
But at þe hardest ȝit or I be dede,
Of my distresse siþ I can no rede
But stond[e] dovmb, stil as eni stone,
Tofore þe goddes I wil me hast anone   690
And complein withoute more sermon.
Þouȝ deth be fin and ful conclusioun
Of my request, ȝit I will assai.'
And riȝt anon me þouȝ[te] þat I say
This woful man (as I haue memorie)   695
Ful lowli entre into an oratorie,
And knelid doun in ful humble wise
Tofore þe goddes, and gan anon deuyse
His pitous quarel wiþ a doleful chere
Sayyng riȝt þus, anone as ȝe shul here: 700

I

'Redresse of sorow, O Citheria,
That wiþ þe stremes of þi plesaunt hete

87

Gladest þe contre of [al] Cirrea
Where þou hast chosen þi paleis and þi sete,
Whos briȝt bemes ben wasshen and of[t] wete   705
In the riuer of E[lic]on þe well:
Haue nou pite of þat I shal here tell.

2

'And not disdeyneþ of your benignite,
Mi mortal wo, O lady myn, goddes,
Of grace and bounte and merciful pite   710
Benig[ne]li to helpen and to redresse.
And þouȝ so be I can not wele expresse
The greuous harmes þat I fele in myn hert,
Haueþ neuerþeles merci of my smert.

3

'This is to sein, O clere heuens liȝt,   715
That next þe sonne cercled haue ȝour spere,
Siþ ȝe me hurten wiþ ȝour dredful myȝt
Bi influence of ȝour bemys clere,
And þat I bie ȝour seruise nov so dere,
As ȝe me brouȝt into þis maledie,   720
Beþ gracious and shapeþ remedie.

4

'For in ȝow hooli liþ help of al þis case
And knowe best my sorow and al my peyne:
For drede of deþ hou I ne der, allas,
To axen merci ones ne me compleyne.   725
Nou wiþ ȝoure fire hire hert[e] so restreyne
(Withoute more, or I deie at þe lest)
That she mai wete what is my requeste:

5

'Hov I noþing in al þis world desire
But forto serue fulli to myn ende   730
That goodli fressh, so womanli of chere,
Withoute chaunge, while I haue life and mynde;
And þat 3e wil me such grace send
Of my seruyse, þat she not disdeyne,
Siþen hir to serue I may me not restreyne,   735

6

'And siþ þat Hope haþe 3eue me herdines
To loue hir best and neuer to repent,
Whiles þat I lyue with al my bisenes
To drede and serue, þou3 Daunger neuer assent.
And hereopon 3e knowen myn entent: 740
Hov I haue vowid fulli in my mynde
To ben hir man þou3 I no merci finde;

7

'For in myn hert enprintid is so sore
Hir shap, hir fourme, and al hir semelines,
Hir port, hir chere, hir goodnes more and more,   745
Hir womanhede and eke hir gentilnes,
Hir trouth, hir faiþ and [eke] hir kynd[e]nes,
With al vertues, iche set in his degre:
There is no lak, saue onli of pite.

8

'Hir sad demening, of wil not variable,   750
Of looke benynge and roote of al plesaunce,
And exemplaire to al þat wil be stable,
Discrete, prudent, of wisdom suffisaunce,
Mirrour of wit, ground of gouernaunce,
A world of beaute compassid in hir face,   755
Whose persant loke doþ þuru3 myn hert[e] race;

9

'And ouer þis, secre and wondre trwe,
A welle of fredome and riȝt bovntevous,
And euer encresing in vertue nwe and nwe,
Of spech goodli and wonder gracious,   760
Deuoide of pride, to pore not dispitous;
And if þat I shortli shal not feyne,
Saue opon merci I noþing can compleyne.

10

'What wonder þan þouȝ I be wiþ drede
Inli supprised forto axen grace   765
Of hir þat is a quene of womanhed?
For wele I wot, in so heigh a place
I wil not ben; þerfor I ouerpace
And take louli what wo þat I endure
Til she of pite me take vnto hir cure.   770

11

'But oone avowe pleinli here I make:
That wheþir so be she do me lyve or deye
I wil not grucch but humb[eli] it take,
And þank[e] God and wilfulli obey.
For (be my trouth) myn hert shal not reneye,   775
For life ne deþ, merci nor daunger,
Of wil and þouȝt to ben at hir desire;

12

'To bene as trwe as was Antonyus
To Cleopatre while him lasted breþe,
Or vnto Tesbe ȝung[e] Piramus   780
Was feiþful found til hem departid deþe.
Riȝt so shal I, til Antropos me sleiþe,
For wele or wo, hir faithful man be found
Vnto my last, lich as myn hert is bounde;

13

'To loue as wel as did Achilles   785
Vnto his last þe faire Polixene,
Or as the gret[e], famous Hercules,
For Dianyre þat felt þe shottes kene.
Riȝt so shal I, [I] sei riȝt as I mene,
Whiles þat I lyve, hir boþe drede and serue,   790
For lak of merci þouȝ she do me sterve.

14

'Nou ladi Venus, to whom noþing vnknowe
Is in þe world, ihid ne not mai be—
For þere nys þing neþir heigh ne lowe
Mai be concelid from ȝour privete—   795
Fro whom my menyng is not nov secre,
But witen fulli þat myn entent is trwe
And lich my trowth, nov on my peyn[e] rwe.

15

'For more of grace þan presumpcioun
I axe merci, and not of duete,   800
Of louli humblesse wiþoute offensioun,
That ȝe enclynce, of ȝour benygnyte,
Your audience to myn humylite
To graunt[e] me þat to ȝov clepe and calle
Somdai relese ȝit of my paynes alle.   805

16

'And siþ ȝe haue þe guerdon and þe mede
Of al louers pleinli in ȝour hond,
Nou of [your] grace and pite takeþ hede
Of my distresse, þat am vndir ȝour bond
So lovli bound—as ȝe wele vndirstond.   810
Nou in þat place where I toke first my wound,
Of pite sufferiþ my helth mai be found—

17

'That lich as she me hurt[e] wiþ a siȝte,
Riȝt so with helpe let hir me sustene,
And as þe stremes of hir eyȝen briȝt   815
Whilom myn hert with woundis sharp and kene
Thuruȝ perced haue (and ȝit bene fressh and grene):
So as she me hurt, nou let hir me socoure,
Or ellis certein I mai not long endure.

'For lak of spech I can sey nov nomore: 820
I haue mater but I can not plein:
Mi wit is dulle to telle al my sore.
A mouth I haue, and ȝit for al my peyne,
For want of woordis I may not nov atteyne
To tell[en] half þat doþ myn hert[e] greue,   825
Merci abiding til she me list releue.

'But þis th'effecte of my mater finalle:
Wiþ deþ or merci, reles forto finde.
For hert, bodi, þought, life, lust and alle,
Wiþ al my reson and alle my ful mynde,   830
And fiue wittes, of oon assent I bind
To hir seruice wiþouten eny strife,
And make hir princesse of my deþ or life.

'And ȝov I prai of routh and eke pite,
O goodli planet, O ladi Venus briȝt,   835
That ȝe ȝoure sone of his deite
(Cupid I mene) þat wiþ his dredful myȝt
And wiþ his brond þat is so clere of liȝte
Hir hert[e] so to fire and to mark,
As ȝe me whilom brent[e] with a spark: 840

21

'That euenlich and with þe same fire
She mai be het, as I nov brenne and melt,
So þat hir hert be [fl]aumed bi desire,
That she mai knowe bi feruence hou I swelt.
For of pite pleinli if she felt   845
The selfe hete þat doþ myn hert enbrace,
I hope of rouþe she would do me grace.'

22

'And þerwithal Venus, as me þouȝt,
Toward þis man ful benyg[ne]li
Gan cast hir eyȝe, liche as þouȝ she rouȝt   850
Of his disease, and seid ful good[e]li:
'Siþ it is so þat þou so humb[e]lie
Wiþoute grucchyng oure hestis list obey,
Toward þin help I wil anon puruey.

23

'And eke my sone Cupide þat is so blind,   855
He shal ben helping, fulli to perfourme
Ȝour hole desire, þat noþing behind
Ne shal be left: so we shal refourme
The pitous compleint þat makiþ þe to mourne,
That she for whom þou soroist most in hert   860
Shal þuruȝ hir merci relese al þi smert

24

'Whan she seþ tyme þuruȝ oure purueaunce.
Be not to hasti, but suffre alway wele.
For in abidyng þuruȝ lowli obeissaunce
Liþe ful redresse of al þat ȝe nov fele,   865
And she shal be as trw as eny stele
To ȝowe allone þuruȝ oure myȝt and grace,
Ȝif ȝe lust mekeli abide a litel space.

93

25

'But vndirstondeþ þat al hir cherisshing
Shal ben grovndid opon honeste,   870
That no wiȝt shal, þurugh euil compassing,
[D]emen amys of hir in no degre.
For neiþer merci, reuþe, ne pite
She shal not haue, ne take of þe non hede
Ferþer þen longiþ vnto hir womanhede.   875

26

'Beþe not astonied of no wilfulnes,
Ne nouȝt dispeired of þis dill[a]sioun;
Lete reson bridel lust bi buxumnes
Withoute grucching or rebellioun,
For ioy shal folov al þis passioun.   880
For who can suffre turment and endure,
Ne mai not faile þat folov shal his cure.

27

'For toforn all she shal þe louen best:
So shal I here, withoute offencioun,
Bi influence enspire[n] in hir brest,   885
In honest wise wiþ ful entencioun,
Forto enclyne bi clene affeccioun
Hir hert fulli on þe to haue rouþe,
Bicause I know þat þou menyst trouþe.

28

'Go nov to hir where as she stant aside,   890
Wiþ humble chere and put þe in hir grace,
And al biforne late Hope be þi guide,
And þouȝe þat Drede would[e] with þe pace—
It sitteþ wel; but loke þat þou arace
Out of þin hert wanhope and dispaire,   895
To hir presence er þou haue repaire.

29

'And Merci first shal þi wai[e] make,
And Honest Menyng aforn do þi message
To make merci in her hert awake.
And secrenes, to further þi viage,   900
Wiþ humble port to hir þat is so sage
Shul menes ben—and I myself also
Shal þe fortune er þi tale be do.

30

'Go forþe anon and be riȝt of goode chere,
For specheles noþing maist þou spede.   905
Be goode of trust and be noþing in were,
Siþ I myself shal helpen in þis nede;
For at þe lest, of hir goodlihed
She shal to þe hir audience enclyne,
And lovli þe here til þou þi tale fyne.   910

31

'Fore wel þou wost (ȝif I shal not feine)
Withoute spech þou maist no merci haue:
For who þat wil of his preve peine
Fulli be cured, his life to help and saue,
He most mekeli oute of his hurtis graue   915
Discure his wound and shew it to his lech,
Or ellis deie for defaute of spech.

32

'For he þat is in myschef rekeles
To sechen help, I hold him but a wrecch.
And she ne mai þin hert[e] bring in peas   920
But if þi compleint to his hert[e] strecch.
Wouldist þou be curid and wilte no salue fecch?
It wil not be: for no wiȝte may atteyne
To come to blis if he lust lyue in peyne.

33

'Therfore at ones go in humble wise 925
Tofore þi ladi and louli knele adoun,
And in al trouth þi woordis so deuyse
That she on þe [may] haue compassioun.
For she þat is of so heigh renoun
In al vertues as quene and souerain, 930
Of womanhed shal rwe opon þi pein.'

And whan þe goddes þis lesson hade him told,
Aboute me so as I gan bihold,
Riȝt for-astonied I stode in a traunce
To sein þe maner and þe covntenaunce 935
And al þe chere of þis woful man,
That was of hwe deedli pale and wan,
Wiþ drede supprised in his owne þouȝt,
Making a chere as þ[ouȝ] he rouȝt[e] nouȝt
Of life ne deþ, ne what so him betide: 940
So mych fere he hade on euere side
To put him forþe forto tel his peyne
Vnto his ladi, oþer to compleyne
What wo he felt, turment or disease,
What dedli sorov his hert[e] did[e] sease; 945
For rouþe of which his wo as I endite,
Mi penne I fele quaken as I write.
Of him I had so gret compassioun
Forto reherse his weymentacioun
That, wel vnneþe þouȝ with myself I striue, 950
I want connyng his peynes to discryue.
Allas, to whom shal I for help[e] cal?
Not to þe Musis, for cause þat þei ar al
Help of riȝt in ioi and not in wo,
And in maters þat þe[m] delite also, 955
Wherfore þei nyl directe as nov my stile
Nor me enspiren, allas þe hard[e] while.
I can no ferþer but to Thesiphone
And to hir sustren forto help[e] me

That bene goddesses of turment and of peyne. 960
Nou lete ȝoure teris into myn inke reyne,
With woful woordis my pauper forto blot,
This woful mater to peint[e] not but spotte:
To tell þe maner of þis dredful man,
Vpon his compleint when he first bigan 965
To tel his ladi, when he gan declare
His hid[de] sorois and his euel fare
That at his hert constreyned him so sore,
Th'effecte of which was þis withoute more:

I

'Princes of iouþe, and flour of gentilesse, 970
Ensaumple of vertue, ground of curtesie,
Of beaute rote, quene and eke maistres
To al women hou þei shul hem gie,
And soþefast myrrour to exemplifie
The riȝt[e] wei of port and womanhed— 975
What shal I say?—of merci takeþ hede:

2

'Biseching first vnto ȝoure heigh nobles
Wiþ quaking hert of myn inward drede,
Of grace and pite and nouȝt of riȝtwisnes,
Of verrai rouþe, to help[en] in þis nede. 980
That is to saie, O wel of goodlihed,
That I ne recch þouȝ ȝe do me deie,
So ȝe list first [to] heren what I saie.

3

'The dredful stroke, þe gret[e] force and myȝt
Of god Cupide, þat no man mai rebel, 985
So inwardli þuruȝout myn hert[e] riȝt
Ipersid haþ, þat I ne mai concele
Myn hid[de] wound, ne I ne may apele
Vnto no grettir: þis myȝti god so fast
Yow to serue haþ bound me to my last, 990

97

4

'That hert and al withoute strife ar yolde,
For life or deþ, to ȝoure seruise alone,
Riȝt as þe goddes myȝti Venus would.
Toforne hir mekeli when I made my mone
She me constreyned, without chaunge, anone   995
To ȝoure seruise, and neuer forto feyne,
Whereso yow list to do me ease or peyne.

5

'So þat I can noþing but merci crie
Of ȝov, ladi—and chaungen for no nwe—
That ȝe list good[e]l[i] tofore I deyȝe,   1000
Of verrey rouþe opon my peynes rwe.
For be my trouþe, and ȝe þe soþe knwe
What is þe cause of myn aduersite,
On my distres ȝe would haue pite.

6

'For vnto ȝow trwe and eke secre   1005
I wole be found, to serue as best I can,
And þerwithal as lowli in ich degre
To ȝow allone, as euir ȝit was man
Vnto his ladi, from þe tyme I gan,
And shal so forþe withouten eny slouþe   1010
Whiles þat I lyue, bi god and be my trouþe.

7

'For leuyr I had to dei[e]n sodeinli
Than yow offend in any maner wise,
And suffre peynes inward priueli
Than my seruise ȝe shuld as nov despise.   1015
For I riȝt nouȝt wil asken in no wise
But for ȝoure seruant ȝe would me accepte,
And when I trespace, goodli me correcte,

8

'And forto graunt, of merci, þis praier:
Oonli of grace and womanl[i] pete   1020
Fro dai to dai þat I my3t[e] lere
3ow forto please, and þerwithal þat 3e,
When I do mys, list [for] to teche me
In 3oure seruyse hou þat I mai amende
From hensforþe and neuyr 3ow offende.   1025

9

'For vnto me it doþ inou3 suffise
That for 3oure man 3e would me reseyue
Fulli to ben, as 3ou list deuyse
And as ferforþe my wittes con conceyue.
And þerwithal, lich as 3e perseyue   1030
That I be trwe, to guerdone me of grace
Or ellis to punyssh aftir my trespace.

10

'And if so be þat I mai not atteyne
Vnto 3our merci, 3it graunteþ at[te] lest,
In 3our seruice, for al my wo and peyne,   1035
That I mai dei3en aftir my bihest.
This is al and som, þe fine of my request:
Oþir with merci 3our seruant forto saue
Or merciles þat I mai be graue.'

11

And when þis benygne, of hir entent trwe,   1040
Conceyued haþ þe compleint of þis man,
Ri3t as þe fressh[e] rodi rose nwe
Of hir coloure to wexin she bigan.
Hir bloode astonyed so from hir hert it ran
Into hir face, of femyny[ni]te: 1045
Thuru3 honest drede abaisshed so was she.

12

And humb[e]l[i] she gan hir eiȝen cast
Towardis him, of hir benygnyte,
So þat no woord bi hir lippes past
For hast ne drede, merci nor pite.   1050
For so demeyned she was in honeste
That vnavised noþing hir astert:
So mych of reson was compast in hir hert.

13

Til at þe last, of rouþe she did abraide
When she his trouþe and menyng did[e] fele,   1055
And vnto him ful goodli spake and seide:
'Of ȝoure [be]hest and of ȝour menyng wele,
And ȝoure seruise so feiþful eueredel
Which vnto me so lowli now ȝe offre,
Wiþ al my hert I þanke ȝow of ȝoure profir: 1060

14

'That for as mych as ȝoure entent is sette
Oonli in vertu, ibridelid vnder drede,
Ȝe most of riȝt nedis fare þe bette
Of ȝoure request and þe bettir spede.
But as for me, I mai of womanhede   1065
No ferþir graunt to ȝov in myn entent
Thanne as my ladi Venus wil assent.

15

'For she wele knowiþ I am not at my laarge,
To done riȝt nouȝt but bi hir ordinaunce:
So am I bound vndir hir dredful charge   1070
Hir lust to obey withoute variaunce.
But for my part, so it be plesaunce
Vnto þe goddes, for trouþe in ȝour emprise,
I ȝow accepte fulli to my seruyse.

16

'For she myn hert haþ in subieccioun   1075
Which holi is ȝoures and neuer shal repent,
In þouȝt nor dede, in myn eleccioun.
Witnes on Venus þat knoweþ myn entent
Fulli to obei hir dome and iugement,
So as hir lust disposen and ordeyne,   1080
Riȝt as she knoweþ þe trouth of vs tweyne.

17

'For vnto þe time þat Venus [list] prouyde
To shape a wai for oure hertis ease,
Boþe ȝe and I mekeli most abide,
To take agre and not of oure disease   1085
To grucch agein, til she list to appese
Oure hid[de] wo, so inli þat constreyneþ
From dai to day and oure hert[is] peyneþ.

18

'For in abiding of wo and al affray,
Whoso can suffre is founden remedie;   1090
And for the best ful oft is made delay
Er men be heled of hir maladie.
Wherfore, as Venus list þis mater guie
Late us agreen and take al for þe best
Til her list set oure hertes boþe at rest.   1095

19

'For she it is þat bindeþ and can constreyne
Hertes in oon, þis fortunate planete,
And can [re]lesen louers of her peyne,
To turne fulli hir bitter into swete.
Nou blisful goddes, doun fro þi sterri sete,   1100
Vs to fortune caste ȝour stremes shene,
Like as ȝe cnow þat we trouþe mene.'

20

And þerwithal, as I myn ey3en cast
Forto perceiue þe maner of þese twein,
Tofore þe goddes mekel[i] as þei past,   1105
Me þou3t I saw with a golden cheyne
Venus anon enbracen and constrein
Her boþ[e] hertes, in oon forto perseuer
Whiles þat þei liue and neuer to desseuer.

21

Saiyng ri3t þus with a benyngne chere: 1110
'Siþ it is so 3e ben vndir my my3t,
Mi wille is þis, þat 3e, my dou3ter dere,
Fulli accepte þis man, a[s] hi[t i]s ri3t,
Vnto 3our grace anon here in my si3t,
That euer haþ ben so louli 3ou to serue: 1115
It is goode skil 3our þank þat he desserue.

22

'Your honour saue, and eke 3our womanhed,
Him to cherissen it sittiþ 3ov ri3t wele,
Siþ he is bound vnder hope and drede
Amyd my cheyne þat maked is of stele.   1120
3e must of merci shape þat he fele
In 3ov some grace for his long seruise,
And þat in hast, like as I shal deuyse.

23

'This is to sein, þat 3e taken hede
Hou he to 3ov most faiþful is and trwe   1125
Of al 3our seruauntis, and noþing for his mede
Of 3ov ne askiþ but þat 3e on him rwe:
For he haþe vo[w]id to chaunge for no nwe,
For life nor deþ, for ioy[e] ne for peyne—
Ay to ben 3ours, so as 3e list ordeyne.   1130

24

'Wherfore ȝe must (or ellis it were wrong)
Vnto ȝour grace fulli hym receyue
In my presence, bicause he haþ so long
Holli ben ȝoures, as ȝe may conceyue
That, from ȝoure merci nov if ȝe him weyue,   1135
I wil myself recorden cruelte
In ȝoure persone, and gret lak of pite.

25

'Late him for trouth þen find[e trouth] agein:
For long seruice guerdone him with grace
And lateþ pite wei[e] doun his pein.   1140
For tyme is nov daunger to arace
Out of ȝoure hert and merci in to pace;
And loue for loue would[e] wele biseme
To yeve agein, and þis I pleinli deme.

26

'And as for him I wil bene his borow   1145
Of lowlihed and bise attendaunce:
Hou he shal bene, boþ at eue and morov,
Ful diligent to don his obseruaunce,
And euer awayting ȝou to do plesaunce.
Wherfore, my sone, list and take hede   1150
Fulli to obey as I shal þe rede.

27

'And first of al, my wil is þat þou be
Feiþful in hert and constant as a walle,
Trwe, humble and meke, and þerwithal secre,
Withoute chaunge in parti or in al.   1155
And for no turment þat þe fallen shal,
Tempest þe not but euer in stidfastnes
Rote þin hert, and voide doublenes.

'And forþermore, haue in reuerence
Thes women al for þi ladi sake,   1160
And suffre neuer þat men do þem offence,
For loue of oon; but euermore vndirtake
Hem to defend, wheþer þei slepe or wake,
And ay be redi to holden champartie
With al[le] þo þat to hem haue envie.   1165

'Be curteis ay and lowli of þi spech
To riche and poure, ai fressh and welbesein,
And euer bisie weies forto sech
All trwe louers to relese of her peyne,
Siþ þou art oon; and of no wiȝt haue disdein   1170
For loue haþ pouer hertis forto daunt,
And neuer for cherisshing þe to mych auaunte.

'Be lusti eke, deuoid of al tristesse,
And take no þouȝt but euer be iocond,
And nouȝt to pensif for non heuynes.   1175
And with þi gladnes let sadnes ay be found,
When wo approcheþ lat myrþ most habound
As manhod axeþ; and þouȝ þou fele smert,
Lat not to manie knowen of þin hert.

'And al vertues biseli þou sue,   1180
Vices eschew, for þe loue of oon.
And for no tales þin hert[e] not remue:
Woorde is but winde þat shal sone ouergon.
Whateuer þou here, be dovmb as eny ston,
And to answere to sone not þe delite: 1185
For here she standeþ þat al þis shal þe quite.

'And where þou be absent or in presence,
None oþirs beaute lat in þin herte myne,
Siþ I haue hir ȝyue of beaute excellence,
Aboue al oþir in vertue forto shine.   1190
And þenk in fire hou men ar wont to fyne
This purid gold to put it in assay:
So þe to preue þou ert put in delay.

'But tyme shal come þou shalt for þi sufferaunce
Be wele apaide and take for þi mede   1195
Thi liues ioy and al þi suffisaunce,
So þat goode hope alway þi bridel lede.
Lat no dispeire hindir þe with drede
But ay þi trust opon hir merci grovnd,
Siþ noon but she may þi sores sound.   1200

'Eche houre and tyme, weke, dai and ȝere,
Be iliche feithful and varie not for lite.
Abide awhile, and þan of þi desire
The time neigheth þat shal þe most delite.
And lete no sorov in þin hert[e] bite   1205
For no differring, siþ þou shalt for þi mede
Reioise in pees þe floure of womanhede.

'Thenk hou she is þis wor[l]dis sonne and liȝt,
The sterre of beaute, flour eke of fairnes,
Boþe crop and rote, and eke þe rubie briȝt   1210
Hertes to glade itroubled with derknes,
And hou I haue made hir þin hertes emperesse.
Be glad þerfore to be vndir hir bonde.
Nou come nere, douȝter, and take him bi þe hond,

'Vnto þis fyne þat, after al þe showres   1215
Of his turment, he mai be glad and liȝt,
W[h]an þuruȝ ȝoure grace ȝe take him to be ȝoures
For euermore, anon here in my syȝt.
And eeke also I wil, as it is riȝt,
Withoute more his langour forto lisse,   1220
In my presence anon þat ȝe him kisse:

'That here mai be of al ȝoure old[e] smertis
A ful relese vndir ioy assured.
And þat oo lok be of ȝoure boþe hertes
Shet with my key of gold so wel depured,   1225
Oonli in signe þat ȝe haue recured
Ȝoure hole desire here in þis holi place,
Within my temple, nou in þe ȝere of grace.

'Eternalli, be bonde of assuraunce,
The cnott [is] knytt which mai not ben vnbovnd:
That al þe goddis of þis alliaunce,   1231
Saturne and Ioue and Mars (as it is fovnd)
And eke Cupide þat first ȝou did[e] wounde,
Shal bere record, and [e]uermore be wreke
On which of ȝou his trouþe first doþe breke: 1235

39

'So þat bi aspectes of hir fers[e] lokes,
Wiþoute merci shal fal[le] þe vengeaunce
Forto be raced clene out of my bokes
On which of ȝow be found[e] variaunce.
Þerfore atones setteþ ȝour plesauns   1240
Fulli to ben, while ȝe haue life and mynde,
Of oon accord vnto ȝoure lyues ende,

40

'That, if þe spirit of nvfangilnes
In any wise ȝoure hertis would assaile
To meve or stir to bring in doubilnes   1245
Vpon ȝour trouþe to giuen a bataile,
Late not ȝoure corage ne ȝoure force fail,
Ne non assautes ȝov flitten or remeve:
For vnassaied men may no trouþe preue.

41

'For white is whitter if it be set bi blak,   1250
And swete is swettir eftir bitternes,
And falshode euer is drive and put abak
Where trouþe is rotid withoute doubilnes.
Wiþout[e] prefe may be no sikirnes
Of loue or hate; and þerfor, of ȝow too   1255
Shal loue be more, þat it was bouȝt with wo.

42

'As euere þing is had more [in] deinte,
And more of pris when it is dere bouȝt;
And eke þat loue stond more in surete
When it tofore with peyne, wo and þouȝt   1260
Conquerid was, first when it was souȝt;
And euere conquest haþ his excellens
In his pursuite as he fint resistence:

43

'And so to ȝow more sote and agreable
Shal loue be found, I do ȝou plein assure,   1265
Wiþoute grucching þat ȝe were suffrable
So low, so meke, pacientli t'endure,
That al atones I shal nov do my cure
For nov and euer ȝour hertis so to bynd
That nouȝt but deþ shal þe [k]not vnbynd.   1270

107

44

'Nou in þis mater what shuld I lengir dwel?
Comeþ at ones and do as I haue seide.
And first, my douȝter, þat bene of bounte wel,
In hert and þouȝt be glad, and wele apaied
To done him grace þat haþ, and shal, obeid   1275
Ȝour lustes euer; and I wole for his sake
Of trouþe to ȝow be bounde and vndertake.'

And so forþewith, in presence as þei stonde
Tofore þe goddes, þis ladi faire and wele
Hir humble seruaunt [to]ke goodli bi þe honde   128(
As he toforne here mekeli did knele,
And kissed him after, fu[l]fillyng eueredele
Fro point to point in ful tristi wise,
A[s] ȝe toforne haue Venus herd deuyse.

Thus is þis man to ioy and al plesaunce   1285
From heuynes and from his peynes old
Ful reconsiled, and haþ ful suffisaunce
Of his þat euer ment[e] wel and would.
And in goode faith, [if] I tell[e] shuld
The inward myrþe [that] dide hir hertis brace,   129(
For al my life it were to lit a space.

For he haþe wonne hir þat he loueþ best,
And she to grace haþe take him [of] pite.
And þus her hertis beþe boþe set in rest
Wiþouten chaunge or mutabilite;   1295
And Venus haþ, of hir benygnete,
Confermed all (what [shal] I lenger tarie?)
This tweyn in oon, and neuere forto varie:

That for þe ioy[e] in þe temple aboute
Of þis accord, bi gret solempnyte   1300
Was laude and honoure within and withoute
Ʒeue vnto Venus and to þe deite
Of god Cupide, so þat Caliope
And al hir sustren in hir armonye
[Gan] with her song þe goddes magnyfie.   1305

49

And al at ones, with notes loude and sharpe
Thei did her honour and her reuerence,
And Orpheus among hem with his harp
Gan strengis touch[e] with his diligence,
And Amphioun, þat haþe suche excellence   1310
Of musike, ay dide his bisynes
To please and queme Venus þe goddes,

50

Oonli for cause of þe affinite
Betwix þese twoo not likli to desseuere.
And euere louer of louȝ and heiȝ degre   1315
Gan Venus pray: fro þensforþ and euer
That hool of hem þe loue may perseuere,
Wiþoute[n] ende in suche plite as þei gonne,
And more encrese þat it of hard was wonne.

51

And so þe goddes, hering þis request,   1320
As she knew þe clene entencioun
Of boþe hem tweyne, haþ made a ful bihest:
Perpetuelli, by confirmacioun,
Whiles þat þei lyue of oon affeccioun
Thei shal endure—þer is no more to sein—   1325
Þat neiþer shal haue mater to compleyne.

52

'So ferforþ euer in oure eternal se
The goddes haue, in oure presscience,
Fulli deuysed þuruȝ hir deite
And holi concludid bi hir influence,   1330
That þuruȝ hir myȝt and iust[e] pr[ovi]dence
The loue of hem, bi grace and eke fortune,
Wiþoute chaunge shal euer in oon [con]tune.'

53

Of which[e] graunt, þe tempil enviroun,
Þuruȝ heiȝ confort of hem þat were present,   1335
Anone was gon[ne] with a melodius sowne,
In name of þo þat trouþ in loue ment,
A ballade nwe in ful goode entent
Tofore þe goddes with notes loude and clere,
Singyng riȝt þus anon as ȝe shal here: 1340

54

'Fairest of sterres, þat wiþ ȝoure persant liȝt
And with þe cherisshing of ȝoure stremes clere,
Causen in loue hertes to be liȝt
Oonli þuruȝ shynyng of ȝoure glade spere,
Nou laude and pris, O Venus, ladi dere,   1345
[B]e to ȝour name, þat haue withoute synne
Þis man fortuned his ladi forto wynne.

55

'Willi planet, O Esperus, so briȝt,
Þat woful hertes can appese and stere,
And euer ar redi þuruȝ ȝour grace and myȝt   1350
To help al þo þat bie loue so dere,
And haue power hertis to set on fire,
Honor to ȝow of all þat bene hereinne,
That haue þis man his ladi made to wynne.

56

'O my3ti goddes, daister after ny3t,   1355
Glading þe morov whan 3e done appere,
To voide derknes þuru3 fresshnes of 3our si3t,
Oonli with twinkeling of 3oure plesaunt chere,
To 3ov we þank, louers þat ben here,
That 3e þis man—and neuer forto twyn—   1360
Fortuned haue his ladi forto wynne.'

And with þe noise and heuenli melodie
W[h]i[c]h þat þei made[n] in her armonye
Þuru3oute þe temple, for þis manes sake,
Oute of my slepe anone I did awake   1365
And for-astonied knwe as þo no rede.
For sodein chaunge, oppressid so with drede,
Me þou3t I was cast as in a traunce:
So clene away was þo my remembraunce
Of al my dreme, wherof gret þou3t and wo   1370
I hade in hert and nyst what was to do,
For heuynes þat I hade lost þe si3t
Of hir þat I, all þe long[e] ny3t,
Had dremed of in myn auisioun.
Whereof I made gret lamentacioun   1375
Bicause I had neuer in my life aforne
Sei[n] none so faire, fro time þat I was borne.
For loue of whome, so as I can endite,
I purpose here to maken and to write
A litil tretise and a processe make   1380
In pr[a]is of women, oonli for her sake,
Hem to comende, as it is skil and ri3t,
For here goodnes, with al my ful[le] my3t.
Prayeng to hir þat is so bounteous,
So ful of vertue and so gracious   1385
Of womanhed and merciful pite,
This simple tretis forto take in gre
Til I haue leiser vnto hir hei3 renoun
Forto expoune my foreseid visioun;

And tel in plein þe significaunce,   1390
So as it comeþ to my remembraunce,
So þat herafter my ladi may it loke.

Nou go þi wai, þou litel rude boke,
To hir presence, as I þe commaund,
And first of al þou me recomavnd   1395
Vnto hir and to hir excellence
And prai to hir þat it be noon offence
If eny woorde in þe be myssaide,
Biseching hir she be not euel apaied;
For as hir list I wil þe efte correcte   1400
Whan þat hir likeþ againward þe directe:
I mene þat benygne and goodli of hir face.
Nou go þi way and put þe in hir grace.

ABBREVIATIONS USED IN
THE NOTES

AH	*Analecta Hymnica Medii Ævi* (ed. Dreves, Blume, Bannister), vols. i–lv, Leipzig, 1886–1922.
BM	British Museum.
Brusendorff	*The Chaucer Tradition* (Brusendorff), Copenhagen, 1925.
CT	*Canterbury Tales.*
Deschamps	*Œuvres complètes d'Eustache Deschamps* (de Queux de Saint-Hilaire, Raynaud), vols. i–xi, Société des Anciens Textes Français, Paris, 1878–1903.
EETS	Early English Text Society.
Godefroy	*Dictionnaire de l'ancienne langue française* (Godefroy), vols. i–x, Paris, 1881–1902.
Hammond	*English Verse between Chaucer and Surrey* (Hammond), Durham, North Carolina, 1927.
Index	*The Index of Middle English Verse* (Brown, Robbins), New York, 1943.
MacCracken	*The Minor Poems of Lydgate* (ed. MacCracken), vols. i–ii, EETS, Extra Series, 1911–34.
ME	Middle English.
MED	*Middle English Dictionary* (Kurath, Kuhn), Ann Arbor, U.S.A., 1956– .
MLR	*Modern Language Review.*
OED	*Oxford English Dictionary.*
OF	Old French.
PL	*Patrologia Latina.*
PMLA	*Publications of the Modern Language Association of America.*
STS	Scottish Text Society.
TLS	*Times Literary Supplement.*

NOTES

1. *Letter to Gloucester*

THERE are seven authorities for this poem: BM MSS. Harley 2255, f. 45b: (H); Harley 2251, f. 6a: (h); Additional 34360, f. 64b: (A). Lansdowne MS. 699, f. 90a: (L). Leyden Vossius MS. 9, p. 204: (Ly). Magdalene College, Cambridge MS. Pepys 2011, f. 78a: (P). Pierpont Morgan MS. 4, f. 75b: (M). *Index* 2825.

Both Hammond and MacCracken print H (with minor variations) as the authoritative text. Although H is a cleaner text there is nothing about it to suggest its absolute authority. The first modern account of the poem was given by Miss E. P. Hammond in *Anglia*, xxxviii (1914), pp. 125 ff. Professor Schirmer's account in *John Lydgate*, pp. 215–16, agrees with Miss Hammond's.

Although six MSS. designate Duke Humphrey as the recipient of the letter, only four provide evidence as to the occasion. P has the title: 'This is the letter that daun Lidgate Monke of Bury sent to Humfrey duke of Gloucestre for making of Bochas'; A and h have the colophon (with minor variations): 'Explicit *littera* Dompni Ioh*n*is Lidgate monachus monasterij *sanct*i Edmundi de Bury miss*a* ad ducem Gloucestrie in tempore translationis libri Bochas*ii pro* oportunitate pecunie'; M has the title: 'This is the copy of þe letter that Dan John Lidgate, Monke of Bury, sent to Homfrey Duke of Glouceter [*sic*] for mony for the makynge of Bochas.'

Miss Hammond's theory was that Lydgate wrote the *Letter* after finishing Book ii of the *Fall of Princes*. The Latin 'in tempore translationis' may be taken to support this theory. In her view, the *Letter* produced such a devastating effect on Duke Humphrey that he paid up. It is this payment, the result of the poem, which is recorded in the Prologue to Book iii of the *Fall of Princes* (ll. 66 ff.):

> Mi purs ay liht and void off al coignage
> Bachus ferr off to glade my corage;
> An ebbe off plente; scarsete atte fulle,
> Which of an old man makth the sperit dulle.
>
> But hope and trust to putte away dispair
> Into my mynde off newe gan hem dresse;
> And cheef off all to make the wethir fair,
> Mi lordis fredam and bounteuous largesse
> Into myn herte brouht in such gladnesse.

But whatever sum Lydgate had been paid at the end of Book II
it was small enough to have been exhausted by the end of Book III.
Lines 3865 ff. record in an apostrophe to Humphrey the poet's
pressing poverty. The *Letter*, to be effective rhetoric, ought to
allude more precisely and more complexly to some other passage
in the *Fall of Princes*. MSS. P and M imply that Lydgate had
finished his translation. The last of Lydgate's envois to the *Fall*
confirms this view. In his envoi to Duke Humphrey, *Fall of Princes*
IX. 3345 ff. Lydgate complains bitterly and at length of his lack
of reward:

> Trustyng ageynward your liberal largesse,
> Of this cotidien shal relevyn me,
> Hope hath brought tydyng to recure myn accesse;
> Afftir this ebbe of froward skarsete
> Shal folwe a spryng flood of gracious plente,
> To wasshe a-way be plentevous inffluence
> Al ground ebbys of constreyned indigence.

The disease and water imagery of this passage connects with much
of the imagery of the *Letter*. It is obvious that Lydgate was paid
an initial sum (*Letter*, l. 19) after the first two books were completed and was not paid again. The final envoi to Book IX convicts
Duke Humphrey of the niggardliness which was so characteristic
of him. Even in Book VIII. 132 ff. Lydgate (speaking through the
disguise of Petrarch) is looking forward to some payment at the
completion of his nine books:

> Yit at the laste, thynk, for thi socour
> Sum roial prince shal quyte thi labour.

> (ll. 146–7)

There is no evidence that Humphrey made final payment. The
unidentified Greneacre was to write later in his *A Lenvoye vpon
John Bochas*:

> No cloth of tyssewe ne veluet crimesyne,
> But lik thi monke, moornyng vnder his hood,
> Go weile and wepe with wofull Proserpyne
> And lat thi teres multeplie the flood
> Of blak Lythey vnder the bareyn wood,
> Where-as [the] godesse hath hir hermytage,—
> Helpe hir to wepe, and she wyll geve the wage.

> (ll. 8–14)

The references, *flood, bareyn, hermitage*, may point to stanza 8 of the *Letter*. Chapter iv, pp. 60–61, of R. Weiss's *Humanism in England during the Fifteenth Century* (1957) gives an account of the unsuccessful efforts of Pier Candido Decembrio to extract payment from the Duke for a considerable amount of translation.

The purse had been the subject of personification in earlier ME verse: complexly personified as the poet's *domina* by Chaucer, and more simply by Hoccleve in his *Regement of Princes*, ll. 4369 ff.; *La Male Regle de T. Hoccleve*, ll. 409–12. Lydgate's treatment owes little to either Chaucer or Hoccleve. Sickness as a metaphor for indigence, medication as a metaphor for a patron's donation were common in medieval verse. Cf. Deschamps, *Balade* 902 ('J'ay par cinq ans esté en maladie') and Hoccleve's *Rondel to Somer*, ll. 39–40. In Lydgate, for the first time, the purse is personified as a consumptive companion to the ailing poet.

1. *and*: 'conj. if '. Cf. Chaucer, *A Complaint to his Lady* 112.

6. *rerage*: 'arrears of payment'. Cf. *Piers Plowman*, B. V. 246.

8. *coignage*: 'coins collectively'. *OED* records the first occurrence of this sense in the *Paston Letters* (1467). *MED*'s only pre-Lydgatian recording of this sense (*c*. 1380) is not a sufficiently clear example.

12. *Bury toun*: Miss Hammond assumed that Lydgate leads the reader to understand that he is writing from Bury St. Edmunds, but the *ther* of l. 18 invites another interpretation. The unit name +town probably indicates the town of Bury St. Edmunds. Lydgate means us to understand that he is writing from the abbey where the living is free.

Dia: the pharmaceutical prefix *dia*- used as a separate noun, 'a medical compound'. Cf. *Piers Plowman*, B. XX. 173.

13. Cf. *Fall of Princes* III. 3846: 'Ther [poetis] purs turnid vp-so-doun.'

17. *ship*: the imagery here is perhaps difficult because two ideas are blended. The first idea is discarded after line 18 and the second element in the similitude occupies the rest of the stanza. The first element is based on a physical image, the gold noble coined under Edward III which bore the image of a ship (cf. Hoccleve, *La Court de bone Compaigne* 29). Lydgate then expands this image visually and numerically for emphasis: *seilis reed of hewe* refers to the colour of gold (cf. Ekkehard IV, *De lege dictamen ornandi* 20, 'Aurum sit purum sit mundum sit rubicundum'). Lydgate next (ll. 19–23) refers either to a thwarted or non-existent ship. This ship allegorizes 'the fortunes of a person's life'.

Cf. Deschamps, *Balade* 223, 'Par ce vaissel no vie est figurée';
Lydgate, *Fall of Princes* III. 3738; Dunbar, *The Tabill of Confession* 165:

> Thow mak my schip in blissit port to arryif
> That sailis heir in stormis violent . . .

The link between the two ship images is associative. Lines 17–18
are a unit; the acc. pronoun refers to *seilis*, cf. h's 'saile . . . hym'.

19. *flood*: 'the flowing in of the tide'. This in the similitude refers
to the initial payment for the translation of the *Fall of Princes*
recorded in the Prologue to Book III. 66 ff. A ground-ebb or total
lack of patronage soon occurs (i.e. directly at the end of Book III.
3865 ff.). The ground-ebb image may have been suggested by
Hoccleve's *Regement of Princes*, 668–9.

23. *custom*: 'tax levied on imports'. An example of the figure
litotes. There is no cargo to be taxed.

25. *the Tour*: the Mint in the Tower of London. Cf. John Stow,
A Svrvay of London (1603), p. 52: 'In the yeare 1344. King Edward
the 3. in the 18. yeare of his raigne, commaunded Florences of gold
to be made and coyned in the Tower. . . .'

26. *countirpeys*: *OED* and *MED* define 'a counterweight'. The
sense here would seem to include the scales to which the *countirpeys* belongs.

28. *cotidian*: 'a recurring fever'. Cf. *Fall of Princes* IX. 3345 ff.

29. *Sol and Luna*: 'the sun and the moon' and 'gold and silver
pieces of money'. The word-play is developed from Alchemical
terms; cf. Chaucer, *CT* G. 826: 'Sol gold is and Luna silver we
threpe.'

30. *cros*: 'coins generally'. Cf. Hoccleve, *Regement of Princes* 685.
The allegory disappears at this point. 'Cros' and 'preent of no
visage' are more direct images for coins bearing a cross or royal
likeness.

35. *ernest-grote*: 'money paid as an instalment for purchase'.
Cf. 'ernest-penny'.

36. *Bargeyn*: 'compact', in apposition to 'ernest-grote', which is
the symbol of the business agreement. Cf. the reading of P: 'As
bargeyn. . . .'

37. *callyd to the lure*: a phrase taken from falconry and applied
fig. to mean 'under the control of'. Lydgate uses variations of the
phrase in connexion with Fortune. Cf. *Fall of Princes* IV. 972,
1076; V. 2959.

38. *Indigence*: personified in *Fall of Princes* III. 77 and *Thebes* 863:

> Treason, Pouert, Indigence and Nede
> And Cruell Death in his rent wede.

40. *receyt*: (*a*) 'a remedy', (*b*) 'a sum of money'.

41. *sugre-plat*: *sucura crustalis*, a sweet lozenge for medicinal use.

43. *Boklerys-bury*: Bucklesbury. Cf. John Stow, *A Svrvay of London* (1603), p. 262: 'This whole streete called Buckles bury on both sides throughout is possessed of Grocers and Apothecaries.'

46. *Aurum potabile*: 'drinkable gold'. *OED* defines as 'gold held in a state of minute subdivision in some volatile oil, formerly in repute as a cordial'.

47. *quint-essence*: *OED* defines for this passage as follows: 'The fifth substance supposed to be that substance of which heavenly bodies were composed and to be actually present in all things. . . .' This definition does not fit the passage. Two senses not recorded by *OED* until the sixteenth century are being played on here: (*a*) some chemical tincture used as a restorative or balm, (*b*) substance in its purest form, i.e. money, not promises or token payments.

51. *attamyd*: (OF *atamer*). This vb. has a wide semantic area in ME (cf. Modern French *entamer*). The sense here would seem to be 'to broach'.

52. *nichil habet*: a legal phrase. The return made by the sheriff to the exchequer in cases where the party named in the writ had no goods upon which a levy could be made.

53. *tisyk*: 'phthisic', usually applied to consumption, sometimes extended to include asthma.

58. H reads *soyl*. hA read *sail*, 'chamber'.

59. *pyle*: Lydgate probably plays on two words: (1) 'a cushion', used for devotional purposes; (2) 'the side of a coin opposite to the *cross* or face' (Med. Lat. *pila*: 'the under iron of the minting apparatus with which the money was struck').

reclus: 'what is shut up', 'store'.

60. *seyntuarye*: 'a box containing relics'. The object is appropriate since a reliquary might be expected to contain images.

63. *lectuarye*: 'electuary', 'a medicine consisting of powder or other ingredients mixed with honey, jam or syrup' (*OED*). In practice the concoction could be sweet or sour, depending on the formula.

2. *On the Departing of Thomas Chaucer*

THERE is only one authority for this poem, a Shirley MS., BM MS. Additional, 16165, f. 248a. *Index* 2571. The rubric reads 'Balade made by Lydgate at þe Departyng of Thomas Chaucyer on Ambassade into France'. Thomas Chaucer (1364–1434), son of the poet (Manly, *TLS*, 3 August 1933), married Maud Burghesh *c.* 1391–5. Alice, their only child, was born 1404. Thomas was M.P. for Oxfordshire and Speaker for Parliament on a number of occasions. Under Henry V he was frequently employed on government diplomatic missions (1414, 1417, 1420). He served in the field for Henry during the years 1417–19. He was Chief Butler to Henry IV, V, and VI.

Although Miss Hammond, Dr. T. B. Ruud (*Thomas Chaucer*, Minneapolis, U.S.A. (1925)), Professor MacCracken, and Professor Schirmer date this poem October 1417, when Chaucer was commissioned to treat with the ambassadors of the French king for a truce and final settlement of the war (*Rotuli Nor.* 1: 167. 169–170), Brusendorff may be right in dating it 4 June 1414, when Chaucer was sent to treat with the ambassadors of the Duke of Burgundy on the subject of a marriage with Catherine of Valois (*Issue Rolls*, Easter, 2 Henry V. Die Jovis xxj, die [*sic*] Junis). The major objection to October 1417 is that Chaucer (*Issue Rolls* 624, m. 5) was paid £182 in June 1417 for 'going with the king upon the voyage which he is soon to make'. If he sailed with the military expedition in July he was already in France. When he was commissioned for the October mission he had no water to cross. It is entirely possible that the poem may refer to his diplomatic activities in 1420. After 12 July 1420 Chaucer was again sent to France (he had returned home in 1419) to treat with the Lieutenant of Brittany and others for the observance of the king's final peace with France (*Cal. Norman Rolls*, D.K. 42 Report, App. 375).

If there was a recognized medieval genre of Propemticon (a poem wishing a friend a safe voyage) it was little practised in English or French. Deschamps's 'Propemticon' balade 1040, 'Sur le départ du roi' (? 1386), although it makes use of epithets, personification, prayer, and panegyric, has no structural relation to Lydgate's poem. Lydgate's work probably owes its first section (stanzas 1–3) to Horace's Propemticon, 'Ad Navem qua vehebatur Virgilius' (*Odes* 1. iii):

> Sic te diva potens Cypri,
>> Sic fratres Helenæ, lucida sidera,
> Ventorumque regat pater,
>> Obstrictis aliis præter Iapyga,
>
> Navis, quæ tibi creditum
>> Debes Virgilium, finibus Atticis
> Reddas incolumen precor . . .

The codified exordium (cf. Statius, *Silvæ* III. ii), with its mythological invocations to Venus, Castor and Pollux, Aeolus and Iapyx culminating in a direct prayer, is exactly paralleled by Lydgate's invocations to Luna and Neptune ending in a direct prayer to God. It is in no way odd that Lydgate should have known Horace. His own MS., Laud Misc. 233, contains a *florilegium* of Horace on ff. 121a and 123a, though the *Epistles* only are represented in this collection.

1. *Lucina*: Luna. Cf. *Troy Book*, Prol. 132. Cf. Chaucer, *CT*, F. 1045 ff.:

> Youre blisful suster, Lucina the sheene,
> That of the see is chief goddesse and queene
> (Though Neptunus have deitee in the see
> Yet emperisse aboven hym is she),

and Douglas, *Æneid*, Prol. III. 1 ff.:

> Hornyt Lady, pail Cynthia not bricht,
>
> . . . . . .
>
> Schipmen and pilgrymys hallowis thi mycht.

8. *expleyte*: 'to prosper'. A Lydgate coinage, an example of aureation. The verb has probably been coined directly from Latin *explet-*, the past part. stem of explēre. Examples quoted by Godefroy would seem to indicate that Latinate spellings (*expleict-*, *explet-*) of *esploitier* existed at this time in OF. This sense of the ME vb. seems to derive from OF.

12. *meynee*: 'refinne'.

29–30. *Ceres*: (MS. *certes*). The goddess of agriculture is commonly described by poets and mythographers as crowned or ornamented with the harvest, standing in a chariot drawn by dragons. Cf. Ovid, *Metamorphoses* v. 642 ff., where Ceres gives her chariot stored with seeds to Triptolemus.

34. (MS. *with*) which makes nonsense of the grammar and ruins the compliment to Chaucer. Chaucer is the real source of wine, Bacchus is only his agent.

38–39. Cf. Shakespeare, *Timon of Athens* I. ii. 104 ff.

43. *Molynes*: William de Moleyns 1377/8–1425. He was a commissioner of array in Buckinghamshire in 1399 and 1403, a justice of the peace 1403, 1419, 1422. In 1414 he was styled knight. He held the manors of Cippenham, Beachendon, Stoke Poges, and Henley-on-Thames (the last until 1417, when it was exchanged for the manor of Dachet). There is a brass of Sir William and his wife Margery (*née* Whalesborough) in the chancel of Stoke Poges (cf. G. Lipscomb, *History and Antiquities of Buckinghamshire*, vol. iv, p. 566). Thomas Chaucer became the custodian of William de Moleyns's granddaughter Eleanor after his son's death (*Cal. Pat. Rolls* 1429–36, p. 156).

50. The MS. glosses *la femme Chaucer*, i.e. Maud, daughter and coheiress of Sir John Burghersh, lord of the manor of Ewelme. There is a brass of her in the church at Ewelme. Cf. *Oxford Journal of Monumental Brasses*, vol. i, pp. 11–14.

tender creature: cf. Chaucer, *Legend of Good Women* 1370.

51. *Sainte Eleyne*: St. Helena, mother of the Emperor Constantine, who visited Palestine (Eusebius, *Vita Constantini* III. 42 ff.). However vague medieval geography was, India was never confused with Palestine (Isidore, *Etymologiae* XIV *passim*). Lydgate here probably employs the rhetorical figure *abusio*. India, a specific distant region, is generalized to signify any remote region, standing here for Palestine. Cf. Virgil, *Georgics* II. 467 ff., where Tempe, originally in Thessaly, is generalized to signify any beauty spot (Servius says of this passage: 'Tempe propriae sunt loca amoena Thessaliae, abusive cuiusvis loci amoenitas').

52. *shul*: (2nd plur.). Cf. *Siege of Thebes* 1607.

54. *amonge*: 'all the while'. In l. 65 *euer amonge* does not have its usual sense of 'every now and then' but means 'perpetually'. Cf. *MED ever* 9(d).

56. *Goddes soule*: the MS. wrongly underlines *to hem*. *Goddes soule* perhaps translates the opening of the famous prayer of thanksgiving, *Anima Christi*.

57. Thomas Chaucer's principal manor was at Ewelme (acquired by marriage). He was M.P. for Oxfordshire in the Parliaments of 1400–1, 1402, 1405–6, 1407, 1409–10, 1411, 1413, 1414, 1421, 1422, 1425–6, 1427, 1429.

59. The *repetitio* of 'farwel' in this stanza is a rhetorical feature borrowed from an amatory genre, the farewell to a mistress. Cf. R. H. Robbins, *Secular Lyrics of the XIV and XV Centuries* (1952),

nos. 197, 202–5 ; R. Steele, *The English Poems of Charles of Orleans*, EETS (1941), no. 60; Deschamps, *Rondel* 577 and *Virelay* 754. This feature had already been used by Deschamps for poems addressed to cities: *Rondel* 552, à Bruxelles, *Rondel* 640, à Troyes, *Balade* 871, à Paris.

68. *Saint Julyan*: Thomas Chaucer is identified with 'Saint Iulian the gode Herberour'. This refers to ll. 22–42. Lydgate is characterizing Thomas Chaucer through his father's portrait of the Franklin in *CT*, A. 339–56:

> An householdere, and that a greet, was he;
> Seint Iulian he was in his contree.
>
> .   .   .   .   .   .
>
> His table dormant in his halle alway
> Stood redy covered al the longe day.
> At sessiouns ther was he lord and sire;
> Ful ofte tyme he was knyght of the shire.

3. *Balade Sente to the Shirrefs Dyner*

THERE is only one authority for this poem, a Shirley MS., Bodley MS. Ashmole 59, f. 62b. *Index* 2170. The poem is prefaced by Shirley's rubric, which provides some information as to the place, occasion, and form of presentation:

> Nowe here nexst folowyng ys made a balade by Lydegate,
> sent by a poursyuant to þe Shirreves of London, acompanyed
> with þeire breþerne vpon Mayes daye at Busshopes wod,
> at an honurable dyner, eche of hem bringginge hys dysshe.

The text of the poem is marred either by bad copying or bad textual tradition. The poem and rubric have been noticed by R. Withington, *English Pageantry*, Cambridge, U.S.A. (1918), vol. i, 106 ff.; W. F. Schirmer, *John Lydgate*, 102 ff.; G. Wickham, *Early English Stages 1300–1660* (1959), vol. i, 191 ff. The poem was noticed earlier by John Stow in his *Svrvay of London* (1603), 99–100. The stanzas of the poem that he quotes are from the Ashmole MS., which was once in his possession. Stow provides probable identification of the place of performance:

... of these Mayings, we read in the raigne of *Henry* the sixt, that the Aldermen and Shiriffes of London being on May day at the Bishop of Londons wood in the parish of *Stebunheath* [Stepney], and hauing

there a worshipfull dinner for themselues and other commers, *Lydgate*
the Poet that was a Monke of Bery, sent to them by a Pursiuant a
ioyfull commendation of that season. . . .

A side-note particularizes the place in Stepney: 'Bishops wood |
Bishops hall | by Blethenhall greene |.'

The form of presentation is difficult to deduce from the evidence
provided by the poem and rubric. Dr. Wickham, following
Withington, notices the indoor nature of the poem and observes
that the personifications do not speak. The Pursuivant describes
and explains: speech and action are distinct. There is no dramatic
action, simply a presentation performed by the personifications.
Taking the poem and rubric together, the following explanation
is possible: (1) The occasion is a dinner; (2) the diners are seated;
(3) their plates are in front of them; (4) the personification of
early Spring presents two things: (*a*) physical descriptions of the
season, and (*b*) tidings which are moral generalizations arising
out of the nature descriptions (compare especially link-stanza 7,
where the two elements are fused together for emphasis); (5) the
personification of May performs the same role: May in stanza 12
presents 'prosperous plesaunce', which is exemplified by the
nature description of stanzas 13 and 14.

The 'mumming' resembling the action of this poem is contained
in the verses that record the presentation of 'sotleties' (courses
accompanied by a place favour) at the coronation dinner of Henry
VI in 1432 (MacCracken, ii. 623). The Sotleties poem (attributed
to Lydgate) has a simple progressive structure: each place
favour (described in detail in the MS.) is described and explained
by one eight-line stanza. After each presentation the course,
presumably, was eaten. In our poem the situation is very much
the same. The diners are seated, their plates are ready. The
Pursuivant comes before the table and announces two personifications who are to present abstract tidings, and (it would seem) are
to present something concrete, something which is correlated with
the tidings and with the situation. If there is any connexion
between the words of the poem and the action, the personifications
presented actual or artificial May boughs and flowers intended as
'sotleties' (place favours) to be placed on or near the diners'
plates.

The structure of the poem seems diffuse and repetitive, but
closer examination reveals an attempt at interweaving the repre-
sentation and presentation. There is an overall progression from

Ver (who presides over March and April) to May (who presides over the day and the following season). Verbal repetition abounds: 'lusty', 'swote', 'ermonye', 'lustynes', and one instance of *polyptoton* in stanza 13: 'lustely' and 'lusty'. The core of the poem is announced in stanza 15 by a complete change in imagery and quickening of rhythm. In this stanza earthly harmony and unity are related to a heavenly Parnassus, where the Muses, Venus and Cupid, and Orpheus weave an elaborate song of praise for the season. A similar harmony tableau is presented in the *Temple of Glas*, ll. 1299–312, in which the same figures praise Venus and Cupid, who are presented as the agents of durable true affection (1313–14). The tableau in this poem seems to be Lydgate's own poetic amalgam, deriving its elements from three places: (1) Chaucer's *Hous of Fame*, 1203, for the figure of Orpheus; (2) Chaucer's *Parlement*, for the idea of the closing rondel of praise; (3) *Troilus* III. 1807 ff., for the grouping of Venus, Cupid, and the Muses in connexion with a celebration of universal Love.

2. MS. reads *hast*. Shirley has read þ in his exemplar as long *st*, assuming the first verb in the sequence to be 2nd sing., with *Flora* in the vocative. Stow silently emends to 'hath'.

7. Ver is not a common personification in ME verse. The season was not personified in classical Latin poetry, although there is a possible instance in Claudian's *De Bello Getico* 166 ff. She appears as an extended example of *prosopopoeia* in Alcuin's *Conflictus Veris et Hiemis*, and thereafter appears often in Medieval Latin verse (cf. Alan of Lille, *De Planctu Naturæ*, pr. 1 and m. 3). In ME her existence before Lydgate's popularization is thin. There is, for example, only one reference to her in Gower (*Confessio Amantis* VII. 1014) and one in Chaucer (*Troilus* I. 157).

9. *vertu vegytable*: 'the basic vital power of growth exerted by the vegetable soul'. Cf. *Reson and Sensuallyte* 2747 and Fairfax MS. 16, where *virtus vegetativa* occurs as a marginal gloss. Although the Latin phrase does not seem to have been recorded, it occurs in OF. Cf. Bruno Latini, *Il Tresors* II. i. vi: *Des trois Puissance l'ame*: 'L'ame de l'ome a trois puissances. L'une est vegetative et ce est commun as arbres as plantes, car il ont ame vegetative aussi comme li home ont.' Lydgate sometimes uses the word *vertu* by itself as an equivalent of 'vertu vegetable': cf. *Troy Book*, I. 3910, 3923; IV. 3367.

10. The MS. reads *trascends*. The stroke has been omitted over the *a*. Stow silently expands to 'transcends'.

9–14. Lydgate in his descriptions of spring often shows a scientific interest in certain botanical processes. Cf. *Troy Book* I. 3915 ff.; and N. E. Enkvist, *The Seasons of the Year* (1957), 126 ff. for an account of Lydgate's treatment of the seasons.

15. *swaged*: 'diminished', used of frost. Cf. *Troy Book* II. 5067 ff.

24. MS. reads *sugre*. It is just possible that Lydgate intended an attributive use of the n. But such a use would be unique in ME. *sugred* is a favourite past part. adj. of Lydgate's.

27. Cf. G. Tilander, *Romania*, lvi (1936), pp. 267–75 for the origin and development of the vb. *proygne*.

51. *þe hede*: Lydgate refers obliquely to the late classical and medieval image of the body politic. Cf. *Fall of Princes* II. 827–903 for a complete allegory of the corporate image (probably derived from John of Salisbury's *Polycraticus*). For an account of this image see A-H. Chroust, 'The Corporate Idea in the Middle Ages', *Review of Politics*, viii (1947).

55. The MS. reads *beo* although the sense requires *haue*. The succour derives from the judges' action. The Commons are not their own protection.

88. MS. reads *enemye*, which is badly written over the back of an erasure. The form in Shirley's exemplar was probably 'ermonye'. The contraction for *r* has disappeared from the first *e*. The second *e* is a misreading of *o*, and *m* and *n* have got transposed.

92. MS. reads *Topyted*. Shirley has miswritten *o* for *a*. Cf. *Troy Book* I. 1659 ff. This is an example of Chaucer's influence on Lydgate's vocabulary: cf. *Book of the Duchess* 258 ff.:

> . . . and al hys halles
> I wol do peynte with pure gold
> And tapite hem ful many folde . . .

92. *motleys*: 'garment of grass and many-coloured flowers'. Cf. *Fall of Princes* VI. 183 ff.:

> The erthe is clad in motles whiht and rede;
> Whan Estas entrith with violettis soote,
> The greuis greene, and in euery meede
> The bawme fleteth, which doth to hertis boote.

The origin of this n. probably springs from Lydgate's translating of *Les Échecs Amoureux* (*Reson and Sensuallyte* 105 ff.):

> Dont la terre est si orgueilleuse
> Et si se cointoye et se pare
> Quil samble quelle se compare

> Au ciel destre mieulx estellee
> Pour ce quelle est enmantellee
> De son verd *mantel pincele* . . .

100. *Citherra*: 'Venus'. Chaucer always uses the form *Citherea* (although *CT*, A. 2215 might be more regular metrically if 'Cithera' were read). Lydgate uses both forms of the word. ME *Cithera* probably reflects the influence of the poetic collateral form *Cythere, -es* used in post-classical Latin verse. The epithet derives from the island of Cythera. Cf. Servius *ad Æn* x: 'Insula est contra Laconicam Veneri consecrata.'

102. *wellis*: Lydgate here refers to the rivers Helicon and Hippocrene, sacred to the Muses. Lydgate's geography of Parnassus agrees with Chaucer's. Basic information about Parnassus came to medieval poets from two sources, Servius's commentary on Virgil and Isidore's *Etymologiæ*. In Servius's commentary on *Georgics* III. 290 ff. we are told 'Per Parnassi ardua, Eliconem et Citheronem montes musis dictatos significat'. Again, on *Æneid* x Servius notes: 'Parnassus mons est Thessaliæ iuxta Boeotiam . . . qui in duo finditur iuga Citheronem Liberi et Heliconem Apollinis et Musarum. Ex quo fons manare dicitur quem Pegasi ungula protulisse fertur qui vocatur Ippocrene.' In Isidore, *Etymologiæ* XIV, Servius's notes are repeated with the following elaboration: 'Hic [Mt. Parnassus] in duo finditur iuga Cirra et Nisa.' The medieval view of Parnassus from these accounts would suppose that Parnassus was directly next to Boeotia, where the river Helicon was located. The division of Parnassus itself into two ridges, one of which was called Helicon, would encourage close geographical identification. Thus, when Chaucer writes (*Anelida* 15 ff.)

> Be favorable eek, thou Polymia
> On Parnaso that with thy sustres glade,
> By Elicon, not fer from Cirrea . . .,

in terms of medieval geography he is being perfectly accurate.

103. *hem*: Venus and Cupid.

106. Lydgate has combined two passages from Chaucer: *Hous of Fame* 1201 ff.:

> Ther herde I pleyen on an herpe
> That sowned bothe wel and sharpe,
> Orpheus ful craftely . . .

and the translation of Boethius's *De Consolatione* III. m. 12. 21 ff.:

'. . . and ther he tempride his blaundyssinge songes by resouninge strenges . . .'.

4. *An Exclamacioun of the Deth of Alcibiades*
(*Fall of Princes* III. 3655–82)

THE *Fall of Princes* was commissioned by Humphrey, Duke of Gloucester, in *c.* 1431 and finished in 1439. The work, based chiefly on Boccaccio's Latin prose *De Casibus Virorum Illustrium*, stretches to 36,365 lines, in nine books. The increased encyclopedic quality and genuine reforming zeal towards Princes owe not a little to Laurent de Premierfait's French version. The envoi summaries to many of the histories were added by Lydgate at the insistence of Duke Humphrey (II. Prol. 146 ff.). The poet's insights into the concept of Fortune and human motivation are inconsistent and eclectic. They are scarcely combined into an intelligible pattern. The same disjointed quality may be seen in the author's attitude to pagan society and antique ideals of conduct. Sometimes Lydgate displays a pronounced Christian bias (Constantine VIII. 1170 ff.; Theodosius VIII. 1891 ff.), at other times he shows an appreciation of individual stoic heroism (Marcus Scævola, II, 918 ff.; Alcibiades, III. 3284 ff.; Cato, III. 1226 ff.). It should be noted that much of the range of Lydgate's sympathy is the result of the historian's task of incorporating the material of his Authority. Whatever Lydgate's additions and abridgements, the *Fall* lacks formal shape. It is Chaucer's Monk's collection of tragedies considerably filled out. The universal chronology is retained, if not in strict sequence, at least in scope; we begin at Adam and end with King John of France. It would be tempting to see the poet in this work moving towards a distinct and influential appreciation of the spirit of the Renaissance, but the evidence is not convincing. The main contributions of the *Fall* to the sixteenth century lie in (1) the provision of the material in intelligible English; (2) the dramatic quality of some of the writing; (3) the 'medieval' poetic diction which first caused Sackville to attempt an imitation and later provided a method for Spenser's archaistic style.

This *exclamatio* is Lydgate's invention and owes nothing to his two main sources, Boccaccio or Laurent. Given the character of Alcibiades depicted in his sources, these verses, which record the death of ideal knighthood, would have been impossible. Both Boccaccio and Laurent delineate a flawed example of knighthood. Lydgate has removed all grounds for criticism. This passage forms an analogue to the *Troy Book* III. 5423–502, where Lydgate laments the death of Hector. The language is elevated according to the rhetorical practice of *exclamatio* but it is not aureate. The poetic texture derives from Chaucer's *Troilus* IV. 1546 ff.; v. 543 ff. Reminiscence of Chaucer provides the points of departure for stanzas i and ii, but stanzas iii and iv (which are poetically more interesting) are original and take many elements from non-literary sources. The infernal deities inveighed against in this passage play an integral role in the tragic action of the *Fall of Princes* (cf. I. 776, 3815, 4207, 5018; V. 908; IX. 2865). In Book III. 3956 ff. Lydgate describes Tyrants as 'ministris to Parchas sustren thre' and 'verray cosyns . . . Vnto the woode Furies infernall'.

The MSS. of the poem are numerous. For a complete list consult *Index* 1168. This text is based on Bodley MS. Bodley 263, f. 188b but readings have been incorporated from other Bodley MSS., notably Rawlinson C. 448, Hatton 2, and e Museo i.

1. *lyues threde*: cf. Chaucer, *Troilus* IV. 1546; V. 7.

3. Alcibiades was murdered by an act of arson. The method of murder provided his funeral pyre (l. 17).

4. The same sentiment is expressed in Lydgate's lament for Hector (*Troy Book*, III. 5476): 'Ʒe [Parcæ] were to hasty, allas, why were Ʒe so.'

5. *web of knihthod*: 'garment of knighthood'. The image has been developed from 'lyues threde'. Lydgate has probably been assisted by Chaucer's notion expressed in *Troilus* III. 733 ff.:

> 'O fatal sustren, which, er any cloth
> Me shapen was, my destine me sponne . . .'

Chaucer's conceit emphasizes the earliness of Fate's ordinance. Lydgate is interested in the Fates as the creators and destroyers of a perfected Being.

8. *Styx*: one of the infernal rivers (as in *Troilus* IV. 1540 and *Fall of Princes* I. 5013–19).

10. *you thre*: Lydgate here addresses the Furies, Alecto, Megaera, and Tisiphone (cf. *Fall of Princes* I. 5027 ff.). Their genealogy is based on Ovid, *Metamorphoses* IV. 451–2 and Chaucer, *Troilus* IV. 22. Chaucer describes the Furies as complaining in eternal torment (as in *Fall of Princes* I. 5027 ff.), but here Lydgate repre-

sents them as silent. The characterization is derived from Virgil, *Aeneid* VI. 264–5:

> Di, quibus imperium est animarum, umbræque silentes
> Et Chaos et Phlegethon, loca nocte tacentia late,

where infernal gods, spirits, and infernal places are addressed together. The shades are voiceless according to Servius, for 'secreta infernorum semper silentia'.

12. *Lethum*: *Lethe*, river of oblivion. In Virgil, *Aeneid* VI. 714–15, its waters are regarded as beneficial (as in Dante). Lydgate regards them as the active enemy of renown and reputation. The poetic impulse is affected by Chaucer, *Troilus* V. 543: 'O thow lanterne of which queynt is the lyght.'

13. *merour*: 'a speculum', 'a book which contains the true reproduction of something'; hence the vb. 'speke' in line 14. Cf. Chaucer, *Legend of Good Women*, Prol. G. 307.

16. Cf. Lydgate, *The Cok hath Lowe Shoone* (MacCracken, ii. 813), l. 103: 'Thersites wrecchyd, Ector moost wourthy knyght.' Thersites as a type of ignoble conduct does not occur in either Guido de Columnis or Benoît de Sainte-Maur. As an exemplary figure he occurs in Gower, *Confessio Amantis* VII. 3581 ff. and *Mirour de L'Omme* 2337 ff.; Evrard, *Laborintus* ll. 371–2.

18. I have kept the MSS. reading *To*, although the sense requires *Ye*.

18–19. The metaphoric identification of heroic men with cedars and laurels, knaves with furze, is probably derived from the *Rota Virgilii*, the medieval rhetorical schematization of subject-matter for inclusion in the three styles of narrative. The trees suitable for description in the *stylus gravis* (epic or tragedy) are the cedar and the laurel. The tree appropriate for the *stylus humilis* (eclogue) is the beech. The satiric nature of the comparison here requires a more pointed contrast, hence 'furze'. Compare Gavin Douglas, *Aeneid*, Prol. IX. 44 for *cedir* and *rammale* ('shrub') as examples of the high and low styles of narrative. The comparison of military character to the same trees is used by Shakespeare in *Titus Andronicus* IV. iii. 45: 'Marcus we are but shrubs, no Cedars we....'

19. *pall*: 'to make dim', an aphetic form of *appall* used of a person's honour or reputation. Cf. Chaucer, *CT*, A. 3053.

22. Cf. *Troy Book* II. 882: 'Or Parchas made hem [kings etc.] passyn into fate.'

27. *defied*: 'consumed'. Used here only in Lydgate to refer to

dissolution by fire. The vb. usually refers to dissolution by weather or water.

28. *stellified*: 'placed in heaven'. Cf. *Temple of Glas*, l. 135. This is the surprise note in the passage and justifies the addressing of infernal places earlier. Alcibiades, according to Lydgate, is not destined for the seats of oblivion.

5. *A Tale of Froward Maymond*

T H E R E are four authorities for this poem: Bodley MS. Laud Misc. 683, f. 54b: (N). BM MS. Harley 2251, f. 14a: (H). Lansdowne MS. 699, f. 88b: (L). Leyden Vossius MS. 9, p. 101: (V). The text is based on N but readings from other MSS. have been used. The alternative title given in L and V is *Descripcio Garcionis. Index* 36.

This is the most polished example of Lydgate's satiric manner. Maymond was a traditional medieval name for a bad servant (cf. 'Davus', Matthieu of Vendome, *Ars Versificatoria*, sect. 53). The name appears to have originated in Petrus Alfunsi's *Disciplina clericalis* xxvii, 'exemplum de Maimundo servo'. This eleventh-century collection of anecdotes about social types provided material for similar verse stories about Maymond (cf. the late thirteenth-century Anglo-Norman verse version, 'De Maimound mal esquier', in Bodley MS. Digby 86, ff. 94a–95a, or OF 'De Maimon le Pereceus' (*Fabliaux et Contes*, vol. ii. 166–71). If Lydgate's idea for the figure of Maymond came from the *Disciplina* (there was a fourteenth-century MS. of it in the library of the Abbey of Bury St. Edmunds) his satiric details of the portrait owe nothing to Alfunsi or later verse versions. Lydgate has taken the name and the basic associations only. His poetic texture derives from Chaucer, the *Cook's Tale*, in the description of Parkin Revelour.

3. *precious*: this is the first recorded example of the sense 'something worthless'.

cast: other MSS. read *castith*. I have kept the reading of H. Compare other uses of the preterite in the poem.

5. *tournebroche*: 'a boy whose office was to turn the spit', 'a turnspit'. This is the first recorded example in ME literature.

Hogge of Ware: Roger Hodge of Ware (Hertfordshire), the Cook in Chaucer's *Canterbury Tales*. Cf. *CT*, A. 4336. Lydgate accepts the host's picture of Roger as a dishonest, unskilled cook.

7. *Iakke Hare*: Lydgate seems to have been responsible for the

creation of this satiric type. Lydgate's *Testament* 668–9 (Mac-Cracken, i. 329):

> Wilfull, rekles, made stertyng as a hare
> To folowe my lust, for no man wold I spare

explains the appropriateness of the animal imagery.

8. Cf. the seventh order of knaves in Awdeley's *Fraternitye of Vacabondes*: 'Rince Pytcher is he that will drinke out his thrift at the ale or wine.'

10. *sloggy*: 'indolent'. Cf. Chaucer, *CT*, I. 705.

11. *gentil*: 'a reveller well-born in the family of vices'. His moral genealogy is given. Cf. Chaucer, *CT*, A. 647.

13. *Wecok*: I have found no other occurrence (or explanation) of this name in ME.

17. *Chekrelyk*: ? an otherwise unrecorded name for a type of knave who pilfers food from dishes returned from table. *MED* defines 'go-after-the-leavings'. But 'relik' in the sense 'leavings' is not recorded until the sixteenth century.

18. *lypet*, 'a bit' (cf. Dialect *libbet*). This is the only recorded example of the n. in ME.

19. *Fafynticol*: no other example of this name is recorded.

20. *Of euery brybe the caryage for to make*: 'to undertake the get-away with the loot'.

27. *vernysshed*: cf. Chaucer, *CT*, A. 4149:

> Wel hath the millere vernysshed his heed;
> Ful pale he was for dronken and nat reed.

29. Cf. Lydgate, *The Order of Fools*, l. 132 (MacCracken, ii. 449) and *Roman de la Rose* 18242: 'E deus chandelles sembler d'une.'

35. Other MSS. read *shake*. H reads *take*.

47. *ale-stakes*: 'a stake or pole set up before an alehouse.'

49. *iousy*: the first recorded example of the adj. 'juicy'. *OED* defines as 'succulent', but the meaning here seems to be 'soggy'. Cf. Lydgate, *A Mumming at Hertford*, l. 39 (MacCracken, ii. 675).

50. *Vnthrift*: compare the twenty-second order of knaves in Awdeley: 'Vnthrift, is he that wil not put his wearing clothes to washing, nor black his owne shoes, nor amend his own wearing clothes. This rechles knaue wyl alway be lousy. . . .'

51–53. Maymond's habit of leaving the door open is mentioned in the *Disciplina*.

Rigg: *OED* defines as 'ridgel' ,'an animal which has been improperly neutered'. MS. V has in the margin *nota canis*. *Rigg* is here a dog's name.

Togace: not recorded in *OED*. H has an interlinear note *þe cat*.

out-het: 'over-heated'.

6. *The Rebuilding of Troy*

(*Troy Book*, II. 479–710)

THERE are nineteen MSS. of the *Troy Book* (*Index* 2516) but only four MSS. are essential for establishing a text: BM MS. Cotton Augustus A. iv: (C). Bristol MS.: (B). Bodley MSS. Digby 232: (D2); Rawlinson C. 446: (R1). The present text is based on C, with readings from D2.

The *Troy Book*, drawing on a number of sources (chiefly Benoît de Sainte-Maur's *Roman de Troie* and Guido de Columnis's *Historia Destructionis Troiæ*), was commissioned in October 1412 by Henry V. It was probably intended originally by both patron and poet as a 'Mirror for Princes'. Lydgate, although he employed strict chronological sequence according to the rules of the *stylus naturalis* proper for history, intended the poem as an encyclopedia of military, political, and moral observations where historical material and poetic imagination are freely mixed. Three main interests are pursued at length by the poet: (1) scholarly accounts of all relevant mythological and historical material drawn from a wide range of sources; (2) criticism of political discord, especially when rulers embark on active policies of war; (3) Fortune and the ultimate theme of the vanity and impermanence of human ambition. These would appear to be the normal and legitimate interests of an educated author of the period. There is no need to see Lydgate obliquely lecturing Henry for his French policy.

After eight years' labour Lydgate finished the *Troy Book* in 1420. Whatever recurring themes and interests are traceable in the poem, the expanded chronological structure (inherited from Benoît and Guido) engulfs the digressions and moralizations. No distinctive shape or formal plan survives the exhaustive treatment accorded to every aspect. Lydgate creates no sense of perspective, no foreground or background. It is an episodic composition of a kind paralleled in the visual arts by the full-page serial illuminations for' Universal Histories' so popular in the fifteenth century.

The rebuilding of Troy was a popular subject for fifteenth-century illuminators. For a beautifully executed depiction see Bodley MS. Douce 353, f. 43b of *La Vraye Ystoire de Troye*, and Plate 19 in Scherer, *The Legends of Troy* (1963).

1–10. Compare Guido de Columnis, *Historia Destructionis Troiæ* v (ed. N. E. Griffin, Cambridge, Mass., 1936): 'Sed demum lacrimarum imbribus fluuialibus excollatis, amaro corde satisfactionis quasi recepta quiete, post depositos gemitus et lamenta, longo examinatio consilio, placuit Troyam euersam iterum instaurare.'

10–32. Cf. Guido: 'Hinc est quod quesitis undique fabris et peritis in hedificandis artibus et marmoreis celaturis, lapidariis, et doctissimis architectis omnis generis, marmora natiuis diuersimode insignita coloribus mirabiliter coegit instruere.' Lydgate expands and particularizes freely.

33–44. This excursus is added by Lydgate. For Pygmalion as an exemplary figure of the sculptor see the *Roman*, 16177 ff. The Middle Ages seems not to have known Pliny's account of Apelles (*Naturalis Historia* xxxv. 79–97). Their source of information was Walter of Chatillon's epic the *Alexandreis*. Walter was a curriculum author (cf. Douglas, *Palis of Honoure* ii. st. 15: 'Thare wes Galterus and Boetius'). Apelles makes two appearances in the *Alexandreis*; in Book iv. 178 ff., where he builds a tomb for Darius's wife, and Book vii. 381 ff., where he constructs Darius's tomb. Walter, possibly for aesthetic reasons, changes Apelles's nationality from Greek to Hebrew. His authority for this may rest on a misreading of Horace, *Satires* i. v. 100. Horace's 'Iudæus Apella' may have produced Walter's:

> . . . structum quem schemate miro
> Erexit celeber digitis Hebræus Apelles.

(iv. 178–9)

Walter, vii. 383–4:

> . . . niveo quæ marmore structa
> Ingenio docti super ædificatur Apelles

is the common source for Lydgate and for Chaucer, *CT*, D. 498–9:

> As was the sepulcre of him, Daryus,
> Which that Apelles wroghte subtilly.

45–56. This is an amplification of ll. 10–32 in Lydgate's redundant manner.

55–58. Cf. Guido: 'Quam in ea magnitudine et fortitudine fabricare decreuit quod nullos hostiles timere posset insultus et in suorum offensionem hostium uere posset erigi ceruicosa.'

59–80. Cf. Guido: 'Et sic amotis ruderibus et ruinosis locis purgatis in quibus consedit prima Troya, mirabilis longitudinis et latitudinis sub dei Neptuni nomine ciuitatem erexit quam eodem nomine Troyam uidelicet censuit appellari. Fuit autem huius secunde Troye ambitus longitudinis trium dierum latitudinis coequalis.'

81–83. Cf. Guido: 'A terre igitur superficie usque ad summum eius superhedificata sunt menia in mirabili compositione murorum circumquaque cubitorum altitudine ducentorum.'

83. *maskowed*: 'machiolated', provided with openings between corbels supporting a projecting parapet.

84–88. Cf. Guido: '. . . quorum superficies erat marmoreis incrustata lapidibus in uariorum diuersitate colorum ut intuentium aspectibus blandirentur.'

88–91. Cf. Guido: 'Nec ante fundationem eius aut postea nunquam legitur condita ciuitas tante magnitudinis, tante pulcritudinis, aut similis speciei.'

92–97. Cf. Guido: 'In murorum itaque ipsorum circumgiratione corone non multum vna turris distabat ab alia que super muros eosdem excrescenti altitudine imminebant.' 'In the circumgirding crown of its own walls stood a separate tower at not too great a distance from the others which in their rising height hung over the same walls.' Lydgate has taken Guido's figurative crown literally.

95. *bretexed*: 'furnished with a breastwork'.

98–115. Cf. Guido: 'Introitus autem et exitus ciuitatas ipsius fuit in sex ianuis institutus, quarum una Dardanides, secunda Tymbrea, tercia Helias, quarta Chetas, quinta Troyana, et sexta Athenodes vocabantur. Quelibet portarum ipsarum bellicosis fuerat firmata turribus per latera et in celaturis marmorearum imaginum circumquaque decora.'

116–18 and 128–30. Cf. Guido: 'Quarum quelibet amicis intrare uolentibus placidos permittebat ingressus et superbe resistentie quibuslibet inimicis duros et fortes minabitur accessus.' The reference to artillery has been added by Lydgate.

119–27. The details of wild animal decoration on the outside of have been expanded and transferred from Guido's mention decorations on buildings within the city walls. Cf. Guido:

'. . . totum etiam marmoreis firmatum lapidibus in mirificis ymaginum ferarum et hominum celaturis.' In the description of animal imagery in stone-work Lydgate established a sixteenth-century fashion. Compare Stephen Hawes, *The Passetyme of Pleasure* (the tower of Doctrine):

> But the fayre toure so moche of rychesse
> Was all about sexangeled doubtles,
> Gargeylde with grehoundes and with many lyons
> Made of fyne golde with diuers sundry dragons.
>
> (ll. 361–4)

And William Nevill, *Castell of Pleasure*:

> This royall castell was on eche syde quadraunt,
> Gargaled with goodly grehoundes and beste many one:
> The tyrannous tygre, the stronge and myghty elephaunt
>
> (ll. 226–8)

131–4. The details of the gates, portcullises, and bolts have been added by Lydgate. There is no mention of them in Guido (nor later in Lefevre or Caxton). Shakespeare, *Troilus and Cressida*, Prol. 17–18:

> And Antenonidus with massie Staples
> And corresponsiue and fulfilling Bolts . . .

is remembering Lydgate.

135–55. Expanded from Guido: 'Infra uero ciuitatem eandem instructa fuerunt infinita palatia et in ea infinite domus ciuium formosis hedificiis fabricate, que ciuitatem eandem ornabant in multarum latitudine platearum.'

141. *enbowing*: 'arched work'. A Lydgatian formation.

vergis; a unique n. in ME. *OED* quotes Parker's definition 'shafts of columns'. J. H. Parker, *A Glossary of Terms* (1850), p. 510, quotes this passage, claiming that *verge* is a French architectural term. Godefroy, unfortunately, records no use of the n. in an architectural context in OF. The general sense of *verge* in ME and OF is 'rod'. It may refer to some kind of rod moulding on the inside of an arch. The term is not recorded by L. F. Salzman, *Building in England down to 1540* (1952).

142. *vowsing*: 'vaulting'. A Lydgatian coinage from OF vb. *vouser* + English suffix *-ing*.

143. *copurnyng*: the reading of D2. C reads *caxening*. *Coporon*, *copron*, *coporne* is a term of masonry meaning some cut stone in the form of a coping, a cornice, or the capital of a column. Salzman

(p. 109) quotes examples in accounts from 1368 to 1444. Bergen, following *OED*, emends to *koyning*. *MED* follows Bergen.

144. *vynnetts*: 'running ornaments of leaves and tendrils'.

147–55. An example of the rhetorical figure *occupatio*.

156–67. Cf. 'In ipsarum uero lateribus platearum innumerabilibus super columpnis marmoreis arcubus circumuolutis erectis, sub ipsorum hedificiis eleuatis, liber et cotidianus gradientibus patebat incessus, ut nec a uentorum rabie nec ad ymbrium rore celesti uexarentur inuitis aspersionibus gradientes.'

161. *frontel*: *MED* (following Bergen) defines 'the front of a building' and quotes only this passage. This sense is not properly recorded until 1789. Lydgate means little more than 'front', following the general sense of the n. in OF and Medieval Latin.

reclinatories: 'a covered place provided with a half-seat'. Lydgate has coined this word from OF or late Latin.

165. *deambulatories*: 'covered walks'. A Lydgate coinage from Medieval Latin. Compare Douglas's translation of *Aeneid* VII. 177 ff. in the description of Latinus's palace:

> Within the cheif deambulatour on raw
> Of forfaderis gret ymagis dyd stand
>
> (VII. iii. 62–63)

There is no hint of such an architectural arrangement in Virgil. The extended use of precise architectural terms in late Latin poetry was first established by Sidonius Apollinaris in his poem on the Castle of Pontius Leontius (*Carmen* XXII).

168–72. The interest in drains and sanitation is Lydgate's. The plumbing in medieval monastic houses tended to be of superior quality.

175–82. Lydgate's town planning derives from Guido: 'Per plateas enim, ipsas mechanicarum artium locate fuerunt proprie stationes, in quibus earum operarii, per certa loca districti, cotidianis operibus et uenalibus artificiis insudabant.' The economic *raison d'être* for the arrangement is not in Guido.

7. *As a Mydsomer Rose*

THERE are seven authorities for this poem: BM MSS. Harley 2255, f. 3b: (H); Harley 2251, f. 15a: (h). Bodley MS. Ashmole 59, f. 31b: (A). Trinity College, Cambridge MS. R. 21, f. 300a: (T). Jesus College, Cambridge MS. 56, f. 25a: (J). Cambridge University MS. Hh. 4. 12, f. 86a: (C). Huntington HM 140 [*olim* Phillips MS. 8299], f. 86b: (P). *Index* 1865.

Two distinct versions of the poem survive. Version *a* (which is probably earlier) exists only in A, a Shirley MS. Although A is more regular metrically it lacks the polished eighth stanza and at several points shows grammatical ineptness. It contains several independent touches, e.g. the refrain shows greater variation and the conclusion is managed by descriptive emphasis rather than the rhetorical adhortation of the *b*-version. Version *b* (probably the revised copy) exists in six MSS. Although H was selected as the best text by Professor MacCracken, it has no absolute claim to textual authority. One test case will indicate the necessity for an 'open' text. At line 60: 'Tellus and Imo be dullyd of ther cheere', there is wide MS. disagreement about the second mythological figure. JT read *Ymo*, h reads *Iuno*, P reads *Yone*, and H reads *Imo*. MacCracken, presumably, assumed that JT's *Ymo* supported H and so retained *Imo*. There is no such figure. H's *Iuno* and P's *Yone* point to Lydgate's original figure, *Ioue* (Jove). The same scribal miswriting occurs in Chaucer's *Troilus* v. 207 in BM MS. Add. 12044. Lydgate's stanza describes the changeableness of the earth and the heavens. Jove was a common designation for the heavens in classical and medieval Latin verse. The identification of Jupiter with *æther* is the subject of two long notes in Servius's commentary on the *Æneid*. Christian writers, too, were aware of the identification: cf. St. Augustine, *Civitate Dei* 7. 23: 'primum, qui omnes fructus agriculturæ cælo et terra continet, Jovem et Tellurem.'

The poem has been classified by MacCracken and Schirmer as a 'little homily with proverbial refrain'. Certainly, the general structure resembles that of other Lydgatian poems so classified. But this poem is more ambitious and more complex than the other examples of this genre. There are eight stanzas of the usual *exemplum* type, followed by a middle section of *catalogue* (Lydgate's favourite rhetorical scheme) cast in the grammatical formula of 'ubi sunt' (stanzas 9–12). The *conclusio* consists of three stanzas where the contrasting examples emerge gradually into poetic contradiction. The concluding refrain is not merely a variation but a change of image and emphasis; the final stanza is not just an ultimate definition by example but a more complicated treatment of the rose of the refrain—the natural rose raised to an allegorical power.

In the concluding section a paradox is presented, for the Christian martyrs of stanzas 13–14 are not symbolized traditionally by the rose, yet Christ's 'martyrdom' is so symbolized. Christ, the universal type of Christian suffering, is the rose 'of Iericho that greuh in Beedlem'. In the *a*-version ordinary martyrdom and the Passion were merged into a single, overlapping image through the original link-refrain 'þere martirdame as lyke þe rede roose'. In the *b*-version the revised refrain 'Ther blody suffraunce was no somyr roose' presents a surface contrast between the Passion and martyrdom. The 'It' ('Ther blody suffraunce') in the last stanza carefully rejects only the attributive noun 'somyr' in the contrasting refrain: 'It was no *summer* rose. . . . It was the rose that grew in Bethleham.' The poetic activity which translates the natural rose, symbol of organic decay, into the highest expression of martyrdom through the traditional symbolism of Christ, the rose of Jericho, and, further, translates the new image into a meditational emblem, is original and unparalleled elsewhere in medieval poetry.

1–8. Diversity of gifts is not properly a proof of changeability. Cf. Lydgate's *Benedictus Deus* 1–8 (MacCracken, i. 7) for a more logical use of the argument.

7. This line has been emended along lines suggested by the reading of h: 'Som man hath wisdom and some hath eloquence.'

8. *mydsomer roose*: cf. Lydgate, *That Now is Hay Some-tyme was Grase* 17–24 (MacCracken, ii. 809). Although classical poets were aware of the rose's short-lived beauty (Horace, *Odes* II. iii. 14) the rose as a type of worldly mutability seems to have originated in medieval Latin verse: cf. Alan of Lille, *Omnis mundi creatura* 7–11:

> Nostrum statum pingit rosa
> Nostri status decens glosa
> Nostræ vitæ lectio.
> Quæ dum primo mane floret,
> Defloratus flos effloret.

Lydgate uses variations on this refrain elsewhere. Cf. *Fall of Princes* IV. 2002: 'Al stant on chang: record vpon king Darie', and *The World so Wyd* 118 (MacCracken, ii. 734): 'Al stant on chaung: now los and now wynnyng.'

11. *colourys*: 'coloured petals'. Cf. Lydgate, *Look in thy Merour* 115 (MacCracken, ii. 765): 'Sharp thornys hid somtyme vndir

roosys.' This is an example of the rhetorical figure *metonomy*, where quality has been substituted for substance. Lydgate has been assisted here by Chaucer's word-play in *CT*, F. 723: 'Colours ne knowe I none. . . . But swich colours as growen in the mede. . . .'

12. Cf. Chaucer, *Hous of Fame* 272. This proverb derives from Alan of Lille's collection, *Parabolæ*: 'Non teneas aurum totum quod splendet ut aurum.'

13. *stokfyssh*: a name for cod and other fish cured by splitting open and drying hard without salt. A codfish bone here appears to be an example of contraries which may never agree. Cf. the glow-worm in Lydgate's *The Cok hath Lowe Shoone* 47 (MacCracken, ii. 813): 'A fowle gloowerme in dirknesse shewith a lyght.'

18. Cf. Chaucer, *CT*, A. 1491: 'The bisy larke, messager of day. . . .'

30. *verdite*: C reads *mater*. 'Verdite', used by Chaucer in the *Parlement* to mean little more than 'an opinion', is here further weakened in sense to mean 'the act of singing'.

33. Cf. Lydgate, *Isopes Fabules* ii, *The Tale of the Wolfe and the Lambe*, 260 ff. (MacCracken, ii. 574):

> Lyke þy fadyr, þou art false and double
> And hym resemblest of dysposicion,
> For he was wont my water here to trouble . . .

Although the wolf's claim against the lamb derives from the fables of Gualterus Anglicus, the notion of an animal parliament or court of law (such as the one in Lydgate's *Debate of the Horse, Goose and Sheep*) does not seem to have been part of the fable tradition. Lydgate, in the introduction of an animal assembly in the *Debate* may have been the originator of the impulse which led to Henryson's *Trial of the Fox*.

43. *kalends*: 'calendar'. The earliest instance of this sense of the n. recorded by *MED*. MS. A reads *kalende*, h *kalendis*. The other MSS. read *Kalenderys*.

aureat noumbre: the 'aureus numerus', the number of the lunar cycle by which the date of Easter is calculated.

prime: the golden number.

48. A's refrains begin to show a greater use of variation: 'For al in chaunge stant lyche a midsomer roose.'

52–56. The *a*-version (A) reads here:

> Soone affter þat þe clowdes assemble in feere   52a
> And night foloweþe, it is wele seene to here;

It chaungeþe offt what thing þat men purpose,
Leve þis [s]ooþe, beo it far or neere,   55a
For þe worlde chaungeþe as a midsomer roos.

This is the first major difference between the *a*- and *b*-version. In the *a*-version the antithesis to the example of pleasantness (49–51) is split up into two kinds of statement: (*a*) physical image (52–53), and (*b*) generalization arising from the image, where the grammar does not make it clear how the generalization is related to the physical image. In fact, 54a is not really connected with the imagery but is an additional thought on the subject thrown in (much like l. 23). The generalization of 54a unfortunately explains the whole *exemplum*, thereby making the refrain redundant. The three fillers in ll. 53a and 55a do not contribute much to the grammatical strength of the passage. In the *b*-version the two halves of the *exemplum* are neatly balanced, and in each half the sun acts as the unifying image; there is no anticipatory generalization and the refrain is not anticlimactic.

60. *Tellus and Iove*: 'earth and sky'. Cf. *Troy Book* iv. 6957 and *Fall of Princes* i. 2628, 'Tellus which of the erthe is guide'. For *Iove* compare Horace, *Odes* i. i. 25: 'Manet sub Ioue frigido Venator.'

62. *gery March*: cf. Chaucer, *Troilus* ii. 765.

65–95. This is a long passage of catalogue using the *ubi sunt* motif. The list of exemplary figures is for the most part conventional. Cf. Deschamps, *Balade* 368, 'Ilz sont tous mors, ce monde est chose vaine', where his list includes David, Salemon, Alixandre, Julles Cesar, Godefroy, Jason, and Charlemaine. Absalon occurs in Deschamps's *Balade* 427. Some of the figures are treated in the *Fall of Princes*: Pirrus in iv. 3745–898; Alisaundre, iv. 1604–2170; Sardonapal, ii. 2234–338; Tullius, vi. 2948–3276. St. Chrysostom, Homer, and Seneca are not commonly included in mutability catalogues.

72. A's refrain reads: 'Al is in chaunge lyche a midsomer roos.'

82. *Tullius*: Marcus Tullius Cicero. Cf. *Fall of Princes* ii. 2455 ff.:

First in Rome, be souereyn excellence,
Off rhethorik Tullius fond the flours,
Ple and diffence off subtil oratours.

83. *Crisistomus*: St. John Chrysostom. Cf. Lydgate, *The Pain and Sorrow of Evil Marriage* 40 (MacCracken, ii. 456), and Godfrey

of Viterbo, *Pantheon*: 'Eo tempore Joannes Chrysostomos, qui interpretatur os aureum. . . .'

86. *Senek*: Lucius Annæus Seneca the Younger, philosopher and dramatist. Lydgate's explanation in the story of Oedipus (*Fall of Princes* I. 3578 ff.):

> Cause off this siknesse and these maladies,
> As the goddis pleynli han disposid,
> And Senek writ eek in his tragedies,
> Thouh the cause be secre and iclosid . . .

gives an indication of what he means here by 'mysterys'—i.e. 'riddles or enigmas connected with divine authority': the oracle and plague in *Oedipus*, the ghost of Tantalus in *Thyestes*, etc.

88. A's refrain reads 'þey beon far chaunged as a somer Roos'.

89. *dozepeers*: in the romances the twelve peers or paladins of Charlemagne. Lydgate is probably not referring to any specific historical tradition.

91. *Vowes of the Pecok*: cf. Lydgate, *A Praise of Peace* 159 (MacCracken, ii. 785):

> Vowes of the Pecok, the Frenssh makith mencioun,
> Pryde of the werrys moost contrary vnto pees.

The reference is to Jacques de Longuyon's Alexander romance, *Les Vœux du Paon*. The vows referred to were the martial boasts of the heroes in the Great Battle of Epheson which were made to a peacock. The episode occurs in ll. 3840–4357 of the OF (cf. R. L. G. Ritchie, *The Buik of Alexander*, STS, iii. 249–76). The custom of vowing to a bird of mystical or heraldic significance to perform some high deed seems to have become a knightly exercise in the early fourteenth century. Jacques' peacock was roasted.

92. *nine worthies*: Joshua, David, and Judas Maccabaeus; Hector, Alexander, and Julius Caesar; Arthur, Charlemagne, and Godfrey of Bouillon. They are listed in Lydgate's *That now is Hay Some-tyme was Grase* 65–84 (MacCracken, ii. 809).

99. *Theban legioun*: cf. Lydgate, *Fall of Princes* VIII. 831 ff.:

> Bothe these tirauntis [Diocletian and Maximian] wrouhte be assent,
> Vndir whos swerd many [a] martire deies,
> Slayn in Octodorun, the legeoun of Thebeies.

Lydgate is probably following Jacobus ab Voragine's *Legenda Aurea*, chapter cxli. The Emperor Maximian (Cæsar from 286 to 305) took an army into Gaul, during Diocletian's persecution, which included a wholly Christian Theban Legion (from Thebes in Egypt) commanded by Mauricius. When the Legion refused to sacrifice to pagan gods it was massacred by Maximian at Aganum (now St. Maurice-en-Valois).

100. *Roda[n]us Ryuer*: the Rhone. Cf. *Legenda Aurea*: 'Quod sancti milites audientes octo miliaribus ab exercitu secesserant et in quodam loco amoeno, cui Aganum nomen est, juxta Rhodanum consederunt.'

104. *stage*: 'station' with a strong secondary play on 'stage' signifying the *castata*, the scaffold of the martyrs.

109. The MSS. in the *b*-group read *Lawrer* (laurel) which may be correct. But 'laurel' makes strange sense with the vb. 'founded'; it adds another plant, which obscures the antithesis between roses and lilies. A reads *pawtiers*, 'the altars'. This would seem to glance at the Legion's refusal to sacrifice at pagan altars.

112. A: 'þere martirdame was lyke þe rede rose.'

113. Cf. Lydgate, *A Seying of the Nightingale* 113 ff. (Mac-Cracken, i. 221):

> Hees wowndes fyve for man he did vncloose
> Of hondes, of feet, and of his fayre syde;
> Make of þees fyve, in þyn hert a roose

Cf. Rabanus Maurus, *Allegoria in Sacram Scripturam*: 'Rosa est coetus martyrum, ut in libro Ecclesiastici (24. 18) "Quasi palma exaltata sum in Cades et quasi plantatio rosæ in Jericho".' The comparison of Christ's wounds with roses is a commonplace of medieval religious writing. Cf. *The Meditation on the Life and Passion of Christ* 315–16 (ed. C. d'Evelyn, EETS (1921), p. 11):

> Strengthe of loue þat is so feer
> Haþ mad þy body a red roser.

For a full treatment of this subject, cf. Douglas Gray, 'The Five Wounds of Our Lord', *Notes and Queries* (1963), pp. 50 ff., 82 ff., 127 ff., 163 ff. Perhaps Lydgate's addition to this imagery is the creation of a single five-petalled rose (common in medieval iconography) out of the five wounds.

116. A reads:

> þe sunne was derke almoste with bright beeme
> Whane Ihesu Christ fyve wellis list vnclose,
> Called þe Ryver with þe red streme:
> To Paradyse-wardes vnto Ihesu oure Roos.

8. *A Balade in Commendation of Our Lady*

THERE are two MS. authorities for the poem: Bodley MS. Ashmole 59, f. 36b: (A), and BM MS. Sloane 1212, f. 101a–2b: (S). *Index* 99. The Sloane MS. is a fifteenth-century MS. (? of the second half of the century) which has fly-leaves made up from a dismembered Lydgate MS. of an earlier date. These leaves contain: on f. 1 a fragment of the *Temple of Glas* (ll. 736–54); f. 2 *Temple of Glas* (ll. 98–162); f. 3 a fragment of *A Defence of Holy Church* (ll. 1–56); f. 4 another fragment of the *Temple of Glas* (ll. 439–505 of the 'Compleynt' in the *GS version). All the fragments of the *Temple of Glas* substantially represent the *GS version. F. 101a begins with the last nine lines of a poem which the colophon identifies as 'Pallas the dowtyr off Jupiter, goddesse, and gouernour of Venus derre'. This 'verse epistle' may have been by Lydgate. The *Commendation* follows after the colophon and is without title. The poem is assigned to Lydgate by John Shirley in the Ashmole MS.: 'a devoute balade by Lidegate of Bury, made at the reverence of oure lady, Qwene of Mercy.' Like so many of Shirley's copies of Lydgate's poems the Ashmole version is a shorter, probably earlier, draft which exhibits distinctive words, phrases, and lines. The Sloane copy is an expanded and more polished version. Unfortunately, the scribe of S either had an indifferent exemplar or was a poor copyist. This text is based on S but is corrected by A at various points. This is not a happy solution, since A represents a wholly different version.

This is probably Lydgate's finest religious lyric and affords an example of his aureate style. On the whole, the Marian lyrics are of good literary quality. In this poem the use of Chaucer, *Troilus* v. 1849–55 (contrasting erotic love with religious) is skilful. This reworking of Chaucer is probably intended to recall Lydgate's secular adaptation of the passage in *A Complaynt of a Loveres Lyfe*, ll. 400–6. Lines 106–12 of the *Commendation*, which provide the religious parallel to ll. 5–7, are structurally effective. The enigmatic quality of many of the images of the Virgin derives from Alan of Lille, *Anticlaudianus*, v. 487–99, which is the source for ll. 1–63:

> Hec est stella maris, uite uia, porta salutis,
> Regula iusticie, limes pietatis, origo
> Virtutis, uenie mater thalamusque pudoris,
> Ortus conclusus, fons consignatus, oliua 490

Fructiferans, cedrus redolens, paradisus amenans,
Virgula pigmenti, uinaria cella, liquore
Predita celesti, nectar celeste propinans,
Nescia spineti florens rosa, nescia culpe
Gracia, fons expers limi, lux nubila pellens,   495
Spes miseris, medicina reis, tutela beatis,
Proscriptis reditus, erranti semita, cecis
Lumen, deiectis requies, pausacio fessis.

Both Skeat and Schirmer put forward the view that the *Commendation* owed much of its structure and diction to Chaucer's *ABC to the Virgin*—that Lydgate 'accentuated' an 'eloquence inherited from Chaucer'. The *Commendation* little resembles Chaucer's poem or Deguileville's original prayer. The exordium, with its contrast between secular and religious love, is traceable to no known original in this genre. The personal tone and style of the speaker is radically different. The wickedness which Chaucer asks the Virgin's aid in suppressing is not present in the *Commendation*. Chaucer's penitent prays purposefully in an 'abcedial' formula of petition and invocation. His style is provided by the initial letter of each stanza. In Lydgate the humble poet attempts in waves of liturgically inspired eloquence to describe the Virgin. His 'style' forms an essential part of the poem's shape: the plot of the poem is the poetic effort of describing. Characteristically, the poem ends with a return to humility when Lydgate finally asks (l. 136) 'why haven't I the skill and knowledge to describe her?'. The moderate extension of the syntactic period is well managed. The invocatory style owes more to Alan than to Chaucer. Lydgate's 'aureat' experiments in religious verse made possible the flamboyant Marian Balades of Dunbar and the enigmatic *Annunciation* attributed to Henryson in the Gray MS.

The structure of the *Commendation* is simple, in two parts: PREFACE (including the figures *contentio, correctio, invocatio*) and ORATIONES. The descriptive material used for the prayers is drawn from five main sources: (1) Alan of Lille's *Anticlaudianus* v. 487–99; (2) the Vulgate; (3) authorities of the Church; (4) liturgical tradition; (5) vernacular religious works. In many instances it is impossible to tell source from analogue. The references to authorities of the Church given below are made according to the arrangement in *PL*.

5–7. Cf. Chaucer, *Troilus* v. 1849–55.

12. This glances at *Troilus* II. 8–10.

21. This probably means kneeling before an image of the Virgin. Cf. Lydgate, *The Fyfftene Ioyes of Oure Lady* (ii), 22–28 (Mac-Cracken, i. 260) ; *Ave Maria*, 7–8 (MacCracken, i. 280) ; *The Image of Our Lady (passim)* (MacCracken, i. 290) where Lydgate specially refers to a copy of a painting attributed to St. Luke hung in St. Maria del Populo. The copy given to Bury St. Edmunds appears to have been a benefaction of Ralph Gelebronde at the instigation of the Archdeacon, John Thornton.

22–23. Cf. *Anticlaudianus* v. 487: 'Hec est stella maris.' This image was popular in liturgical and devotional tradition. Cf. Adam of Persenia, *Mariale* (Sect. 127), 'Stella maris Maria est necessaria in hujus incertitudinis pelago naviganti.' 'Stella Maris' was supposedly the meaning of the name 'Maria' (cf. St. Anselm, *Super Ave*, Sect. 8).

26. *Anticlaudianus* v. 487: 'uite uia.' Cf. St. Hildefonsus, *De Corona Virginis* IX.

27. Cf. Chaucer, *ABC to the Virgin*, 14 ; Adam of Persenia, *Mariale* (Sect. 127): 'Portus est totius misericordiæ mundo naufragium patienti.' Lydgate's manuscript of Alan may have read *Portus salutis* here.

[*up*] *to ryve*: cf. *MED ariven* vb., 'to come into port'.

29. *Anticlaudianus* v. 488: 'Regula iusticie.' Cf. St. Anselm, *Super Ave Maria*: 'Regula perfectionis.'

rote of holynesse: developed from Isa. xi. 10: 'there shall be a root of Jesse'. Cf. St. Bernard, *Sermones Super Salve* III: 'Radix benedictionem.'

30. Both MSS. read *lyne*, which Skeat translated 'cheering course', commenting that this was 'very obscure'. It is perhaps less obscure if we assume that the word should be **ly[m]e*, modelled on the Latin n. *limes* and taken from Alan, *Anticlaudianus* v. 488, 'limes pietatis', 'path of compassion'. The n. is common in Latin Hymns; cf. *AH*, vi, no. 17: 'Limes æquitatis.'

31. *Anticlaudianus* v. 488–9: 'origo Virtutis.'

32. Cf. Lydgate, *Ave Regina Celorum* 41 (MacCracken, i. 291): 'Hayle, condute of comfort, with watyr crystall.' St. Bernard, *Sermo in Nativitate Beatæ Virginis Mariæ* (68), 1014, 1019: 'aquæductus desiderabilis.'

33. Cf. Hymn, *Salve Regina, Mater misericordiæ*.

34. Cf. Canticles iii. 4.

36. *Anticlaudianus* v. 490: 'Ortus conclusus.' A favourite image of the Virgin derived from Canticles iv. 12: 'Hortus conclusus,

soror mea, hortus conclusus, fons signatus.' Cf. Paschasius Radbertus, *Expositio in Matthæum* II. i. (96): 'Itaque hortus conclusus,
quia uterus Virginis modis omnibus integer atque incorruptus fuit.
Hortus autem est appellatus, quia universæ deliciæ paradisi in eo
effloruerunt, et signatus est venter pudoris, ubi fons emicuit
nostræ redemptionis.'

37. *Anticlaudianus* v. 490: 'fons consignatus.'

38. Ibid. 490–1: 'oliua Fructiferans.' Cf. Ecclus. xxiv. 19:
'Quasi oliva speciosa in campus', and Adam of Persenia, *Fragmenta Mariana* (155): 'In his campis est oliva fructifera, mater
misericordiæ, virgo Maria.'

39. *Anticlaudianus* v. 491: 'cedrus redolens.'

42. Cf. St. Bernard, *Ad Beatam Virginem Deiparam* (Sect. 4):
'O lampas lucentissima.'

43. *Anticlaudianus* v. 491: 'paradisus amenans'. Cf. Canticles iv.
13 and St. Bernard, *De Laude Mariæ Virginis* (702): 'paradisus
omnium deliciarum'.

44. *Anticlaudianus* v. 492: 'virgula pigmenti.' Cf. Canticles iii. 6,
and St. Peter Damian, *Sermo* XLVI: 'Beata quippe Maria sicut virgula fumi ex aromatibus ascendit, quia ex vitæ suæ virtutibus in
interni semper incensi recitudinem proficere studuit. . . . Et bene
virgula fumi hæc dicitur quæ per virgam quoque Aaron mystice
figuratur.' Cf. *AH*, vi, no 24.

45. *Anticlaudianus* v. 492: 'uinaria cella'. Alan's 'wine cellar'
becomes in Lydgate a 'wine cellar coloured with vermilion'. The
adj. (formed on OF *envermeiller*) may have been suggested by
Jer. xxii 14: 'Ædificatio mihi domum latam et coenacula spatiosa;
qui operit sibi fenestras et fiat laquearia cedrina, *pingitque sino-
pide*.' The phrase 'uinaria cella' was popular in Latin hymns; cf.
AH, iii. no. 2: 'Cella fragrans unguentorum | Cellaque vinaria.'

46. *Anticlaudianus* v. 492–3: 'liquore Predita celesti.'

47. Cf. Ecclus. xxiv. 20.

50. *Anticlaudianus* v. 494: 'Nescia spineti florens rosa.'

51. Ibid. 495: 'Fons expers limi.' Cf. St. Bernard, *Sermo in
Nativitate Beatæ Mariæ Virginis* (68): 'fons indeficiens, qui
universam irrigat superficiem paradisi.'

52. *propyne*: Lydgate coinage modelled on the Latin vb. Cf. Jer.
xxv. 15: 'Sume calicem . . . et propinabis de illo cunctis gentibus.'

53. *Anticlaudianus* v. 495: 'Lux nubila pellens.' Perhaps we
should read *n[u]b[i]le* ?

54. Ibid. 496: 'medicina reis.' Cf. Adam of Persenia, *Fragmenta*

Mariana (133): 'poenitentium Medicina' and *AH*, i, no. 77: 'Peccatorum medicina.'

57. Cf. St. Bernard, *Deprecatio et Laus elegantissima Beatam Virginem*: 'Protectrix vitæ.'

tutele: 'guardian'. A Lydgatian coinage from *Anticlaudianus* v. 496: 'tutela beatis.' Cf. Adam of Persenia, *Mariale*: 'tutela mundi.'

58. *Anticlaudianus* v. 497: 'Proscriptis reditus.'

59. Ibid.: 'erranti semita'. Cf. St. Hildefonsus, *De Corona Virginis* v: 'via errantium.'

sequele: 'followers'. A Lydgate coinage formed on Latin *sequela*.

60. *tente*: Cf. *Chaucer's ABC to the Virgin* 14. The origin of the constr. *wery* + past part. is discussed by T. F. Mustanoja, *A ME Syntax*, 1. 562.

pawsacioun: 'pause', 'intermission'. A Lydgatian coinage from *Anticlaudianus* v. 498: 'pausacio fessis.'

62. MS. S's reading is not corrupt. Cf. *Anticlaudianus* v. 498: 'deiectis requies', 'rest for the dejected'.

64. *itinerarie*: 'way', 'route'. Cf. Adam of Persenia, *Mariale* (49): 'Per mentem et uterum Virginis complevit suæ itinera æternitatis.'

65. *bravie*: 'reward', 'prize' (Latin *bravium*). Cf. I Cor. ix. 24. Cf. St. Hildefonsus, *De Corona Virginis* xxi: 'bravium laborantibus.'

66. *dyorne denarye*: 'daily pay'. This has been coined from Matt. xx. 2: 'conventione autem facta cum operariis ex denario diurno.'

68. Cf. Lydgate, *Regina Celi Letare* 1–2 (MacCracken, i. 293).

69. *palestyr*: a fig. use of the n. 'wrestling school'.

71. Cf. St. Hildefonsus, *De Corona Virginis* ii: 'martyrum suavitas.'

72. *donatyff*: 'offering', 'gift'. A Lydgatian coinage from the Latin n. *donativum*. This is a rare, if not unique, expression as applied to the Virgin.

73. *aureolle*: 'The crown or reward given to virgins, martyrs, or preachers.'

78. *turtyl*: Canticles ii. 12. Cf. Lydgate, *Ave Jesse Virgula*, 30 (MacCracken, i. 299).

79. Canticles ii. 14. Cf. St. Hildefonsus, *De Corona Virginis* xviii: 'columba plena gemitu.'

80. Cf. Adam of Persenia, *Mariale*: 'Philomela dulcis.'

82. Cf. Lydgate, *To Mary, Queen of Heaven* 26 (MacCracken, i. 284): 'Of Phebus vprist, massageer most enteer.'

83. *Phebus*: mythological equivalent for biblical 'Sol justitiæ' (Mal. iv. 2).

85. *ruby*: cf. Dunbar, *Rois Mary*, l. 42: 'Haile redolent ruby, riche and radyuss!' and *AH*, i, no 204: 'Rubor carbunculeus/ Fulgens claritate.'

87. *dyamaunt*: cf. Lydgate, *Ave Regina Celorum* 37 (MacCracken, i. 291): 'A dew diamant, most precyous of pryse.' Cf. Carleton Brown, *Religious Lyrics of the XVth Century*, no. 28, l. 49.

92. *safyr*: cf. Lydgate, *To Mary, Queen of Heaven* 13–15:

> O Saphir loup al swellyng to represse,
> Off cankred sores and venymous feloun,
> In gostly woundes be ther gouerneresse

lowp: a type of sapphire; *ewage*: a sea-coloured sapphire.

98. S: '*þan* reemis', A: 'with hert ful trewe'. This probably refers to the gem imagery. *ewe* ('hewe') = (a) external appearance of the face ('visage' l. 94), (b) colour of the gem. [*b*]*eemis* = (a) 'radiance', (b) gleams of the gem.

102. *to thee was obvmbrid*: the vb. and the dative use of the personal pron. are modelled on the Latin of Luke i. 35: 'Et virtus Altissimi obumbrabit tibi.' The phrase was popular with Latin hymn writers.

ll. 106–9, refer to the prophecy of Isa. xxvii. 6.

110. Jer. xxiii. 5: 'suscitabo David germen iustum.'

111. *ground*: 'foundation'. Isa. xxviii. 16.

113. *viole*: cf. *Adam of Persenia, Mariale*: 'vas miraculorum.'

vitre inviolate: cf. St. Hildefonsus, *Sermo* III: 'Solis radius specular penetrat, et soliditatem ejus insensibili subtilitate pertrajicit, si talis videtur intrinsecus, qualis extrinsecus. Itaque, fratres, nec cum ingreditur violatur, nec cum egreditur dissipat, quia in ingressu et egressu ejus specular integrum perseverat. Specular ergo non rumpit radius solis; integritatem Virginis ingressus aut regressus vitiare poterat Deitatis?'

118. Isa. lxv. 9.

swete Sunamyte: Canticles vi. 12: 'Revertere, revertere Sunamitis, revertere, revertere ut intueamur te.' Cf. St. Rupertus, *In Cantica Canticorum* VI. vi–vii: 'Ergo tu, o Sunamitis, o filia principis, corde et corpore es casta, mente et carne integra et incorrupta, cognitione et opere munda.'

119. *mesure my mournynge*: cf. St. Hildefonsus, *De Corona Virginis* VIII: 'O miserorum refrigerium.'

margarite: cf. St. Bernard, *Super Salve* II: 'margarita pretiosa.'

120. Isa. xlvi. 13.

121. *punycall pome*: 'pomegranate'. Cf. Canticles iv. 3.

122. *auryat vrne*: Heb. ix. 4. Cf. St. Bernard, *Super Salve* III: 'urna aurea' and *AH*, i, no. 7.

book and bo[u]n: MS. S reads *book and born*. Skeat suggested 'body and bone', but this rendering interrupts the probable syntactical connexion with the next line. *book* is perhaps the past part. form of the vb. 'bake' (referring to the imagery of John vi. 58) *boun* is perhaps the ME adj. 'ready', 'prepared'. If so, then we should translate 'was prepared'.

123. *agnelet*: a Lydgatian coinage. Cf. St. Jerome, *In Ezechielem* XIV. xlvi, for 'agniculus' as applied to Christ.

125. *lyoun*: the Lion of Judah. Cf. Rev. v. 5.

128. *Cockyl*: cf. Hugo of St. Victor, *Sermo In Annuntiatione*: 'Concha margaritafera.'

129-30. Exod. iii. 2: 'Apparuitque ei Dominus in flamma ignis de medio rubi; et videbat quod rubus arderet, et non comburetur.' Cf. Henryson, *The Annunciation*, ll. 39-40.

> The low of luf haldand the hete,
> Vnbrynt full blithlie birnis.

131. Cf. Lydgate, *The Life of Our Lady* II. 879-900.

132. The fleece of Gideon (Judges vi. 37 ff.). A favourite devotional image.

133. S's 'And fructifyeng fayrest the yerde of Aaron' is unsatisfactory. The rod of Aaron, another favourite image (Num. xvii. 8). Cf. Adam of Persenia, *Mariale* (19): 'Ipsa est virga Aaron, quæ sine succo floruit, fronduit, et nuces protulit, quia beata Dei mater sine viro Salvatorem concepit et peperit.'

134. *arke*: the ark of Noah. Cf. St. Bernard, *De Beata Maria Virgine Sermo* (6): 'Siquidem arca Noe significavit arcam Ecclesiæ: arcam foedaris, arcam gratiæ, sanctitatem, scilicet, Mariæ?'

probatyk piscyne: 'the sheep-cleansing pool of Bethesda'. A phrase formed directly on the Latin of John v. 2: 'Est autem Iersolymis probatica piscina quæ cognominatur hebraice Bethsaida.'

135. *Aurora*: another favourite image of the Virgin. Cf. Lydgate, *To Mary, Queen of Heaven*, l. 25 (MacCracken, i. 284). Cf. Adam of

Persenia, *Mariale* (127): 'Ipsa est quippe aurora consurgens, quæ tenebras arguit quæ malis terminum, quæ finem ponit erroribus, et veri luminis radios administrat.'

136. *Columpne and base*: cf. St. Hildefonsus, *De Corona Virginis* v: 'columna et firmamentum veritatis.'

abime: 'hell'. Presumably the column stretches from hell to heaven since Mary's power extends over both places (she is titled Queen of Heaven, Earth, and Hell). Cf. St. Bernard, *Sermo: In Dominica Infra Octavam Assumptionis Beatæ Mariæ Virginis*: 'Jure ergo Maria sole perhibetur amicta, quæ profundissimam divinæ sapientiæ, ultra quam credi valeat, penetravit abyssum.'

140. *tabernakyll*: cf. St. Peter Damian, *Rhythmus* LXIII, ll. 41–42:

> Ventris habitaculum Rex regum intravit,
> Cujus tabernaculum sibi dedicavit.

9. *A Defence of Holy Church*

THERE are two MS. authorities: BM MS. Sloane 1212, f. 3a–b: (S) which contains ll. 1–56 only; and BM MS. Harley 1245, f. 182b: (H). *Index* 2219. S is a fragment (see p. 143 for an account of the manuscript) and is not a particularly careful copy. H is a complete version representing a careful copy in a well-produced copy of the *Fall of Princes*. The *Fall* ends on 182b, and after the colophon the *Defence* (without title) begins in the same hand as that of the *Fall*. Although the *Defence* lacks a colophon the poem would seem to be complete, since 183b is blank. On internal evidence there is nothing to suggest that the poem breaks off. MacCracken, i. xv and Schirmer, *John Lydgate*, p. 134, n. 3 are too hasty in supposing that the poem is incomplete. Robbins in the *Index* lists the poem as complete.

The occasion for which the poem has been composed is obscure. If we follow Schirmer's dating, *c.* 1431, we must identify the royal figure with Duke Humphrey (Lieutenant and Warden of England in the King's absence from April 1430 to January 1432) and associate the heresy with the Lollard uprisings in Oxford, Salisbury, and London in the spring of 1431. Lydgate draws our attention to the role played by Duke Humphrey in suppressing the risings in ll. 400–13 of the Prologue to Book I of the *Fall of Princes*. In view of the association of the poem with the *Fall* in MS. H this is an

attractive possibility. On the other hand, Lydgate may have
written the poem on the occasion of the more serious Lollard
risings in London in 1413–14, and in that case the royal person
addressed is the young King Henry V (see F. E. Jacob, *The
Fifteenth Century, 1399–1485*, pp. 129–34). Lydgate uses the same
form of address and sentiment in his envoi to Henry V in the
Troy Book: 'Most worþi prynce, of knyȝthod sours and welle.'
The presence of the poem in MS. S which may very well pre-date
1431 must be taken into account. If we take the expression
'thy corone' in line 95 in its usual sense, then the reference is to
Henry V. Cf. *Balade to Henry VI* 81 ff. for conclusive proof.

The poem is a curious combination of symbols of the Church and
references to the history of Israel which suggest allusions to contemporary events and persons. After the succession of linking
images of the Church (the bride of Christ, the daughter of Zion,
the exiled of Psalm cxxxvii, the ark of Noah, the ark of the
Covenant, Israel), which contains a panegyric on the young
king's saving of the Church (ll. 1–77), the poem indulges in a
series of warnings and exhortations to the king urging vigilance
and extreme severity. The 'peace-loving Lydgate' presumably did
not believe in mercy or forbearance in matters of religious disorder.
Lines 127–30 indicate that the subversive doctrines should be
identified with Lollard opinions.

The rime-royal stanza pattern is subordinated to expanded and
suspended syntax in the form of a more Latinate, periodic, sentence structure. If the poem may be assigned to the years 1413–14,
Lydgate became interested in Latinate syntax early in his poetic
career. Unfortunately, it would seem to have been a minor, inter-
mittent interest. The beneficial tightness of periodic syntax was
never generalized from this poem or the *Life of St. Giles* to the
repetitious flow of his usual narrative style. In ll. 134–47 the
syntactical smoothness, rhetorical clarity, and felicitous 'classical'
phrasing ('With smale worms hym fretyng manyfolde') exemplifies
and justifies Warton's comment (*History of English Poetry*):
'. . . he is the first of our writers whose style is clothed with that
perspicuity, in which the English phraseology appears at this day
to an English reader.'

The metrical control of the poem is extremely good and several
unusual scribal contractions are recorded in H and S (with minor
variations): 'Talefft' (23), 'to have left', and 'Tamade' (12), 'To
have made'. If these forms represent Lydgate's pronunciation

(and clearly 12 and 23 are regular 5-stress lines only if so pronounced) then we must think again about Lydgate's metre in the light of elisions and colloquial contraction. This is complicated, since the recording of many such contractions was not ordinary scribal practice in the fifteenth century.

7. *Cristis spouse*: 'Sponsa Christi', Rev. xxi. 9–10.

douhtir of Syoun: Lam. i. 6; Cf. Bede, *In Matthæi Evangelium Expositio* iii. xxi: 'Filia Sion civitas est Jerusalem, et significat Ecclesiam fidelium, quæ est filia superiæ Jerusalem, quæ est mater omnium nostrum. . . .'

10. The reference to Jerusalem seems to be used also to suggest a capital city, i.e. London. Lydgate's use of scriptural types of the Church is not consistent at an 'allegorical' or a 'poetic' level. The various images are used precisely at the level of argument or illustration. At the poetic level they are merely associated.

12. *Tamade*: 'to have made'.

14–25. The imagery of the exiled Jerusalem derives from Ps. cxxxvi (Vulgate) blended with the 'weeping mother' type of Lam. (cf. Lydgate, *The Vertues of the Mass* 65–72 (MacCracken, i. 87)). Cf. St. Augustine's *Enarration* on Ps. cxxxvi, where Babylon is identified with the temporal Church on earth, Jerusalem with the eternal Church. This distinction seems valuable here, although Babylon's river is probably meant to suggest the Thames as well.

17. *her children*: Lam. ii. 10.

19–25. Ps. cxxxvi. 2: 'In salicibus in medio eius, suspendimus organa nostra', 'We hanged our harps upon the willows in the midst thereof.' St. Augustine interprets: 'Habent organa sua cives Hierusalem, scripturas Dei, præcepta Dei, promissa Dei. . . .' Lydgate takes a similar line, shading the meaning more naturally towards the music and liturgy of the Church.

24. *salwys olde, foule and thikke*: St. Augustine explains: 'Salices enim sunt Babyloniæ ligna infructuosa, pasta in temporalibus voluptatibus. . . .' Lydgate's adaptation contrasting 'newe' and 'olde' perhaps suggests a return to a primitive, crude kind of religious ceremony.

25. *orgnes*: this represents the Vulgate *organa*, 'musical instruments'.

30–32. This Babylonian captivity (perversion to heretical notions) is to be distinguished from the 'temporal exile' of ll. 15–25.

31. *Nabugdonosor*: cf. Rabanus Maurus, *De Universo Libri* III. i: 'Nabuchodonosor . . . typum tenet diaboli, qui hæreticorum plebem erroris captivitate devictam ab Hierusalem, hoc est, ab Ecclesia in Babyloniam, id est, ignorantiæ confusionem abduxit.'

34. *Zorobabell*: Zech. iv. 9; Hag. i. 1–2. He was the son of Salathiel, of the tribe of Judah, who under Darius rebuilt the temple and restored the walls of Jerusalem. Cf. Bede, *In Esdran et Prophetas Allegoria Expositio* II. vi.

Neemye: Neh. i–vii. Cf. Bede, *In Esdran* III. xv: 'Nehemias interpretatur Latine consolator Dominus, vel consolator a Domino, qui cum renovaverit muros Jerusalem, et populum Dei ab hostium insultatione liberatum, in divinæ legis observantia sublimaverit.'

48. *Noees shipp*: the ark of Noah, a favourite symbol of the Church. Cf. St. Augustine's *Enarration* on Ps. ciii (Vulgate).

50–51. The classical references seem out of place here, even if some contemporary reference may have been intended.

56. *Armonye*: Gen. viii. 4. The reference is to Mount Ararat, see Isidore, *Etymologiæ* XIII. viii: 'Ararath mons Armeniæ in quo arcam historiæ post diluvium resedisse testatur.' Cf. *MED Armenie* n. for the common spelling 'Armonie' for 'Armenie'.

59–67. Gen. viii. 5–11.

60. *dowe*: 'dove' (MS. *do we*).

70. 1 Sam. iv.

75–77. This warning may make use of the imagery of Jer. xxxi. 35. But the usual medieval allegorizations identified the Church with the moon and Christ with the sun. If the imagery (and interpretation) was in Lydgate's mind it has been applied here in a spirit of extreme secularization.

76. *betrassh*: 'deceive' (*MED bitraishen* 2a). The unusual fig. ext. of the vb. in this context makes the ordinary senses of the vb. inappropriate. 'Disgrace' is perhaps a better rendering.

78–81. 1 Sam. xxiii. 7–14.

82–84. Jer. xxiii. 28–31; *Balade to Henry VI* 86.

85–88. 2 Sam. v. 8 [=Liber Secundus Regum].

86–91. For the identification of the blind and lame specifically with heretics see Isidore, *Allegoriæ Quædam Scripturæ Sacræ*, Sect. 137. 144–7.

106–12. 1 Sam. xxviii. 18.

113–16. 1 Sam. xv. 32–33.

117. 1 Sam. xv. 8–9.

Galgalis: 1 Sam. xv. 33: 'And Samuel hewed Agag in pieces before the Lord in Gilgal.'

118–19. 1 Sam. xv. 28.

120–1. 1 Kings xviii. 40.

127–30. The Lollards were much repelled by the institutional aspects of the Church. They especially despised 'worship' of images and relics. Cf. Jacob, *The Fifteenth Century*, pp. 282–3.

paramenteȝ: 'ornaments' (late Latin *paramentum*).

134–43. The last two stanzas seem to show a shift in emphasis, almost as if the young king himself were being rebuked in advance, lest he might think of expropriating Church property.

135. *Antiochus*: 2 Maccabeus ix; Chaucer, *CT*, B². *3800–15.

142. *chare*: 'chariot'.

144. *Baltasar*: Dan. v; Chaucer, *CT*, B². *3373–436.

146. Babylon returns us to the setting of the opening stanzas.

10. *Life of Our Lady* (ii. 519–903)

THE *Life of Our Lady* is edited by J. A. Lauritis, R. A. Klinefelter, and V. F. Gallagher in Duquesne Studies (Philological Series), vol. 2, 1961. The MSS. and their relation are described and discussed in the Introduction, pp. 11–56. The *Life* appears to have been a popular work and thirty-seven more or less complete MSS. are extant. *Index* 2574. None of the MSS. is without errors, omissions, or transpositions. There are two outstanding MSS.: the textually superior Durham Univ. MS. Cosin V. ii. 16: (D) (the basis of Fr. Lauritis's text), and Bodley MS. Hatton 73: (B3). I have taken D as the basis of this text, although B3 is attractive in view of its early date, richness of production, and probable royal ownership (see f. 121b where 'Quene Margarete' presumably refers to Margaret of Anjou).

The poem has been associated by modern scholarship with Henry V's patronage, but it is more likely that Henry only suggested the subject to Lydgate and urged him to set about writing it (see the wording of the King Harry rubric: 'at the excitacioun of Kyng Harry'). It is impossible to date the poem. Had it been expressly commissioned by Henry V, Lydgate (after his usual manner) would probably have mentioned it. The only clear reference to an actual person is a tribute to Chaucer (II. 1628–55) regretting that the poet was no longer alive to guide and correct the work. It may be suggested that Lydgate's literary relations with Chaucer (as far as this work is concerned) are not personal. Chaucer's *opus* rather than Chaucer himself provided Lydgate with a model and guide for this kind of religious 'biography'. If we compare the *Lyf of St. Cecile* as it appears in *CT* with the *Life of Our Lady* there are many points in common: (1) the rime-royal stanza form; (2) the use of Prologue; (3) extended use of lyrical invocation; (4) use of etymological and interpretative material as a form of digression. Lydgate probably consulted Chaucer's poem as a basic guide for the form and style of his own work, and had good reason to lament that Chaucer could not provide him with more. In any case, the work as it now stands has no obvious connexions with secular or religious patronage. One is tempted to date the poem after the death of Thomas Chaucer in 1434, when Lydgate had returned to a more cloistered existence.

The *Life* (5,932 lines, in six books) has no basic narrative unity. But the mixture of prayers, invocations, narrative passages, digressive explanations, and lyrical meditations is not entirely haphazard. The whole work may be thought of as organized around the Christmas Cycle; its principal points of interest are the major feasts of the Cycle: Nativity, Circumcision, Epiphany, and Purification. The feasts are chronologically presented through delayed and suspended narrative movement, embellished and emphasized by aetiological excursions and symbolic interpretations. The whole movement marks a psychological progression which begins (Book I, Prologue) in the dark spiritless inertia of Advent and emerges by means of history and remembrance into the light and spiritual illumination of Candlemas. The poem seems to have been designed as a kind of Christian *Fasti* intended for reading during the Christmas Cycle. Schirmer says of the *Life* that it 'has no claim to be judged as a narrative work but postulates a new elevated majestic style, in which the divine is placed at a distance from the every day' (p. 154). Yet the poem's structure may represent an attempt to synchronize the occasion of its being read with the events and symbolism celebrated in the Christmas Cycle. In this event, it would be very much in touch with the 'every day' and would bear some resemblance to Prudentius's *Cathemerinon*.

The present extract follows closely on the narrative section (455–97) dealing with the Annunciation, based on Luke i. 26–38. It appears to be composed of common liturgical, biblical, and exegetical themes and has no more specific original.

3–7. Cf. St. Hildefonsus, *Sermo* III; Lydgate, *Commendation* 113 and note.

11. *paleys prynci[p]all*: Cf. St. Peter Damian, *Sermo in Nativitate*: 'Palatium Regis æterni' and *AH*, i, no. 50: 'Summi regis palatium.'

12–20. Cf. Prov. ix. 1: 'Sapientia ædificavit sibi domum excedit columnas septem'; Paschasius Radbertus, *Expositio in Matthæum*, II, 1 (95c): 'Et ideo sibi ipse columnas scidisse recte dicitur, dum eadem potestate cum Patre manens æternus, dedicavit Mariam et per eam sibi univit Ecclesiam, cui septem principalia dona Spiritus sancti divisit.'

14. Cf. St. Hildefonsus, *De Corona Virginis* VIII: 'Verbi Patris sanctum reclinatorium puella dulcis, gratia plena'; Canticles iii. 10.

22–28. These lines reflect the common application of Canticles vii. 4: 'Collum tuum sicut turris eburnea' to the Virgin, blended with the temple of Solomon in 1 Kings v–vii.

29–32. Several images have been blended together: (1) the wall of the New Jerusalem (Rev. xxi. 18); (2) a comparison of the Virgin to a castle (cf. Alan of Lille, *Sermo* II: 'Hæc est castram seu castellum . . .'); (3) the temple of the vision of Ezekiel (referred to in ll. 50–56). Cf. Ezek. xl–xliv, especially xliv. 2: 'Et dixit Dominus ad me: Porta hæc clausa erit: non aperietur, et vir non transibit per eam: quoniam Dominus Deus Israel ingressus est per eam, eritque clausa principi.' The passage from Ezek. had been applied to the Virgin: cf. St. Hildefonsus, *De Virginitate Perpetua Sanctæ Mariæ* III: 'Hæc in Ezechiele domus Dei est, cujus pudoris integerrima claustra, ad Orientem consistens porta semper est clausa'; cf. *AH*, i, no. 21: 'Porta clausa permanens.'

43–49. A blending of a sacred image, 'concha margaritifera' (cf. *Commendation*, 128 and note), with natural history: 'Gignitur autem de coelesti rore, quem certo anni tempore conculae hauriunt' (Isidore, *Etymologiae* XVI. x).

50–56. These lines refer to the vision of Ezekiel (cf. note to ll. 29–32). I do not know why Lydgate should refer to the north gates of the temple (l. 51) when Ezek. xliv. 1–4 identifies the locked gate with the east: 'Et conuertit me ad viam portae sanctuarii exterioris, quae respiciebat ad Orientem: et erat clausa.'

57–63. The fleece of Gideon; cf. *Commendation*, 132 and note.
59. *he*: Gideon.
Madian: Midian, cf. Judges vi–viii.

66–67. The Midianites worshipped Baal.

71–77. Cf. Heb. ix. 4: '. . . in qua vrna aurea habens manna . . .', and *Commendation*, 122 and note.

78–81. It is difficult to see what Biblical altar Lydgate has in mind.

88. *sterres in the frosty nyght*: a Chaucerian tag, cf. *CT*, A. 268, found in various contexts in fifteenth-century verse.

92–105. Cf. i Kings x. 18–20 [Lib. III Regum]: 'Fecit etiam rex Solomon thronum de ebore grandem: et vestiuit eum auro fuluo nimis, qui habebat sex gradus, et summitas throni rotunda erat in parte posteriori: et duae manus hinc atque inde tenentes sedile: et duo leones stabant iuxta manus singulas. Et duodecim leunculi stantes super sex gradus hinc atque inde: non est factum tale opus in universis regnis.' The association of this image with the Blessed Virgin reflects the common moral interpretation of the passage. Cf. *Glossa Ordinaria*: 'Per quem significatur virgo Maria, in cuius gremio Christus sedit tanquam in throno nobilissimo recipiens trium regum homagia.' Cf. *AH*, i, no. 7: 'Thronus es Salomonis.'

106–23. Cf. Rev. xii. 1: 'Et signum magnum apparuit in caelo: mulier amicta sole, et luna sub pedibus ejus, et in capite ejus corona stellarum duodecim.' The detailed interpretation reflects a blend of several commentaries. For the identification of the woman with the Blessed Virgin *vide* Andreas Caesareae, *Commentarius in Apocalypsin*, Cap. 33. The allegorizing of the sun as Christ is a commonplace; the moon's identification with the primitive Church is probably the result of commentaries which identify the moon with *Synagoga*: cf. Andreas, 'luna vero, id est, Judaeorum Synagoga'.

124. Cf. Canticles viii. 9–10.

127–33. These lines announce the future accent on proof taken from natural history. But Lydgate first dwells on the power of God to intervene in history (ll. 134–61).

137–40. The gates of Antioch; cf. Acts xii. 10.

146–7. Matt. xxviii. 1–7; Mark xvi. 1–6; Luke xxiv. 1–12; John xx. 1–17.

150–2. Cf. Acts xii. 5–9.

162–5. Lydgate's copy of St. Hildefonsus must have contained a passage or work not now included in his known or attributed works as collected in *PL*. Although Dr. Galagher (p. 683) refers us to *PL*, xcvi, I can by no means trace any reference to a tree which bears birds in cols. 53–110. Cf. note to l. 358.

169–72. Cf. St. Ambrose, *Hexameron* v. 20; 64–65: 'Negantur enim vultures indulgere concubitu, et conjugali quodam usu nuptialisque copulae sorte misceri, atque ita sine ullo masculorum concipere semine, et sine conjunctione generare, natosque ex his in multam aetatem longaevitate procedere; ut usque ad centum annos vitae eorum series producatur, nec facile eos angusti aevis finis excipiat. Quid ajunt, qui solent nostra ridere mysteria, cum audiunt quod virgo generavit, et impossibilem innuptae, cujus pudorem nulla viri consuetudo temerasset, existimant partum? Impossibile putatur in Dei Matre, quod in vulturibus possibile non negatur? Avis sine masculo parit, et nullus refellit: et quia desponsata viro Maria virgo peperit, pudori ejus faciunt questionem.' Lydgate's own MS. Laud Misc. 233, contains a fragment of the *Hexameron* (fol. 112a).

176–80. Cf. Pliny, *Naturalis Historia* ii. 98. 211: 'Iuxta Harpasa oppidum Asiae cautes stat horrenda uno digito mobilis, eadem, si toto corpore inpellatur, resistens.'

190–3. Cf. Pliny, *Naturalis Historia* ii. 98. 211: 'In Taurorum paeninsula civitate Parasino terra est qua sanantur omnia vulnera.'

194. Cf. *The Minor Poems of the Vernon MS.* Part i, ed. C. Horstmann, EETS (1892), no. 23, ll. 673 ff. (p. 79):

> Heil noble eorþe of grace
> Þorwh ȝiftus wel arrayed,
> To bringe forþ fruyt in luytel space

This translates the Latin 'Ave terra gracie fecundata' of a hymn attributed in the MS. to Albertus Magnus. Cf. *AH*, iii, no. 2: 'Gaude fructuosa tellus.' Cf. Ps. lxvi. 6 (Vulgate).

197–203. Cf. Ezek. xlvii. 12.

204–8. Cf. Pliny, *Naturalis Historia* ii. 106. 228: 'In Dodone Iovis fons cum sit gelidus et inmersas faces extinguat, si extinctae admoveantur accendit.'

218–21. Ibid. ii. 106. 230: 'In Falisco omnis aqua pota candidos boves facit.'

239. *high[e] cristall hevyn*: owing to Lydgate's habit of using the adjs. 'cristal' and 'cristalline' interchangeably, it is probable that the phrase here refers specifically to the crystalline heaven, the ninth sphere.

240. *firmament*: the eighth sphere, the sphere of the fixed stars.

241. *golden axltre*: the polar axis of the universe, with the northern pole star visible and the hypothetical southern pole star invisible (*vide* Virgil, *Georgics* I. 241–3; Macrobius, *Commentum* I. 16. 4–5).

sterres seven: the reference is vague. The phrase can refer to the Pleiades or the Great Bear.

242. *Cithera*: the planet Venus.

243. *reed Mars*: cf. Macrobius, *Commentum* I. 19. 19; Alan of Lille, *Anticlaudianus* IV. 414–25.

256. *myghty chayne*: the chain of the Elements, made up of the four contraries, which binds together the physical structure of the universe. Cf. Macrobius, *Commentum* I. 6. 22.

274–80. The tables of testimony given to Moses; cf. Exod. xxxi. 18; xxxii. 15–16. This image had been associated with the Immaculate Conception, *vide* St. Augustine, *Sermo* XIV: 'Ergo qui scripsit lapideas tabulas sine stylo ferreo, ipse grauidauit Mariam spiritu sancto. . . .'

281–7. The burning bush of Exod. iii. 2. Cf. *Commendation*, 129–30 and note.

288–91. The rod of Moses which turned into a serpent (Exod. iv. 2–4). For the interview with Pharaoh cf. Exod. vii. 9–12. This example and those following, to line 343, seem to stress the power of God manifested in miracles, not necessarily relating the miracle or example with traditional symbols of the Virgin. This type of proof had been used by St. Hildefonsus, *De Virginitate Perpetua Sanctae Mariae* IX.

292–4. Cf. Num. xx. 8–11.

295–8. Cf. Judges xv. 19.

299–303. Cf. Joshua iii. 13–17.

304–5. Cf. Num. xxii. 21–31.

306–7. Cf. 2 Kings vi. 5–7.

309–10. Cf. Apocrypha, Bel and the Dragon, 33–40.

323–9. Cf. Joshua x. 12–13.

323. *Gabeon*: Gibeon.

325. *Achalon*: the valley of Ajalon.

330–3. Cf. 2 Kings xx. 8–11.

331. *Ezechye*: Hezekiah; *orlage*: 'sun-dial'.

333. *Isaye*: Isaiah.

337–40. Cf. John vi. 1–14.

344–5. *be*: cf. *The Minor Poems of the Vernon MS*. Part i, ed. C. Horstmann, EETS (1892), no. 23, l. 913 (p. 89): 'Makyng hony þou art þe Beo', which translates the Latin 'Apis mella faciens' of a hymn attributed in the MS. to Albertus Magnus.

354. Cf. *AH*, i, no. 15:

> Tu sacratum manna,
> Coeli roris canna.

358. *barnacle*: 'the barnacle goose'. Cf. Pierre de Beauvais, *Bestiaire* (ed. C. Cahier and A. Martin, *Mélanges d'archéologie, d'histoire et de littérature* (Paris, 1851), vol. ii, p. 216).

365. *worme*: cf. Vincent of Beauvais, *Speculum Naturale*, 20. 68: 'Vermes dicuntur proprie, qui nascuntur ex putredine, itaque de carne, vel de terra nascuntur, sine coitu, et concupiscentia.'

372–3. *Sagitarrius*: cf. Bartholomaeus Anglicus, *De Proprietatibus Rerum*, 8. 18 (*Le Grand Proprietaire de toutes choses*, translated by Jean Corbichon, Paris, 1556): '. . . ce signe est appellé Sagittaire, car ainsi que le Sagittaire souuent traict et iette les Saiettes, aussi le Soleil quand il est en celle partie du Zodiaque il nous enuoye gresle, pluye et neige ainsi comme saiettes ou flesches.'

11. *A Complaynt of a Loveres Lyfe*

THERE are eight authorities for this poem: Bodley MSS. Fairfax 16, f. 20b: (F); Tanner 346, f. 48b: (T); Bodley 638, f. 1b: (B); Digby 181, f. 31a: (D); Arch. Selden B. 24, f. 120b: (S). Magdalene College, Cambridge MS. Pepys 2006, p. 1: (P). BM MS. Additional 16165, f. 190b: (A). Asloan MS., ff. 243a–6b and 293a–300b: (X). *Index* 1507.

It is impossible to construct a detailed, extensive classification of the MSS., given the nature of the MS. variations. E. Krausser's classification (*Anglia*, xix, pp. 216–23) is meticulous but misleading, since his lists of similarities within MS. groups assume that all variations recorded and classified are connected and meaningful. A (a Shirley MS.) is a unique (probably earlier) version of the poem. It has independent minor variations throughout and lacks the poet's prayer to Venus (ll. 610–51), thereby eliminating the poet's slight implication from the human dilemma. S derives from another early, but definitely worse, copy. The important prayer to Venus now appears, but ll. 113–26 (necessary to narrative continuity) are missing. S has many eccentric, bad readings throughout and shares many bad readings with A. P shares many of the common readings of MS. group FBTD, but is marred by excessive mechanical mistakes and omissions. B is a defective MS. lacking ll. 1–467 and seems chiefly dependent on F. X is a late MS. dependent on the Chepman and Myllar print. D is a fairish MS. which seems to have been copied from an exemplar showing signs of revision from an earlier to a later form. For example, at line 81 the early AS MSS. read *gan spring*. The later TP group read *cam spryngynge*. D has *gane sprynge*, corrected in the same hand to *came spryngynge*. F is a good, reliable MS. marred by occasional mechanical faults. It preserves a few authoritative readings. For example, at line 52 F reads *celured* (supported by A's *syloured*, a variant spelling), where TPD read *coloured* (with variations). But F retains a number of bad readings preserved only in the early AS group, e.g. *out-sterte* (16), *hondes* (97), and *gan syng* (81), which is a mistake for AS's *gan spryng*. T is an equally good MS. marred by occasional mechanical errors. It makes little difference whether one adopts F or T as the basis of a composite text. Both F and T share bad readings, e.g. *may not* (54), *colours* (126), *clepe* (285), *in partyng(e)* (419). I have used F as the basis of the text. Corrections are usually incorporated from T, occasionally from AS.

A Complaynt of a Loveres Lyfe (which came later to be called *The Complaint of the Black Knight*) is generally assumed to be one of Lydgate's early works and is assigned to the years 1398–1412. Although there is no external evidence for dating, it clearly belongs to a period of Lydgate's development characterized by close Chaucerian imitation and use of the *persona* of an actual lover. After 1412 (probably as a result of writing the *Troy Book*) the *persona* of the poet in Lydgate's work becomes less conventional, more autobiographical, and more religiously assertive. Correspondingly, the non-religious verse becomes more imitative of the literary style employed by Chaucer's Monk in *CT*. The flat, over-explanatory, measured seriousness of the Monk's style seems to have been deliberately cultivated by Lydgate, who, at various times, commanded greater range of tone.

The style of the poem is a blend of Chaucer's *Complaint unto Pity* and *Troilus*. Lydgate borrows an obvious feature (for narrative pattern) from the *Book of the Duchess* in the overheard complaint, setting, and concealed poet. But he turns this formulation, used in OF verse, into a simple device for framing a complaint. This technical regression nullifies Chaucer's important addition: the interplay of poet-figure and lover. Lydgate makes no attempt to criticize or modify the lover's state of mind or attitude. The poet-figure in the *exordium* and the *envoy de quare* is represented as a disappointed lover—a role supported by a possible reading of the Preface of the *Book of the Duchess*. The visit to a park and the description of the *locus amoenus* draws on Chaucer's *Parlement*, but Lydgate openly rejects that poem's *significaciones*, insisting that this is reality not dream. Lydgate's natural park is identifiable with Chaucer's idea of Nature and contrasts with the erotic condition. It is wholesome and restorative. The Knight's mental condition, although resembling that of the poet, is extreme and unreasonable. Although his *servise* is represented as honourable, true, and chaste, the Knight plainly describes his *peyn and wo* in erotic terms (ll. 453–65). In the end, he accuses Nature as well as Cupid and Venus (ll. 491–511).

No profound paradox in the nature of love is postulated by Lydgate. His Venus is perfectly respectable and reasonable. She does not belong to the wrong side of the moral world. Further, Lydgate's account of the process of loving (the relation of man, woman, and society) draws heavily, perhaps excessively, on Guillaume de Lorris's account in the *Roman*, especially Amors's speech to L'Amant. The more complicated speculations and objections of Jean de Meung (or Chaucer, for that matter) do not seem to have registered. Thus the lover's pains, problems, and contradictions are all ultimately resolvable on application to the stellar Venus. The poem ends optimistically with the poet's prayer to Venus, which draws on *CT*, A. 2221 ff.

Although Lydgate has realistically described the physical torment and mental anguish of the Knight, there is no moral conflict presented. The poem is medieval polite verse and belongs to the graceful versifying tradition of the *Complaint unto Pity* and the so-called *Complaint of Venus*. In the *Temple of Glas* (closely related to this poem) Lydgate moves on a further stage in presenting a love conflict—a conflict which draws on certain key phrases from Chaucer's *Complaint of Mars*. But Lydgate in this poem shows no interest in the sources of erotic psychology or the moral and metaphysical implications of the theme.

The Knight's complaint is the weakest part of the poem; it degenerates into an over-long exercise in certain rhetorical figures (especially juristic similitudes and grammatical schemes). On the other hand, the 'frame' (consisting of the *descriptio loci* and the closing prayer to Venus) is well-written and economical.

1. *Flora*: cf. Lydgate, *Siege of Thebes*, Prologue 13:

> Whan that Flora the noble myghty quene
> The soyle hath clad in newe tendre grene . . .

3–4. Cf. Chaucer, *Troilus* II. 50 ff.

5–6. *Lucifer*: Lydgate is remembering Chaucer's rendering of
Boethius, *De Consolatione Philosophiæ* 3, m. 1: '. . . and aftir that
Lucifer, the day-starre, hath chased away the dirke nyght . . .'
blended with the *Romaunt* 2636–40 (*Roman* 2501 ff.):

> 'A slowe sonne! shewe thin emprise!
> Sped thee to sprede thy beemys bright,
> And chace the derknesse of the nyght,
> To putte away the stoundes stronge,
> Whiche in me lasten al to longe.'

12. *Seint Iohn to borowe*: literally 'with St. John for a surety'.
In Chaucer (*Complaint of Mars*, l. 9) a phrase used at parting.

Hope: see the account of *Hope* in the *Romaunt* 2766–87 (*Roman*
2621–39).

13. *Daunger*: cf. *Romaunt* 3015–22, 3130–8 (*Roman* 2825–32,
2920–5). Cf. C. S. Lewis, *The Allegory of Love*, Appendix II.

17. Cf. Chaucer, *Troilus* IV. 432: 'But Troilus, that neigh for
sorwe deyde.'

25–30. Cf. Chaucer, *CT*, A. 1493 ff.:

> And firy phebus riseth up so bright
> That al the orient laugheth of the light,
> And with his stremes dryeth in the greves
> The silver dropes hangynge on the leves.

28. *persaunt*: one of Lydgate's favourite adjs. Cf. *Romaunt* 2809:
'Hir laughing eyen, persaunt and clere', which translates the
Roman's 'les iauȝ riantȝ' by way of *Roman* 8953 ff.: 'Car lins a la
regardeure Si fort, si perçant e si pure.'

34. *golde-borned*: a Lydgatian compound based on Chaucer, *CT*,
F. 1247: [Phoebus] 'shoon as the burned gold with stremes
brighte.' Chaucer was describing a hot, summer sun.

36. Cf. *Romaunt* 134; *costey*: 'to skirt'.

42. *grene stoon*: cf. Chaucer, *Parlement* 122: '. . . a park walled
with grene stone. . . .' Chaucer's meaning is uncertain but his
'grene ston' may refer to a precious stone, either emerald, beryl,
or jasper. Compare Chaucer's rendering of Boethius, *De Consolatione Philosophiæ* 3, m. 10: 'Indus . . . candidus miscens virideis

lapillos', 'Indus . . . that medleth the grene stones with the white'. Similarly, Lydgate, *Pur le Roi* 394 (MacCracken, ii. 630), describes a mimic castle, built in honour of Henry VI's entry into London, as 'bilt of iasper grene'. Lydgate means to emphasize the differences between the garden of lines 42 ff. and other poetic pleasure gardens which employ allegory or myth to prefigure a paradox or contradiction in the pleasure. The legend over the gate in the *Parlement* (ll. 127–40), defining two opposed concepts of Love, demands an attitude on the part of the visitor. Chaucer is shoved (l. 154) through the gate by Scipio Africanus. In Lydgate's park any one may freely enter. The well in this park is not the well of the *Roman* (originally Narcissus's) or any other mythological well. Lydgate's park is, in itself, wholesome, ordered nature. The water of the well alters the poet's health in the same way that the sleep into which Chaucer falls in the *Book of the Duchess* restores the poet-dreamer's health and vitality. Compare the 'sanatyf' properties of the Garden of Deduit in Lydgate's *Reson and Sensuallyte* 5150 ff.:

> That yf ther wer in any londe
> A man ybrent with lovys bronde,
> Or with his dredful arwe woundyd,
> Yf he were ewrous to be soundyd,
> This place wer most convenient
> Vn-to his amendement: (5187–92)

Some of the exemplary figures which later are to form part of the Knight's proof of the harshness of Venus's law of Love are here shown transformed into objects of pleasure and delight in the catalogue of trees.

52. *celured*: 'covered over'. Formed by Lydgate from the ME n. 'celure', 'a canopy'. Cf. Lydgate's coining of the technical term 'celature' from Medieval Latin *celatura* in the *Troy Book* iii. 5628.

52–56. The roof of boughs which protects the flowers from the sun's heat is an optional feature of the *locus amoenus*. Cf. Horace, *Odes* ii. 15. 9–10; Statius, *Silvæ* ii. 1. 154–5; Claudian, *De Raptu Proserpinæ* ii. 105–6; Achilles Tatius, *Clitophon and Leucippe* ii. A. 24–25; *Romaunt* 1395–1400 (*Roman* 1367–74).

57. Cf. *Romaunt* 131; *Pur le Roy* 19: 'The eyre attempred, the wyndis smoth and pleyn.'

62. *Take*: 'to begin to grow'. Cf. *Pur le Roy* 400.

63. *redy for to shake*: 'ready for shaking', a substantival infinitive.

64–74. Lists of trees were a rhetorical feature in Late Antique and Medieval poetry, and most lists possess distinct features that declare their origins. The mere mention of names of trees (as in the *Roman* 1289 ff.) seems too vague for classification. The heavily formalized tree catalogue, which consists of name of tree+ epithet of characteristic use (cf. Joseph of Exeter, *Ilias* I. 510–11: 'interpres laurus, vaga pinus, oliva Consilians') derives ultimately from Statius, *Thebaid* VI. 98 ff., via Claudian, *De Raptu Perserpinæ* II. 107 ff. The catalogue, which employs at least four devices (epithet of colour+name, mythological origin+ name, epithet of quality+name, simple name) derives from Ovid, *Metamorphoses* X. 90–104. Lydgate's catalogue here follows the Ovidian rhetorical scheme, with the addition of new subject-matter. Only line 73, 'oake with mony a younge acorne' may owe anything directly to Ovid: cf. *Metamorphoses* X. 94: 'curvataque glandibus ilex'.

64. Cf. Chaucer, *CT*, A. 2062: 'Ther saugh I Dane y-turned til a tree.'

65 *holsome pine*: Cf. Bartholomæus, *De Proprietatibus Rerum* 17.121: 'Also this tree is good to all thinge that is kept and con- tynewyd there under...', or the *De Laudibus Divinæ Sapientiæ* VIII. 71–72: 'Rebus servandis sub ea manet optima nutrix Pinus.'

68–70. *Phyllis* and *Demophoon*: Cf. Ovid, *Heroides* II; Chaucer, *Legend of Good Women* VIII; Gower, *Confessio Amantis* IV. 731– 878. Classical tradition had it that Phyllis was turned into an almond tree. Cf. Servius, *ad Ecl.* V. 10: '... conversa est in arborem amygdalum sine foliis.' Boccaccio, *Genealogiæ Deorum* XI. 25, follows Servius. Her transformation into a filbert tree seems to have originated in Gower's account in the *Confessio*, ll. 866–70:

> . . . Phillis in the same throwe
> Was schape into a Notetre,
>
> .   .   .   .   .
>
> And after Phillis Philliberd
> This tre was cleped in the yerd . . .

72. *motele*: 'garment'.

77. Cf. *Romaunt* 110–15.

78. In the *Roman* 1527 the gravel is 'plus clere qu'argenz fins' (*Romaunt* 1557).

80. *softe as veluet*: this detail derives from the *Romaunt* 1417–20. Guillaume described the grass as 'bassete e drue' (*Roman* 1393).

82. *sute of trees*: 'a number of trees planted and shaped in the

same style'. This is the first instance of the n. in this sense recorded in *OED*. In the *Romaunt* 1391-3 (*Roman* 1365 ff.) the trees are planted in uniform rows. In the *Roman* it is the branches of the pine tree planted by the well of Narcissus which cast a shadow over the well (1498-9: '. . . la fontaine Que le pins de ses rains covroit'). In the *Romaunt* 1510-11 the source of the shadow is not clearly specified.

87-98. A series of negative comparisons, a variation of the rhetorical figure *contrarium*.

87. *Well of Narcissus*: cf. *Roman* 1537 ff. (*Romaunt* 1549 ff.).

90. *greyn of deth*: cf. *Roman*, 1588 ff.:

> . . . Cupido
> Sema ici d'Amors la graine
> Qui toute a teinte la fontaine.

This is translated in the *Romaunt* 1616 ff.:

> . . . daun Cupido,
> Hath sowen there of love the seed
> That help ne lith there noon, ne red,
> So cerclith it the welle aboute.

The seed of love sown on the brink of the well refers back to the alluring properties of the grass which invite the lovers to embrace (ll. 1417 ff.):

> About the brinkes of these welles,
> And by the stremes overal elles,
> Sprang up the grass, as thicke yset
> And softe as any veluet,
> On which men myghte his lemman leye,
> As on a fetherbed to pleye;

Lydgate substitutes death for love in the imagery. The change conflates two separate ideas in the *Roman*: (1) the aetiological digression which explains the origin (though not the function) of the well; (2) the subsequent function of the well in the education of the lover. Guillaume imagined Cupid's seed of love as a 'laz environ tendre' for inducing young men and women to love mutually, in contrast to Narcissus who loved only himself. Either Lydgate is here simply referring us to the myth of Echo and Narcissus (Ovid, *Metamorphoses* III. 356 ff.), incidentally using details from the *Roman*, or he is purposely rejecting the erotic tendencies encouraged by *fine amour*. Much of Lydgate's love ethic borrows imagery and ideas from the *Roman* but Lydgate always recoils from any erotic implications (compare especially ll. 658–62).

91–92. *pitte of the Pegace*: 'fons Pegaseus', the Hippocrene, a fountain in Boeotia sacred to the Muses, according to Late Antique and Medieval geography located on the Heliconian peak of Parnassus. It was fabled to have been created by a stroke of Pegasus's hoof (cf. Ovid, *Metamorphoses* v. 256 ff.; Servius, *ad Æn.* x. 163). These lines derive from Persius, *Prologue to the Satires* 1–3:

> Nec fonte labra prolui caballino
> Nec in bicipiti somniasse Parnaso
> Memini, ut repente sic poeta prodirem.

This passage was used by Chaucer, *CT*, F. 721 ff., and apparently was a favourite of Lydgate's: cf. *Troy Book*, Prologue 45; *Fall of Princes* III. 15–16. There was an eleventh-century MS. of Persius and Juvenal in the library of the Abbey of Bury St. Edmunds.

94. *welle of pure chastite*: Lydgate seems to be following Hyginus's account of the myth of Diana and Actæon. Ovid, *Metamorphoses* III. 161, does not name the fountain or identify it with a moral quality. Hyginus (a second-century Latin grammarian and author), *Fabulæ*, 181, identifies the fountain as Parthenius in Gargaphia in Boeotia. The association of the spring with chastity may have been suggested to Lydgate by Servius's note on Mount Parthenius (*ad Ecl.* x. 57): '... dictus a virginibus, id est, ἀπὸ τῶν παρθένων ...'

111–12. Cf. *Romaunt* 1515–16 (*Roman* 1481–2).

119. *holtys hore*: this phrase occurs in the *Romaunt* 6996 where it translates the *Roman's* 'boschages' (11702). In the *Romaunt* it is used of unpleasant, wild, and deserted places.

124. Cf. Chaucer, *Parlement* 229: 'Her names shul noght here be told for me.'

125–6. For a similar setting compare Chaucer, Prologue to the *Legend of Good Women* (G) 203–4. Cf. *Troilus* II. 1702 for the phrase 'erber grene'.

126. [*clourys*]: The MSS. read *colours*, with the exception of W, which has *turves*. Cf. Lydgate, *The Churl and the Bird* (MS. Ly), 51 (MacCracken, ii. 468): 'Clouryd with newe turves grene' and *Order of Fools*, 52 (MacCracken, ii. 449). It is impossible to bench with colours. The word should be the ME. n. *clour*, 'turf'. Cf. *A Parliament of Birds* (*Journal of English and Germanic Philology*, VII. 105):

And in an erber sote and grene
Þat benchede was with chourys newe

(ll. 9–10)

127. *floures ynde*: 'dark blue flowers'. This phrase is found in the *Romaunt* 67 where it translates the *Roman* 63 (MSS. Za., L): 'flores indes'.

129. The symbolism (if any was intended) of the holly and the woodbine is vague. The MSS. vary considerably over the first plant (TF *hulfure*; A *haselle*; S *lorere*; C *hoser*). This would suggest confusion or indecision. The plants are probably meant to suggest no more than the idea of constancy.

130–1. Cf. Chaucer, *Book of the Duchess* 445. Lydgate's lover is dressed in black and white. The colours worn, like those of the lady in the *Temple of Glas*, have a general moral significance. Cf. Lydgate, *My Lady Dere* 99 ff. (MacCracken, ii. 420):

> And summe in token of clennesse,
> Weren whyte. . .
> But I, allas, in blak appere,
> And alwey shal, in sorowe and dred,

The colours worn by the lover in this poem testify to his chastity and anguish.

147. *shroud*: 'conceal'. The first recorded instance of the vb. in this sense. 'Shroud' is one of Lydgate's favourite verbs. He uses it in at least four new senses. Cf. *OED*'s readings and Bergen's glossary to the *Troy Book*.

151. *fortune and . . . eure*: a glossing phrase like the *Romaunt*'s 'inde and pers' (67). After Lydgate 'fortune and eure' enjoyed some popularity. Cf. *Court of Love* 634, and *Kingis Quair* 10. 2.

167. Cf. Chaucer, *CT*, B.² *1865: 'And gruf he fil al plat upon the grounde.' *desolate*: 'uninhabited'. Cf. Chaucer, *Anelida* 62.

168. Cf. *Temple of Glas* 401: 'That þei wiþ derknes were waped and amate.'

176–82. The rhetorical figure *invocatio*. The use of *dubitatio* (a subdivision of *apostrophe*) has been imitated from Chaucer, *CT*, B.² *3853 ff.:

> Who sal me yeven teres to compleyne
> The deth of gentillesse and of franchise?

The figures addressed by Lydgate are not necessarily derived from *Troilus* I. 669 and IV. 1139, but the form of the appeal is close in structure to *Troilus* I. 6 ff.:

> Thesiphone, thou help me for tendyte
> Thise woful vers, that wepen as I wryte.

Lines 181–2 are reworked from *Troilus* IV. 12–14.

183–9. This digression combines two elements: (1) *Troilus* I. 12–14, which provides for the identification of the author's mood with his subject; (2) the critical commonplace of the desirability of the author being able to suffer the emotions which he wishes to arouse in the reader. Cf. Quintilian, *Institutio Oratoria* VI. ii. 26: 'Summa enim, quantum ego quidem sentio, circa movendos adfectus in hoc posita est, ut moveamur ipsi.'

190–203. Lydgate habitually indulges in humility formulae. The simile of the scribe establishes experience or reality as Lydgate's literary authority. The figure of the 'scrivener' is an unusual if not unique image for the poet in ME literature.

215. The conventional posture of the distraught lover; cf. *Troilus* II. 1305–6.

218–23. The rhetorical scheme, *anaphora, parison, suspensio*, recalls Chaucer's opening lines of the *Parlement*. In Lydgate's hands it turns into a kind of catalogue. The four stanzas (218–45) which describe the lover's physical state are linked by a kind of repetition in which one word in the last line of each stanza is picked up in the first line of the following stanza. The key words are: *grounde, hote*, and *colde*.

224. Cf. Chaucer, *Complaint unto Pity* 106.

227. *chest*: 'receptacle'. Skeat refers to *Troilus* V. 1368: 'cheste of every care'. But the image is perhaps more complicated. Chaucer's 'chest' refers to Troilus's whole body. Lydgate's identification of 'chest' and 'brest' is coloured by an earlier lexical identification in late Latin where 'thorax' is glossed by 'archa' or 'capsum' (cf. Commodianus, *Instructiones* 76). In ME the same situation is reflected in the *Ormulum* 8972. Lydgate uses this expression again in *Life of Our Lady* II. 417: 'My breste, Receyte and cheste of wrecchednesse.'

229. Cf. *Troilus* II. 811 ff. where the alternations of hot and cold in the heart correspond to the psychological alternation of hope and fear. This process is called an *axcess* in *Troilus* II. 1315.

233. The paradox of hot and cold probably derives from *Troilus*

1. 420: 'For hete of cold, for cold of hete I dye.' Cf. Gower, *Balades* IX. 4:

> Jeo ris en plour et en santé languis,
> Jeue en tristour et en seurté m'esfroie,
> Ars en gelée, et en chalour fremis . . .

248. Cf. *Romaunt*, 1883: 'To serve his love with herte and alle.'

250–84. A long 'allegorical' narrative in which the relationship between the knight and the lady is enacted by personifications. The first allegory (250–9) is based on military activities (a commonplace of romantic love: cf. *Romaunt* 3435 ff.). The second (259–84) is juristic. Chaucer uses this kind of allegory in *Complaint unto Pity* 53–91.

257. *Envye*: cf. *Romaunt* 247 ff. (*Roman* 235 ff.).

259. *Trouthe*: personified by Chaucer, *Complaint unto Pity* 74.

260. *Male-bouche*: cf. *Romaunt* 3024 ff. (*Roman* 2833 ff.).

262. *Fals Report*: a Lydgatian personification, as is *Mysbeleve* in the next line.

263. *Fals-Suspecioun*: cf. *Romaunt* 2507 for the phrase. The personification is Lydgate's.

267. *londe*: cf. *Romaunt* 2783: 'Hope kepith his lond and wol abyde.' This economical expression translates, or represents, the French of ll. 2635 ff.:

> Iceste te garantira
> Ne ja de toi ne partira
> Qu'el ne te secueure au besoing.

The English translator's *londe* includes the lover in whom hope abides. This extended application of the n. Lydgate employs to another purpose. The property into which Falsnes has entered is the person of the knight in the lady's estimation—in the allegory, a land which Truth has a right to, since he is what he is, not what the lady imagines him to be.

277. *Cruelte*: a Chaucerian personification. Cf. *Complaint unto Pity* 11.

283. *feyth*: 'formal pledge'. Cf. *Troilus* v. 1675.

285. *c[reke]*: the MSS. show considerable variation here. F reads *clepe*; S reads *cleke*, which perhaps points to what Lydgate originally intended. *OED* and *MED*'s readings for *creke* ('to utter a harsh cry') indicate that in human contexts (as opposed to animal) the vb. implies contempt or foolishness. Cf. (*c.* 1450) Cap-

grave, *Life of St. Katherine* 4. 453: 'Lete hym calle, lady; lete hym crye and creke.' If we allow this emendation Lydgate's use is earlier and without contemptuous reference.

285–8. Cf. Chaucer, *Anelida* 311–12:

> Almighty God, of trouthe sovereyn,
> Wher is the trouthe of man? Who hath hit slayn?

290. Cf. *Temple of Glas* 574; *Troy Book* IV. 1552. Love's chain (*Romaunt* 3178) is here characterized by an adj. originally applied to Cupid's dart by Chaucer, *A Complaint to his Lady* 36: 'Thus am I slayn with Loves fyry dart.'

291. Cf. *CT*, A. 1010: 'Thurgh-girt with many grevous blody wounde.'

294. *drawe alonge*: cf. Chaucer's translation of Boethius, *De Consolatione Philosophiæ* I, m. 1 (31–32): 'myn unpitous lyf draweth a-long unagreable dwellinges in me.' This phrase translates the Latin vb. *protrahit*, 'prolongs'. Lydgate translated ll. 23–29 of this metre of Boethius in the *Fabula Duorum Mercatorum* 743–6 (MacCracken, ii. 486).

309. Cf. *Troilus* II. 778.

330–99. A section composed of catalogues of exemplary figures: (a) true lovers unrewarded; (b) false lovers rewarded.

330. *Palamides*: this would appear to be a reference to the Arthurian Palamides the Saracen, the unsuccessful lover of La Bele Isoude.

345. *Ercules*: Hercules occurs as an exemplary figure on the wall of Venus's temple in the *Parlement* 288, and in *CT*, A. 1943. Lydgate's account of the Pillars of Hercules draws on several types of sources: (a) Chaucer, *CT*, B.² *3307–8:

> At bothe the worldes endes, seith Trophee,
> In stede of boundes, he a piler sette.

(b) Gower, *Traitié* VII. 1. 1–4:

> El grant desert d'Ynde superiour
> Cil qui d'arein les deux pilers fichoit,
> Danz Hercules . . .

(c) Guido de Columnis, *Historia Destructionis Troiae* I (ed. N. E. Griffin, p. 9), states that Hercules set up pillars at Cadez.

354. Cf. *Troilus* I. 517–18:

> Now, thonked be God, he may goon in the daunce
> Of hem that Love list febly for to avaunce.

358. *Phoebus and Daphne*: Cf. *Troilus* I. 659–65; Ovid, *Metamorphoses* I. 452 ff.

359. Cf. Chaucer, *CT*, H. 105: 'Whan Phebus dwelled heere in this erthe adoun.'

365. *Pyramus*: cf. Chaucer, *Legend of Good Women* 724 ff.; Ovid, *Metamorphoses* IV. 55 ff. Pyramus occurs as an exemplary figure on the wall of Venus's temple in the *Parlement* 289. Tristram and Achilles are part of the same collection (*Parlement* 290).

367. *Antonius*: cf. *Legend of Good Women* 588 ff.

368. *Palamovne*: the inclusion of Chaucer's Palamon is odd, but perhaps Lydgate means to indicate the knight's unreasonableness.

372. *Jason*: cf. *Legend of Good Women* 1580 ff.

374. *Tereus*: ibid. 2228 ff.

375. *Aeneas*: ibid. 924 ff.; *Hous of Fame* 240 ff.

380. *Demophoon*: cf. Note to ll. 68–70.

386. *Adonis*: cf. Ovid, *Metamorphoses* X. 542 ff. These lines are reworked from *Troilus* III. 720–1:

> For love of hym thow lovedest in the shawe,
> I mene Adoun, that with the boor was slawe.

Chaucer's factual 'grove' has been developed into the more evocative 'grene shade'. The attractive setting is in contrast to the plight of Venus's devotee. Compare l. 575 for a similar contrast where the knight says that he bleeds 'vpon this colde grene'. Nature allows the knight none of the comforts she had given the ailing poet at the beginning of the poem. Perhaps Lydgate is remembering Ovid's description of the death of Narcissus (*Metamorphoses* III. 502): 'Ille caput viridi fessum submisit in herba.'

393. The usual account of Hippomenes and Atlanta (Ovid, *Metamorphoses* X. 575 ff.) does not tally with the lover's account here.

400–6. These lines are intended to recall *Troilus* V. 1849–54.

404–5. Cf. Chaucer, *Anelida* 270–1:

> Thogh that the swerd of sorow byte
> My woful herte through your cruelte . . .

421. *Lesynges*: 'Lies', personified by Chaucer in *CT*, A. 1927: 'Charmes and Force, Lesynges, Flaterye' are depicted on the wall of Venus's temple.

424. *Fals-Semblaunt*: cf. *Romaunt* 7297 ff. for his portrait.

432. Cf. *Romaunt* 2541–2 (*Roman* 2409–10):

> For they [false lovers] in herte cunne thenke o thyng,
> And seyn another in hir spekyng.

438. Cf. *Romaunt* 1715–926 for the wounding of the lover by Cupid's arrows.

441. Cf. *Parlement* 212: 'Cupide our lord his armes forge and fyle.'

448. Cf. *Anelida* 238 ff.:

> And shal I pleyne—alas! the harde stounde—
> Unto my foo that yaf myn herte a wounde
> And yet desireth that myn harm be more?

449. Cf. *CT*, F. 1038: 'Lo, lord, my lady hath my deeth y-sworn.'

454. For Venus's blindness compare Henryson, *Testament of Cresseid* 134–5:

> O fals Cupide, is nane to wyte bot thow,
> And thy mother, of luve the blind Goddes!

From Henryson's detailed description of Venus in the *Testament* it is clear that the blindness has not been transferred from Cupid to Venus, but from the traditional account of Fortune (Apuleius, *Metamorphoses* VII. 2; Boethius, *De Consolatione Philosophiae* II. pr. 1). E. Panofsky, *Studies in Iconology* (1939), pp. 113–14 suggests that the notion of the blind Venus arose in Germany during the fourteenth century.

460–8. For the conventional iconology of Cupid see Panofsky, *Studies in Iconology*, pp. 95 ff. The fickleness of Cupid's loyalty and its symbolism are a commonplace. Cf. Ovid. *Amores* II. ixa. 5: 'Cur tua fax urit, fugit tuus arcus amicos?'

478. Cf. *Anelida* 242.

487–8. This conceit has been taken from Chaucer, *Troilus* III. 684; *CT*, A. 1564 ff.

491–3. The portrait of Nature derives from Chaucer, *Parlement* 379 ff. For the history of Natura see J. A. W. Bennett, *The Parlement of Foules* (1957), Appendix, *Natura, Nature and Kynde*.

495. The lover here follows Troilus in his despair (*Troilus* v. 207): 'He curseth . . . His burthe, hymself, his fate and ek nature. . . .'

516. *my lyves quene*: cf. Chaucer, *A Complaint to his Lady* 54: 'My hertes lady, and hool my lyves quene.'

525. *charme*: Chaucer had already transferred the magical sense of the noun to the area of the physical pains of love in *Troilus* II. 1313 ff.:

> . . . 'thow shalt arise and see
> A charme that was sent right now to the,
> The which kan helen the of thyn accesse . . .'

540. Cf. *Troilus* IV. 1654: 'Now God, to whom ther nys no cause ywrye.'

558. Cf. *Romaunt* 4610 ff.:

> And make in haste my testament,
> As lovers doon that feelen smerte:
> To Bialacoil leve I myn hert . . .

587. Cf. *CT*, A. 1072: 'And to hymself compleyning of his wo.'

588. *bowes grene*: cf. *Troilus* II. 821.

590. Cf. Chaucer, *CT*, E. 1795: 'Parfourned hath the sonne his ark diurne.' The adjective *diurnal* was coined by Chaucer, *CT*, B^1. 296.

594. Cf. *Troy Book*, Prologue 127 ff. and especially l. 131: 'Passyng the bordure of oure occian.'

596. *rowes rede*: Chaucer, *Complaint of Mars* 2, where the reference is to dawn.

597. *deaurat*: 'gilded over'. A Lydgatian aureation from Late Latin *deauratus*, past part. of *deaurare*.

606. Cf. *Troilus* II. 17–18:

> . . . but prey yow mekely,
> Disblameth me, if any word be lame,
> For as myn auctor seyde, so sey I.

622. Cf. Ovid, *Metamorphoses* IV. 187–9:

> . . . Atque aliquis de Dis non tristibus optet
> Sic fieri turpis. Superi risere: diuque
> Hæc fuit in toto notissima fabula coelo.

Although Arcite (*CT*, A. 2383 ff.) mentions the exposure of Mars and Venus in his prayer to Mars, he suppresses the wider social unpleasantness. The poet's remark seems a little tactless here.

627. Cf. *Troilus* III. 1257: 'Venus mene I, the wel-willy planete!'

645 ff. This is a variation on the 'end of day *topos*' as a device for concluding a poem (cf. E. R. Curtius, *European Literature and the Latin Middle Ages* (1953), pp. 90 ff.). Compare Chaucer's use of the *topos* in the *Legend of Good Women* (F-Prologue), ll. 563–5:

> I mot goon hom (the sonne draweth weste)
> To paradys, with al this companye—
> And serve alwey the fresshe dayesye.

NOTES

663. Cf. the *Romaunt* 3820 ff.

666. As both Professor Schirmer and Dr. Seaton remark, the word 'Princes' may refer to a woman of any high social station.

674 ff. The *envoy de quare* used by Chaucer, Hoccleve, and Lydgate has an interesting literary history. Two main types of poet's address to a personified poem were invented by Classical Latin poets: (1) Horace in the *Epistles* 1. 20 used the conceit of the personified poem (see E. Fraenkel, *Horace*, pp. 356–63) to convey biographical facts, and to satirize his audience. This form in a less subtle, more satiric version appears in Martial (1. 70; III. 4. 5). (2) The second type arises out of the alienation of the poet from his audience. It amounts to a self-directed communication as a result of social and rhetorical isolation. After his exile to Tomis Ovid invented this form as a prologue to his *Tristia.* Book I. i. is a whole poem addressed to itself, where the poem is conceived of as the only friend or intermediary for the poet in Rome. In the *Pontic Epistles* IV. 5, 'To Sextus Pompeius', Ovid extended the form so as to include a description of the long and difficult journey which the poem had to make. This last form perhaps reaches its most complex treatment in Sidonius's *Propempticon ad Libellum* (XXIV), which serves as an epilogue to his poems. It is a combination of several genres acting as a directive for a 'round-robin' circulation of the poet's MS., incidentally showing the route. It ends with a skilful use of the nautical *topos* (poem = ship) in ll. 99–101. This type of verse arising from social isolation or remoteness had been used in an amatory context by Dante, *La Vita Nuova* XII, and by Boccaccio in the ninth part of *Il Filostrato*. Here the poet is denied access to his mistress and he undertakes to send the poem as a conciliator:

> Poi tu, posata aliquanto, te n'andrai
> Alla donna gentil della mia mente:
> *O te felice, che la vederai,*
> *Quel ch'io non posso far, lasso e dolente.*
> E come tu nelle sue man sarai
> Con festa ricevuta, umilemente
> Mi raccomanda all'alta sua virtute,
> La qual sola mi puo render salute.

(Stanza v)

This form, symptomatic of amatory estrangement, is imitated by Lydgate in ll. 674 ff. There is no evidence that Lydgate read

La Vita Nuova or *Il Filostrato* and the intermediate poem (or poems) has not been identified. The *envoi de quare* is much used by Lydgate. It even becomes a stylistic feature of his religious verse.

12. *The Temple of Glas*

THERE are seven more or less complete MS. authorities for this poem, and one fragmentary MS. The more or less complete versions are: Bodley MSS. Tanner 346, f. 76a: (T); Fairfax 16, f. 63a: (F); Bodley 638, f. 16b: (B). Magdalene College, Cambridge MS. Pepys 2006, p. 17: (P); Cambridge University MS. Gg. 4. 27, Part I, A, f. 491a: (G). BM MS. Add. 16165, f. 206b: (S). Longleat MS. 258, f. 1a: (L). The fragmentary MS. is BM MS. Sloane 1212, f. 1, ll. 736–54; f. 2, ll. 98–162; f. 4, ll. 439–505 of the *Compleynt* of the *GS version: (S1). For a more detailed description of this MS. see the notes to the *Commendation of Our Lady*, p. 143. Add. 38179, f. 2a (cf. *Index*) is a late transcript of P. *Index* 851.

One MS. group is composed of G, S, S1. S (a Shirley MS.) is the most complete version of this group. The group represents an early draft of the poem in which the moral situation and the lady's psychology are wholly different and where the end of the poem consists of an extended complaint in the poet's own person, after l. 1379. MS. group FB represents an intermediate draft in which the situation has been altered and the end of the poem changed, but where certain details and the lady's psychology have not been brought into line. MS. group TPL represents the completed draft of the poem, of which T is the most perfect example. T has been chosen as the basis of the text. The poem has been edited by Dr. J. Schick, EETS, Extra Series, lx. A full description of the MSS. with the exception of S1) and their relation is given on xvi–xlix of the Introduction, although their classification and relation are different from that attempted here. For a more radical interpretation of the MS. relations see Dr. Ethel Seaton, *Sir Richard Roos* (1961), pp. 375–83. The authorship of the poem would not seem to be in doubt since Shirley (S, 206b) writes '. . . vne soynge moult plesaunt fait a la request dun amoreux par Lidegate. Le Moyne de Bury.'

The *Temple of Glas*, when compared with *A Complaynt of a*

Loveres Lyfe, shows how cautious Lydgate was when he came to extend the narrative scope and descriptive depth of the Amatory Complaint. He enlarged the genre in terms of description by grafting on certain details of setting from Chaucer's *Hous of Fame*. These borrowings of time and place illustrate Lydgate's characteristic stripping away of Chaucerian complexity, especially of allegory. In this poem Lydgate moves from the *locus amoenus* setting of the *Parlement* and the *Roman* reflected in *A Complaynt of a Loveres Lyfe* to the Temple of Venus in the *Hous of Fame*. Traditionally these 'houses' carried with them a considerable weight of *significaciones* or allegorical detail, which defined the inhabiting personification or concept. Lydgate, aware of the literary and rhetorical tradition, keeps the minimum of significance in the temple setting, cleverly linking the residual allegory with the over-all design of the poem. This design is most visible at three places: (1) the lover's situation and psychology; (2) the resolution as pronounced by Venus; (3) the function of the Planetary Venus as described in the ballade of the rejoicing spirits.

This basic 'connecting' allegory derives from a single philosophical scheme ultimately traceable to Boethius, *De Consolatione Philosophiæ* iv. pr. 2, in which every object of perception and sensation is identified physically, and classified ethically, by its corresponding opposite. Thus, we have no accurate impression of the colour white unless we are able to compare it with black, no real experience of pleasure unless we undergo pain, no notion of 'true love' unless we suffer its opposite—in the case of the lady, an arranged marriage; in the case of the lover, an irresistible yet unrequitable passion. By the same token, the poet, blinded by the sun gleaming on the temple of glass, cannot obtain a view of the temple's interior. Yet the moment a cloud comes over the sun he is able to find his way inside. The symbolism here, that a knowledge of the power and nature of love is obtainable through its frustration and negation, is derived from *Troilus* ii. 764–70, 781, and 862 ff. The identification of Amor with the sun and its blinding properties is supported also by the Prologue to the *Legend of Good Women* (F), ll. 226–40. Further (drawing on *Troilus* i. 638–48), things known by comparison with opposites appear (and at the level of sensation, feel) intensified and enriched by the act of comparing. Thus, ll. 1250 ff., white will appear whiter when it has been compared with black, desires obtained through suffering will be more pleasant than those obtained immediately:

And so to ʒow more sote and agreable
Shal loue be found, I do ʒow plein assure,   1265
Wiþoute grucching þat ʒe were suffrable
So low, so meke, pacientli t'endure . . .

Lydgate, keeping to his variation on the 'end of day' structure
of *A Complaynt of a Loveres Lyfe*, has the Planetary Venus
praised as:

O myʒti goddes, daister after nyʒt,   1355
Glading þe morov when ʒe done appere,
To voide derknes þuruʒ fresshness of ʒour siʒt,
Oonli with twinkeling of ʒoure plesaunt chere . . .

She is the metaphysical resolver of the lovers' anxiety: the final
solution to the night/day, darkness/light, pain/pleasure set of
opposites (609–11, 1210–11, 1215–16, 1342–4).

Amongst these reworkings of convention Lydgate has done one
adventurous thing: he has decided to treat in this genre a triangu-
lar relationship of wife, lover, and husband where the genuine love
is potentially adulterous. Of course, he brings the pain/pleasure
opposition into force in order to prevent the lady and the lover
from entering into the usual social usage, and through degrees of
'daliaunce' end by dishonouring Boethius's and Chaucer's 'faire
cheine of marriage'. Lydgate here is aware of his metaphysical
commitments and is quick to reconcile the lady's chain (marriage)
and the lover's 'fiery chain' (desire) through Venus's golden chain
(love and marriage). Bound by Venus's command, the lady and
the lover must wait honourably for other already fated events to
occur. Presumably the husband (tactfully never individualized)
will disappear from the scene. The true lovers holding hands,
bound by the golden chain, appear to accept this resolution. The
reader is left with no other, wiser insight. This progressive Universe illuminated by guaranteed Hope is not meant by Lydgate
to engage the reader's philosophical interests. It is merely the
result of an allegorical organization which gives the poem a satis-
factory shape. The setting and schematical unity of imagery is
only a design for exhibiting two matching portraits of suffering
and a beautifully composed ballade apostrophe to Venus. This
pattern of cleverly combined elements looks forward to the eclectic
structure of the *Kingis Quair*.

In *A Complaynt of a Loveres Lyfe* Lydgate chose not to involve
the figure of the poet in the lover's suffering, and in the *Temple of*

Glas the poet is still an observer. His most painful moment occurs not in the dream (there is no anguish in the dreamer like that at the end of Book I of the *Hous of Fame*) but when he is awake and cannot quite remember what has happened (ll. 1367–77). Lydgate dared to represent in detail a new, adulterous, situation for the Complaint, but failed to extend his treatment beyond a smooth, socially acceptable expression of the conflict.

1–3. The source is Ovid, *Amores* I. 12. 1–4. Cf. *Romaunt* 2553–64:

> And whanne the nyght is comen, anoon
> A thousand angres shall come uppon.
> To bedde as fast thou wolt thee dight,   2555
> Where thou shalt have but smal delit;
> For whanne thou wenest for to slepe,
> So full of peyne shalt thou crepe,
> Sterte in thi bed about full wide,
> And turne full ofte on every side;   2560
> Now dounward groff, and now upright,
> And walowe in woo the longe nyght;
> Thine armys shalt thou sprede a-bred,
> As man in werre were forwerreyd.

Although Lydgate here appears to identify himself with the conventional figure of the unrewarded lover, the identification is not so absolute as that made in *A Complaynt of a Loveres Lyfe*. The concluding lines and envoi of the *Temple of Glas* do much to blur a clear image of a lover-poet, and move a considerable way towards 'Chaucerian' ambiguity. Lines 1372–91 suggest that it is the lady in the dream to whom the poet has given his heart (cf. especially ll. 1376–80). Line 1392 introduces what at first sight appears to be another lady, a real-life lady. The envoi (ll. 1393–1403) encourages this interpretation until we come to line 1402: 'I mene þat benygne and goodli of hir face.' The epithets have been used repetitiously in the poem of the dream-lady, and the effect of the qualifying 'I mene' is to further cloud the issue. Lydgate creates confusion, for he does not want to associate the poet-figure's pre-sleep anguish with physical desire. The pains of the poet should arise out of the subject-matter of the dream: an essentially adulterous situation where there is a potential conflict of claims—marriage (artificial law) versus true love (natural law). Lydgate lacks the inventive subtlety to create an unobtrusive ambiguity. Line 1 possibly recalls the *Romaunt* 308: 'For sorowe, thought, and gret distresse.'

3. *þis opir nyȝt*: cf. Chaucer, *Book of the Duchess* 45.

4–7. The astronomy is literary, not scientific. Lydgate purposely avoids any tradition of precise dating which would postulate a real situation. The sun, of course, entered Capricorn in December, not Aquarius. Compare the *Kingis Quair* 1–7 for a similar use of literary astrology. The December setting is intended to associate this poem with Chaucer's *Hous of Fame*.

6. Cf. *Hous of Fame* 111–12:

> Of Decembre the tenthe day
> Whan hit was night, to slepe I lay . . .

8. Cf. Chaucer's translation of Boethius, *De Consolatione Philosophiæ* I, m. 5: '. . . the moone pale with hir derke hornes . . .'

12. Cf. *Romaunt* 2562.

16. *Rauysshid in spirit*: 'transported in spirit'. *OED* quotes the *Monk of Evesham*, chapter xiv (ed. Arber, p. 36), as the first example of the phrase, but Lydgate is earlier.

Cf. Chaucer, *Hous of Fame* 119–20:

> But as I slept, me mette I was
> Withyn a temple ymad of glas;

The whole setting recalls the *Hous of Fame*. Cf. ll. 480–91, where the temple of Venus is described as surrounded by a forbidding desert.

19–20. Cf. *Hous of Fame* 1130, where the foundation of the Castel of Fame is: 'A roche of yse, and not of stel.'

20–37. Lydgate alters Chaucer's *significacio* for the glass of Venus's temple in the *Hous of Fame* (brittleness), adopting a new significance via Chaucer, *Troilus* II. 862 ff.:

> 'What is the sonne wers, of kynde right,
> Though that a man, for feeblesse of his yen
> May nought endure on it to see for bright?
> Or love the wers, though wrecches on it crien?
> No wele is worth, that may no sorwe dryen.'

with the addition of *Troilus* II. 764–70 and 778–81:

> 'For love is yet the mooste stormy lyf,
> Right of himself, that evere was bigonne;
> For evere som mystrust or nice strif,
> Ther is in love, som cloude is over the sonne.'

Cf. the *Fall of Princes* VI. 2969–81 where this same imagery is combined with the *topos* of defining by contraries.

36–37. Cf. the description of the Castle of Jealousy in the *Romaunt* 4183: 'The tour was round, maad in compas.'

39. The wicket entry originates in the *Roman* 511–20. Cf. *Romaunt* 528–30:

> Tyl that I fond a wiket small
> So shett, that I ne myght in gon
> And other entre was ther noon.

44 ff. The wall-painting depicting lovers was probably suggested to Lydgate by ll. 284–94 of the *Parlement*. The arrangement of the figures presents some difficulty. Dr. Schick imagined them as grouped according to their physical age. I have followed his punctuation and interpretation, but the parallels which he quotes do not support such a reading. Lydgate's grammar is ambiguous and uncertain. It may well be that the phrase 'of age' means 'maturity', and 'aftir' means 'in the degree that'; so that they were painted as if they were in the prime of life and ranked according to the degree of their fidelity. Lydgate may be misremembering the *Monk's Tale* 3175–7.

50. The reading of prepared complaints is a commonplace of this genre. Cf. Chaucer, *Complaint unto Pity* 43 ff.

53. This parenthetical description of Venus seems to be a passing reminiscence of Chaucer's statue of Venus in *CT*, A. 1955–8.

55–61. *Dido*: a favourite exemplary figure. Cf. Ovid, *Heroides* VII; Chaucer, *Legend of Good Women* 924–1367; *Hous of Fame* 140 ff.

62–63. *Jason and Medea*: cf. Ovid, *Heroides* XII; *Legend of Good Women* 1368–679.

64–65. *Venus and Adonis*: cf. Ovid, *Metamorphoses* X. 503 ff.

67–69. *Penelope*: Ovid, *Heroides* I.

70–74. *Alcestis*: cf. Chaucer, *Legend of Good Women*, Prologue (F), 498–504. The basic fable Chaucer could have got in synopsis form from any number of authors from Servius to Boccaccio. The transformation of Alcestis into a daisy seems to be a Chaucerian myth.

75–76. *Grisilda*: cf. Chaucer, *The Clerk's Tale*.

77–79. *Isault*: cf. *Parlement* 290; Gower, *Confessio Amantis* VI. 471 ff.

80–81. *Thisbe*: cf. Ovid, *Metamorphoses* IV. 55 ff.; *Parlement* 289; *Legend of Good Women* 706–923.

82–85. Theseus: Ovid, *Metamorphoses* VII. 433 ff.; *Legend of Good Women* 1886–2227.

84. for-wrynk[l]ed: 'formed in extreme convolutions'. Cf. *Fall of Princes* I. 2683.

86–90. Phyllis: cf. *A Complaynt of a Loveres Lyfe* 68–70 and note.

92–93. Paris and Helen: cf. *Parlement* 290–1.

94–95. Achilles and Polyxena: cf. *Parlement* 290; Hyginus, *Fabulæ* 110.

97–99. Philomene: *Philomela*. The form Lydgate uses (following Chaucer and Gower) is frequent in Medieval Latin. For the story, see Ovid, *Metamorphoses* VI. 424 ff.; *Legend of Good Women* 2228–393.

100–1. The feast of Lucrece, cf. Ovid, *Fasti* II. 685 ff. Lydgate presumably refers here to the *Regifugium* celebrated on 24 February.

102. Palamon: cf. Chaucer, *Knight's Tale*.

112–16. Phoebus and Daphne: cf. Ovid, *Metamorphoses* I. 452 ff. *arrow of gold*: cf. *Metamorphoses* I. 468–71:

> Eque sagittifera promsit duo tela pharetra
> Diversorum operum. Fugat hoc, facit illud amorem.
> Quod facit, auratum est, et cuspide fulget acuta.
> Quod fugat obtusum est, et habet sub arundine plumbum.

118. Europa: cf. Chaucer, *Troilus* III. 722–5:

> 'O Jove ek, for the love of faire Europe,
> The which in forme of bole awey thow fette,
> Now help! O Mars, thow with thi blody cope,
> For love of Cipris, thow me nought ne lette!'

122–3. Amphitrion and Alcmena: cf. Chaucer, *Troilus* III. 1428; Hyginus, *Fabulæ* 29.

126–8. Mars and Venus: cf. *A Complaynt of a Loveres Lyfe* 389–92 and note.

129–36. Mercury and Philology: cf. Martianus Capella, *De Nuptiis Philologiæ et Mercurii* II, and Chaucer, *CT*, E. 1732–5.

154. The first of several omitted whole lines. This omission is shared by MSS. TPFB. The line has been supplied from *GS.

156. Cf. *Parlement* 136.

162. wanting: 'lack of money'. These are the poor lovers who have divulged their financial position. They are charged with the fault by their mistresses.

201. *Yrendred*: 'handed over'. Cf. *OED render* vb. II. 7.

223-39. Cf. Chaucer, *Complaint of Mars* 218-71.

248. *Pallas*: cf. Lydgate, *Troy Book* II. 2549 ff. for a full description of the goddess. Line 2581 identifies Lydgate's source as Fulgentius's *Mythologicon* or some compilation attributed to him. Cf. 'Albricus Philosophicus', *De Deorum Imaginibus* VIII: '. . . in sinistra vero scutum crystallinum habebat, quod caput Gorgonis a cervice serpentibus monstrose continebat.'

251-2. Cf. *Parlement* 298-301, the description of Nature:

> Tho was I war wher that ther sat a queene
> That, as of lyght the somer sonne shene
> Passeth the sterre, right so over mesure
> She fayrer was than any creature.

270-7. Cf. D. S. Brewer, 'The Ideal of Feminine Beauty in Medieval Literature', *MLR*, lx (1955), pp. 257-69.

299. The Lady's colours prefigure the chaplet of hawthorn boughs and flowers which Venus throws into the lady's lap in ll. 503 ff. The moral significance would seem to be green for constancy and white for chastity.

310. A common French literary phrase (cf. Deschamps, *Lay Amoureux* 206). It came to be used much later as a motto, in England, by the Pastons. But there is no need to see the phrase here as indicating that the poem was commissioned by the family or intended to refer to them (H. N. MacCracken, *PMLA*, xxiii (1908), pp. 128-40).

323. *hauteyn*: 'arrogant'. Cf. Chaucer, *Legend of Good Women* 1120.

331. *woful*: an attributive use of the adj. Cf. Lydgate, *The Churl and Bird* 249: 'Comfortith sorweful, makyth heuy hertis liht' (MacCracken, ii. 468).

335. Although it is never explicitly stated that the lady is married, the context and imagery used to convey the situation make it difficult to imagine otherwise; see line 351 especially.

In MSS. G and S, ll. 335-69 are represented by the following stanzas. For their original interpretative value and the significance of their being removed see Ethel Seaton, *Sir Richard Roos* (1961), pp. 377-8; J. Norton-Smith, 'Lydgate's changes in the *Temple of Glas*', *Medium Ævum*, xxvii (1958), pp. 166 ff.

3a

So that ȝow lyst of ȝoure benygnete,   335
Goodly to seen and shape remedye
On wekkede tongis and on the crewelte
That they compasse thourgh maleys and envye,
To quenche the venym of here felonye,
Wher as they hyndre wemen gilteles: 340
Stynteþe this werre and lat vs leue in pes.

4a

I pleyne also vpon Ielusye,
The vile serpent, the snake tortyvous,
That is so crabbit and frounynge of his ye,
And euere grochynge and suspecyous,   345
Ifret with eysel that makyth hym dispytous
Of euery thing the werste for to deme,
That ther is no thyng that may his herte queme.

5a

Thus is he fryed in his owene gres,
To-rent and torn with his owene rage,   350
And euere frowar[d] and frounynge causeles,
Whos resoun faylyth in elde thourgh dotage:
This is the maner of krokede fer in age
Whan they ben couplyd with ȝouthe: þey can no more
But hem werreyen, which wemen beyeth ful sore.   355

6a

Thus euere in tourment and yre furyous
We ben oppressed (allas the harde stounde!)
Rygh[t] as ȝoure selve were with [Vu]lcanus
Ageyn ȝoure wil and ȝoure herte bounde.
Now for the Ioye, whilom that ȝe founde   360
With Mars, ȝoure knyght, vpon myn compleynt rewe—
For love of Adon that was so frosche of hewe.

338. *knyt*: 'joined by the marriage bond'. Cf. Chaucer, *CT*,
F. 986: 'I wol ben his to whom that I am knyt.'

356–62. Cf. *A Complaynt of a Loveres Lyfe* 228–45 and notes
to 229, 233.

375. *purgatorie*: the first recorded instance of the weakened
sense of the theological term as applied to a psychological state;
but see *CT*, A. 1226.

380. *defence*: 'offence'. Cf. *MED defense* n. 5c.

389. The family relationship of Venus and Saturn and the immediate reason for Saturn's role in the poem derive from *CT*, A. 2443 ff.

391–416. Here occurs the first of many references to the definition of physical and ethical qualities by the doctrine of Contraries. The *locus classicus* for the Middle Ages is Boethius, *De Consolatione Philosophiæ* IV, pr. 2:

. . . quorum alterum demonstratur ex altero. Nam cum bonum malumque contraria sint, si bonum potens esse constiterit, liquet imbecillitas mali: at si fragilitas clarescat mali, boni firmitas nota est.

Cf. *Roman* 21573–4:

> Ainsinc va des contraires choses,
> Les unes sont des autres gloses.

Cf. Chaucer, *Troilus* I. 637–48:

> 'By his contrarie is every thyng declared.
>
> For how myghte evere swetnesse han ben knowe
> To him that nevere tasted bitternesse?
> Ne no man may ben inly glad, I trowe,
> That nevere was in sorwe or som destresse.
> Eke whit by blak, by shame ek worthinesse,
> Ech set by other, more for other semeth,
> As men may se, and so the wyse it demeth.'

395–6. Cf. *Troilus* III. 1011–15, and Boethius, *De Consolatione Philosophiæ* III, m. 2.

398–9. Cf. *Romaunt* 2119–20.

401. Cf. *A Complaynt of a Loveres Lyfe* 168.

407. *dul*: 'to grow weary and bored'. This sense seems to have originated with Chaucer.

410. *Dorigen*: Cf. Chaucer, *Franklin's Tale*.

411. Cf. *Troilus* I. 952: 'And also joie is next the fyn of sorwe.'

436. The brand of Venus was originally Cupid's in classical mythology. Although Prudentius (*Psychomachia* 42–45) had given Libide a pine torch (*pinus*), the transfer of the *fax* to Venus is perhaps due to Alan of Lille, *Anticlaudianus* IX. 233–41:

Ignitam tamen illa [Venus] facem, que fulminis ipsam
Mentitur speciem, que saxa resoluere, cautes
Extenuare solet, ferrum mollescere, rupes
Inflammare, rapit instanter, uibrat in hostem.
Has pugnas, hec bella tremens, hec prelia uitans
Expectare timet iuuenis; fuga consulit illi
Consilioque fuge uenientes effugit ictus.
Fax ignita cadit, expirat in aere, uires
Amittit, dum nulla manent fomenta caloris.

Cf. Guillaume de Lorris, *Roman* 3422 ff. (*Romaunt* 3705 ff.):

Ce est la mere au deu d'Amors,
Qui a secoru maint amant.
Ele tint un brandon flamant
En sa main destre, don la flame
A eschaufee mainte dame;

In Alan and Guillaume the sexual symbolism of Cupid's torch (see
Isidore, *Etymologiæ* VIII. 11) has been preserved in the transfer.
See *CT*, E. 1777. It was Chaucer who softened the erotic emphasis
in his blending of traditional mythological and astrological details
of the goddess in the *Parlement* 112–15. It is Chaucer's ambiguous
Venus of these lines that Lydgate has in mind.

447–53. The beneficial effects of love on moral behaviour were
probably suggested by *Troilus* III. 1744–50, 1787–1806.

463–7. The Judgement of Paris. Cf. Fulgentius, *Mythologicon*
II. i; *Troy Book* II. 2635–792.

494–5. Cf. *Troilus* III. 1224–5.

Between ll. 495 and 496 the following three stanzas occur in
MSS. FBGS. These lines refer to the emphatic figure of 'Ielousy' in
the original stanzas, 3a, 4a, 5a, 6a in MSS. G and S (ll. 335–69).
Cf. notes to ll. 335–69.

25a

And in despit platly of hem alle
That ben to love so contraryous,
I shal hym cherice, what so euere falle,
That is in love so pleyn and vertuous,   500
Maugre alle tho that ben so desyrous
To spekyn vs harm, thourgh grochyng and envye
Of thilke serpent Icallyd Ielousye.

26a

And for hem, lady, (ʒif I durste preye)
Menynge no vengeaunce, but correccyoun: 505
To chastyse hem with torment or they deye
For here vntrouthe and fals suspecyoun,
That deme the werste, in here opynyoun,
Withoute deserte, wherfore that ʒe vouche:
To ponysshe hem dewely for here male-bouche.   510

27a

So that they may stondyn in repref
To alle loueris for here cursedenesse,
Withoutyn mercy, forsakyn at myschef
Whan hem lyste best han helpe of here distresse
And, for here falshed and here doubilnesse,   515
Had in despit—ryght as among foulys
Ben Iayis, Pyis, Lapwyngis and these Oulys.

503–6. In MS. group GSFB (which embodies two earlier drafts of the poem) Venus bestows her own type of garland, that of roses. With variations the GSFB group read:

>   Into hir lap, Roses white and rede   (525)
>   So fressh of hewe, þat wenten enviroun   (526) 505
>   In compas wyse euen aboute hir hede . . .   (527)

'euen', the reading of GS, is altered to *euer* in FB, which indicates the difficulty implied by the recasting of ll. 335–62. As *Troy Book* II suggests, Lydgate was aware of the mythographers' moralization that the roses in Venus's garland signified that the delights of Venus fade quickly. The ever green hawthorn boughs and flowers (recalling Alceste's unfading daisy in the *Legend of Good Women*) support Venus's moral exhortation in ll. 510–23.

524. Cf. *CT*, A. 2265: 'But atte laste the statue of Venus shook.'

530. 'I shall obey you better and better in spite of whatever happens' is the meaning of the motto.

536–44. This short *occupatio* describing sacrifices was probably suggested by *CT*, A. 2906–8, 2919–66.

550. The introduction to the solitary lover is very similar to *A Complaynt of a Loveres Lyfe* 155 ff.

572. The temple setting of the lover's subjection to Venus and Cupid probably reflects Troilus's instant conversion in *Troilus* I. Unfortunately, it plays havoc with Venus's notion of the relationship in ll. 384–90.

578–87. Cf. ll. 223–39. The difficulties of the lady and lover are not unique. Their situation and feelings closely resemble those of the throng in the temple.

606–9. The simile is derived from *Troilus* I. 415–18.

641. Cf. *Troilus* V. 1207: 'Bitwixen hope and drede his herte lay.' The long *thymomachia* which follows recalls *A Complaynt of a Loveres Lyfe* 491–515.

651. *double werre*: 'confusion of mind'. Cf. *Troy Book* IV. 2361.

666. Cf. *Troilus* II. 385.

675. *bitt*: a contracted form of 3 sg. *bideþ*. Cf. *sit* (l. 184) and *list* in ll. 297, 314. The scribe of T misunderstood *bitt* in his exemplar and wrote *bitt* thinking that the contraction mark for *er* had been omitted.

703. *Cirrea*: cf. Chaucer, *Anelida* 17 for the form, and *A Complaynt of a Loveres Lyfe* 91–92 and note for the geography. *Cirra* enters into the medieval map of Parnassus via Isidore, *Etymologiæ* XIV. 8: 'Parnassus mons est Thessaliæ . . . Hic in duo finditur juga Cirra et Nissa.' Cf. Lydgate's translation of this account in the *Troy Book* IV. 6968–70. Cirrha was a town in Phocis at the mouth of the river Pleistus, which descends from Parnassus. The placing of a temple of Venus at Cirrha seems to have been Lydgate's invention.

706. *Helicon*: cf. *A Complaynt of a Loveres Lyfe* 91–92 and note.

716. *cercled*: 'set in the form of a circle'. This merely refers to the physical position of the planet in the order of the spheres (cf. Macrobius, *Commentum* I. 19. 1–7).

732. For the rime *mynde*/*ende*, cf. ll. 1241–2. This rime perhaps reflects variation between ĭ and ī in ME in the class of native words in *-ind*. Cf. E. Dobson, *English Pronunciation 1500–1700*, ii, p. 479. But *mynde* here probably represents an original *mende*, evidenced in South Eastern texts: cf. Confessio Amantis IV. 1961–2.

743. Cf. Chaucer, *CT*, E. 2178: 'Ye been so depe enprented in my thoght.'

755. Cf. *Troilus* V. 816–17:

> Lo, trewely, they writen that hire syen
> That Paradis stood formed in hire yen.

Lydgate, *Troy Book* II. 3671–2:

> Within the cerclynge of hir eyen bright
> Was Paradys compassed in hir syght.

759. *nwe and nwe*: a common phrase, cf. Chaucer, *Troilus* III. 116.

761. For the text of the lover's code of behaviour and the injunction against pride, cf. Amors's words in the *Roman* 2077–264 (*Romaunt* 2175–386).

773. Cf. l. 852.

778. *Antony and Cleopatra*: cf. *A Complaynt of a Loveres Lyfe* 367; *Parlement* 291; *Legend of Good Women* 580–705.

780. *Thisbe and Piramus*: cf. ll. 80–81 and note.

782. *Antropos*: *Atropos*, one of the three Fates. She is imagined by most classical and medieval writers as the sister who cuts the thread of existence (Servius, *ad Æn.* I. 22; *Roman* 19763–71; *Troilus* IV. 1546). *Antropos* is a common form in ME and OF.

785. *Achilles* and *Polyxena*: cf. ll. 94 and note.

787. *Hercules* and *Dejanira*: cf. Ovid, *Heroides* IX; Gower, *Confessio Amantis* VIII. 2559–62.

788. Cf. *Troilus* II. 58.

792–3. Venus is given greater omniscience here than she was in *Troilus* III. 31–35, where she had the power to know all the secrets of lovers. In this passage she comes to resemble Boethius's Jove (*De Consolatione Philosophiæ* v, m. 2).

829. Cf. *Troilus* v. 1319: 'With herte, body, lif, lust, thought and al.'

869 ff. Cf. Minerva's advice to the poet in James I's *Kingis Quair*, stanza 129.

892. 'All these personifications are quite in the style of the *Roman de la Rose*' (Schick).

913–17. Cf. Boethius, *De Consolatione Philosophiæ* I, pr. 4: 'Si operam medicantis exspectas, opportet uulnus detegas'; and *Troilus* I. 857–8:

> 'For whoso list have helyng of his leche,
> To hym byhoveth first unwre his wownde.'

947. Cf. *Troilus* IV. 13–14:

> And now my penne allas! with which I write,
> Quaketh for drede of that I moste endite.

Cf. *A Complaynt of a Loveres Lyfe* 181–2.

952–6. Cf. *A Complaynt of a Loveres Lyfe* 176–9 and note.

958. *Thesiphone*: *Tisiphone*, one of the three Furies. Cf. *Roman* 19832 ff.; Chaucer, *Troilus* IV. 22–24:

> O ye Herynes Nyghtes doughtren thre,
> That endeles compleignen evere in pyne,
> Megera, Ale[c]te, and ek Thesiphone;

Cf. Lydgate, *An Exclamacioun of Alcibiades* 10 and note.

1042 ff. Cf. Chaucer, *Parlement* 442–5:

> Ryght as the freshe, rede rose newe
> Ayeyn the somer sonne coloured is,
> Ryght so for shame al wexen gan the hewe
> Of this formel, whan she herde al this . . .

1106–9. Cf. ll. 1224–5, 1230–1. This golden chain perhaps should be identified with the chain of the four Elements in the macrocosm, and the bond of matrimony in the microcosm (Boethius, *De Consolatione Philosophiæ* II, m. 8; IV, m. 6). The colour has been taken from *Roman* 16785 ff. For a full discussion of this passage and the main sources see J. Norton-Smith, 'Lydgate's Metaphors', *English Studies* (1961), pp. 90–93.

1124 ff. Cf. the notes to l. 761.

1214. Cf. *CT*, A. 3093–5:

> 'Com neer, and taak youre lady by the hond.'
> Bitwixen hem was maad anon the bond
> That highte matrimoigne or mariage . . .

1224–8. Cf. *Roman* 1999–2004 (*Romaunt* 2087 ff.):

> Thanne of his awmener he [Love] drough
> A litell keye, fetys ynowgh,
> Which was of gold polisshed clere,
> And seide to me, 'with this keye heere
> Thyn herte to me now wole I shette.'

1232 ff. These are the 'stellar' gods involved in deciding (so they think) the outcome of the *Knight's Tale* (ll. 2438–78). They are introduced rather gratuitously here.

1250–70. Cf. the introductory notes to this poem (pp. 177–8) and the note to ll. 391–416. The following passage from 'How myschaunce regnythe in Ingeland' (T. Wright, *Political Poems and Songs*, ii (1861), 238 ff.) is very close to Lydgate:

> Wyghte is wyghte[r] ȝyf yt [is] leyd to blake;
> And soote ys swettere aftur bytternesse;
> And falsenesse ys evere drevene abake,
> Where th[e] trou[th]e ys rootyd wytheowte dubbilnesse.
> Wytheowte preef may not be sykernesse;
>
> (ll. 97–101)

1303 ff. Cf. Chaucer, *Hous of Fame*, 1399–1401.

1308–10. Cf. Chaucer, *CT*, E. 1715–17.

1331. Cf. *Troilus* II. 526–7:

> 'O god, that at thi disposicioun
> Ledest the fin, by juste purveiaunce . . .'

1341–61. These lines form a 'balade simple', three turns with refrain and no envoi.

1348. Cf. *A Complaynt of a Loveres Lyfe* 627 ff. and note.

1362–5. The waking of the poet by the ballade of praise to Venus has probably been suggested to Lydgate by Chaucer's 'awakening device' in the *Parlement* 693–5, where the roundel of praise sung by the birds to summer wakes the poet.

1366. Cf. *Romaunt* 3859: 'I was astoned, and knew no red.'

1374. *auisioun*: Lydgate probably means little more than 'dream'. Chaucer in the *Hous of Fame* 7, 40, 48 uses the n. in two senses: (1) in line 40 to mean a 'dream' in general, as here; (2) in ll. 7 and 48 to correspond to Macrobius's *somnium*, 'a dream which requires interpretation'. But see ll. 1389–90, where the 'visioun' plainly requires interpretation.

1379–92. Lydgate's dedication of himself to a future poem in praise of women follows Chaucer's intention in *Troilus* v. 1771–8.

1379. In the G and S MSS. there follow 628 lines of a complaint in octosyllabic couplets, delivered in the person of the poet. It is printed by Dr. J. Schick in his edition of the *Temple of Glas* (see Select Bibliography, p. xviii), Appendix I, pp. 59–67.

1392. On the identity of 'mi ladi' see the notes to ll. 1–3.

1392 ff. None of the MSS. properly indicate the division into an envoi. Cf. *A Complaynt of a Loveres Lyfe* 674 ff. and note.

APPENDIX: AUREATE DICTION

BOTH the ME adj. 'aureat' and the concept of an 'aureate style' are Lydgate's invention. Classical and Late Antique authors had used the adjs. *aureus* and *aureolus* to convey the notion of 'splendid', 'bright', or 'excellent' as applied to physical beauty, mental attainment, or linguistic excellence. In this extended application, the adjs. original association with the metal gold would seem to have been weakened or lost altogether.[1] When Cicero in the *Academia* (II. 38, 119) used the phrase *aureum flumen orationis* in connexion with Aristotle it is difficult to say whether any association with metal or colour still clung to the adj.

Lydgate's coinage, 'aureat', was probably formed on late Latin *aureatus*, recorded once in literary usage (as a *difficilior lectio*) in the poetry of the stylistically influential Sidonius Apollinaris (*Carmen* IX. 295), where the meaning is 'gold-adorned' but does not refer to language.[2] Unlike the earlier *aureus* or *aureolus* Lydgate's 'aureat' is never used without strong metaphoric associations. These associations make it clear that 'aureat' for Lydgate meant both 'eloquent' and 'golden'. Apart from several concrete uses, Lydgate employs 'aureat' in four main metaphoric configurations:

[1] 'rhetoricals kill', 'colours rhetorical', perhaps associated with the art of manuscript illumination. Cf. *Fall of Princes*, Prol. I. 449–66; Prol. IV. 106–8; IX. 3445–9; cf. *Fall of Princes* VIII. 80–81: 'To refourme the rudenesse of my stile With aureate colours of your fresche language' with *Troy Book* II. 192–7:

---

[1] Cf. the similar use of χρύσεος in Greek and the limited application of 'golden' in ME in certain phrases.

[2] Dictionary evidence would seem to indicate that the past part. adj. had some currency in Medieval Latin in non-literary usage. Cf. Guido's *Disciplina Farfensis* (cap. ii): 'Diaconus induat stolas argentatas, atque dalmaticam *aureatam*.'

Al-be þat I ne can þe way[e] goon
To swe þe floures of his eloquence;
Nor of peyntyng I haue noon excellence
With sondry hewes noble, fesche and gay;
So riche colours biggen I ne may
I mote procede with sable and with blake.

and see Dunbar, the *Golden Targe*, ll. 262–70.

[II] 'the spoken sound of eloquent language', associated with botanical 'baum' ('fragrance'): Cf. *Mumming for Mercers* 34–35: 'Throughe þat sugred bawme aureate þey called weren poetes laureate' with *Troy Book* IV. 5202–4: 'His tale gan with sugred wordis swete Making þe baum outward for to flete Of rethorik and of elloquence.'

[III] 'rhetorical inspiration giving rise to eloquence', associated with 'licour' ('influence') or 'dewe': (*a*) extended through 'licour' (*influxus stellarum*) applied to a god, goddess, the Deity, or a Saint; (*b*) extended through 'dewe' ('physical moisture engendered by the moon') applied to a divine power, as in (*a*). Cf. *Fall of Princes* I. 461 ff. Cf. *Life of Our Lady* II. 1628 ff.:

> And eke my maister Chaucer is ygrave . . .
> That made firste to distille and rayne
> The golde dewe-dropes of speche and eloquence
> Into our tunge . . .

with *St. Edmund*, 221: 'Send doun of grace thi licour aureat Which enlumynyth these rethoriciens'; and envoi 12: 'Off Mercurye the aureat influence The tenlumyne dystylled skarsly doun.'

[IV] sense iii+sense i+physical association with 'ink.' Cf. *Troy Book*, Prol. I. 29–35; *St. Margarete* 54 ff.:

> O gemme of gemmes, vyrgyn of most renoun,
> Thy lyf to write be thou my socoure,
> And shede of grace the aureate lycoure
> In-to my penne. . . .

From this evidence it would appear that Lydgate chose to convey his notion of eloquence by means of compound, not complex metaphor. The elements are combined by association in the same way that Tennyson thought of poetic meaning in terms of his 'shot-silk' theory of language. The evidence makes clear the essentially decorative nature of Lydgate's concept of eloquence—the art of applying the *colores rhetorici*.

Although Lydgate's 'aureat' may be rendered by our 'eloquent', his special contribution to Late Medieval style should be isolated. That is, his achievement should be distinguished from Chaucer's more traditional use of the *stylus gravis*, the elevated style. Chaucerian sublimity shows the typical range of poetic interest: syntax, vocabulary, rhetorical schemes, and tropes. On the other hand, Lydgate's interest and achievement emerge as mainly lexical. He was concerned chiefly with importing Latin ns. and adjs. into ME. His borrowing is devoted (according to the meaning of 'aureat') to strictly artistic, rhetorical ends and should be distinguished from other kinds of borrowing, especially of scientific and technical terms from Latin. Dr. Tilgner in his extended treatment of Lydgate's aureate style did not make this distinction.[1] Aureate diction is not necessarily polysyllabic. The disyllable 'nebule' (Vulgate Latin *nebula*) is 'aureat' while the polysyllable 'deambulatorie' is not. Both ns. were introduced by Lydgate directly from Latin into English. In the context of the *Commendation* it is obvious that 'nebule' forms part of a larger attempt to construct an ornate, Latinate liturgical style in English. In the *Troy Book* II Lydgate is merely trying to convey a technically accurate picture of building methods. He himself complains of the lack of such words in English. There is no attempt at any kind or degree of *eloquentia*.

The majority of Lydgate's aureate diction is formed from liturgical or Vulgate Latin and consists of word or phrase 'calques'. The extension of this technique to secular verse (and there are less hard Latin derived words here than is generally

[1] See Select Bibliography, p. xviii. Similarly, Professor Schirmer's list (*John Lydgate*, p. 74) contains an admixture of words, some genuine examples of eloquence, some examples of technical vocabulary, and some mere poeticisms.

supposed) may have been suggested by the religious experiments. This cannot be stated with certainty, since a related chronology of the religious and secular works cannot be established. Aureation produces in ME religious verse a style as richly celebratory as the original Latin.[1] It is highly pointed art language: East Anglian Asiatic. Lydgate never really adapted his florid chantry idiom to the needs of secular poetry. It was left to Dunbar and Douglas to complete the experiment.

[1] It is possible that Lydgate first became interested in a 'liturgical English style' through Edmund Lacy, Dean of the Royal Chapel at Windsor 1414–17, and Bishop of Exeter from 1420. If we allow the strong probability that Lydgate's periods of study at Gloucester College fell in the years c. 1397–1408, it is possible that Lydgate, Lacy, and Henry V became friendly at Oxford. Lacy held college office during the years 1396–9 (he was Bursar and Master of University College), vacating his duties from 1401, but retaining the use of his rooms during 1401–2 and 1406–7. During this period (c. 1398) Henry V was probably in residence in Queen's. His letter concerning Lydgate (M. Dominica Legge, *Anglo-Norman Letters and Petitions* (1941), no. 347, pp. 411–12) testifies to the Prince of Wales's close association with Lydgate. By 1400 Lacy had become a king's clerk and was in attendance upon the King until July 1417. From the evidence provided by rubrics to three religious verse translations, *Benedic Anima Mea Domino* (Trin. Coll. Cambr. MS. R. 3.20, p. 165), *The Eight Verses of St. Bernard* (BM MS. Add. 29729, f. 126b), *Gloriosa Dicta Sunt De Te* (Trin. Coll. Cambr. MS. R. 3.20, p. 1), it would seem that Lydgate, Lacy, and Henry V shared a common interest in liturgical composition. Lacy was much interested in liturgical observances. He applied for Papal permission to institute a new office which he himself had composed in honour of St. Raphael. The office was officially instituted in September 1443. Henry V was sufficiently concerned to stir Lydgate to write the devotional and celebratory *Life of Our Lady*. Henry V and Lacy may well have been the main forces in shaping the direction and style of Lydgate's religious verse.

GLOSSARY

THIS glossary includes words now obsolete or only dialectal, and words used by Lydgate in obsolete or special senses. It does not contain words explained in the notes. An account of Lydgate's grammatical usage is given in J. Schick's edition of the *Temple of Glas*, EETS (1891, reprinted 1924), lxiii–lxxv.

abreyden, to start.
accesse, feverish love sickness.
accorde, in, in harmony.
accorded, reconciled.
adawen, to arise.
aduerten, to consider.
affraye, fear.
affyen, to have faith in.
agre, graciously.
akoyen, to soothe.
algate(s), in all ways; continually; at any rate, nevertheless.
alther, perfect.
alther-last, last of all; **-nexte,** next of all.
amate, dismayed.
amonge, all the while.
and, if.
apayed, to ben wel, to be satisfied; **euel ~,** displeased.
apayren, to spoil; to decay.
Aquarie, the constellation Aquarius.
arechen, to reach out (*past part.* araght).
assigned, assigned for the purpose of absolution.
asterten, to escape; to slip out indiscreetly; **hit shal me nought asterte** (*impers. v.*), I shall not fail.
atempre, moderate, mild.
attelest, at least.
atturney, legal agent (*fig.*).
atwixen, between.
auctor, author, authority.
auter, altar.
avalen, to descend.

aventure, in, in jeopardy.
avisement, legal consultation (*fig.*).
avisioun, vision; dream, cf. note on 12, 1374.
awayte, attendance in a lady's service.
ayenward, in return.

babewyns, grotesque decorative animal figures.
ballaunce, hold the, pass judgement.
barbykans, the outer fortifications of a city.
barkyd, tanned.
barnacle, the barnacle goose.
bataillyng, parapet.
bawm, fragrance; lotion made from oil of balsam; sap.
be(e)n, to be; *pres., 2nd plur.* be; *pres. 3rd plur.* ben, ar(e); *pres. subj., sing. and plur.* be; *imper., sing. and plur.* beth, be; *past part.* ben(e).
b'entaille, (bi+entaille), ? in construction.
bette, (*compar. adv. and adj.*) better.
bihoten, to promise.
bille, petition; poem containing a complaint or request.
blood, spirit.
bobbaunce, display of armed prowess.
bolewerkys, fortifications outside the city walls.
bollyn, swollen with grief.
borow, pledge.

bote, remedy.

brayden, to change.

brede, on, abroad.

breken hert, to disclose one's feelings.

brennen, to burn.

bronten, to rush.

brothir, brother-in-arms.

buglis, buffalo.

but if, unless.

buxumnes, obedience.

can, to know.

canel, drain.

castyng, planning.

cause, in, to blame.

champartie with, holden, to contend against.

charge, weight; have ~, to offer protection.

charmen, to heal by supernatural art (fig.).

chere, face, countenance; glance.

cherisshen, to encourage.

cheuesaunce, profit on the side.

clause, shortly in a, briefly.

clensyng, the act of purifying.

clepen, to call.

closet, bedchamber.

colombe, dove.

colour, outward appearance; complexion (fig.); pretence.

compas, circle.

compleint, anguish.

condicioun, personal character.

conduit, fountain.

confortatiff, cordial.

connen, to be able; conne, (pres. subj. sing.), may.

consigned, confirmed with a seal.

constreint, agony.

contradixion, withouten, without reservation.

contrarien, to oppose.

contunen, to continue.

cope, cloak; outward appearance (? only in Lydgate).

corage, nature, disposition; heart, spirit.

corious, expert.

corrent (attr. n.), running water.

crop, top; blossom.

croun, blossom.

cure, charge, diligence; ~n, (v.) to cover.

cytolle, psaltery, lute.

daister, morning-star.

damnacioun, condemnation.

daren, to be inactive.

daunten, to subdue.

debate, emotional conflict.

debonayre, submissive.

defence, offence.

defyen, to scorn.

deinte, value.

deite, divinity.

delful, doleful.

delyuer, full.

demayne, control.

demenyng, demeanour.

departid, divided; separated.

depeynt, depicted.

depured, purified.

destreynen, to ruin (one's) health.

devisour, designer.

devoider, dispeller.

dillasioun, delay.

discernen, to use discrimination in determining actions.

discuren, to tell (one's) troubles (? only in Lydgate).

disencrece, diminution.

disporte, (n.) entertainment; -n, (v.) to entertain.

dispraven, to corrupt.

divisioun, discord.

do, (aux.) v. cause to; past part. done.

donne, (adj.) dark; ~n, (v). to make dark.

drag, drug.

dressen, to direct; to set in order; (refl. v.) to address oneself.

duryng, remaining unimpaired.

dyghten, to place.

effect, gist.

efte, again; ~ ageyn, once again.

eke, also.

eleccioun, choice.

emprise, purpose, intention; (*pl.*) martial exploits.

enbelysshed, adorned; honoured.

enbracen, to affect.

encombrid, defeated.

ennuyd, renewed.

entaille, sculpture.

entendeth, is inclined to.

entere, devoted.

envie, ill-feeling.

environ, round about.

ermonie, harmony.

estate(s), social, political rank(s).

etyk, a continuous or recurring wasting fever.

e(u)(v)erich, each, every; each one, every one; ~on, each one; every one; one and all.

eure, luck; personal destiny; eurous, happy.

evenlich, evenly; equally.

everydele, (*n.*) everything; (*adv.*) utterly; throughout.

exemplarie, pattern, model.

expert, supreme.

express, (*adv.*) expressly; fully.

extorcyoune, anything obtained by undue exercise of power or authority.

fantasie, romantic inclination.

fere, fire.

feris, companions.

ferles, not burning.

feynen, to make false pretences.

feynten, to fade.

fint, (*pres. 3rd sing.*) finds.

firses, furze, gorse.

fleting, floating.

flitten, to remove.

flon, arrows.

floures, be in, flourishing.

foilys, leaves.

folowen to, to go as an attendant upon.

fonden, to create.

foon, (*n. pl.*) foes.

forecast, overthrown.

fortunen, to prosper.

foyson, bounty.

fraunchise, liberality; privilege of living in a place (fig.).

fressh, (*n.*) young lady; ~ly, (*adj.*) fresh.

froward, adverse; disobedient.

fynen, (1) to end; (2) to refine.

garnement, garment.

gentylesse, gentleness, noble kindness, courtesy.

gery, changeable.

geyn, remedy.

ginnen, to begin; *past, sing.* gann(e); *past, plur.* gunne; gan, (*aux. v.*) did.

gise, customs.

glede, a live coal.

graue, buried.

grene, raw, open (of wounds).

greuaunce, grief.

grisli, fearful.

gropen, to groove, incise.

grucchen, to grumble.

gruffe, in a grovelling position.

guerdon, (*n.*) reward; ~en, (*v.*) to reward.

ha(n), (*aux. v.*) have.

habounde, (*adj.*) overflowing.

halt, (*pres.,sing.*, of *v.* holden) holds.

hard, of, with difficulty.

harlot, rascal.

helping, (*adj.*) helpful.

hem, (*pron., dat., and acc. plur.*) them.

her(e), (*pron., gen. plur.*) their.

hest, promise; command.

(h)estres, apartments.

het, (*past t.* of *v.* heaten) heated.

heuynes, melancholy.

highten, to promise.

hulfere, holly.

iblent, obscured.

ich, (*pron., 1st sing.*) I.

idynged, considered worthy.

iewise, torment.

ifer, together.

ifrore, frozen.

iliche, (*adj.*) alike; (*adv.*) alike; equally.

ilke, same.
imeynt, mixed.
indignacioun, contempt.
innly, (*adj.*) intimate, heartfelt.
iȝolde, taken; captured.

kalendes, the first days of a month according to Roman computation.
kannel, jawbone.
kithen, to make known.
knitten, to bind.
knottis, ornamental knobs or bosses of carved, embossed, or hammered work.
kouthe vnto, familiar with.
kynde, nature; **of kind,** naturally.

lak, defect.
lake, fine linen cloth.
largesse, liberality.
lase, chain.
latoun, a mixed metal of yellow colour.
launde, an open space among woods.
laurer, laurel.
ledne, language.
leemyng, gleaming.
le(e)mys, rays of light.
legys, subjects.
leren, to teach.
letten, to hinder, prevent; to impair.
lever, (*compar. adj.*) rather.
levyn, lightning.
lich, (*adj., adv.*) alike, like.
liklynesse, as by, in all probability.
lissen, to ease.
lit(e), little.
logge, lodge.
lor(e)n, (*past part. of v.* lesen) lost.
lowen, to humble.
lustynesse, pleasure.
lycour, moisture; wine; dew; influence.
lynde, tree (*poet.*).

magnifien, to glorify.
malapert, impudently.

manhoode, valour.
margarete, pearl.
masen, to bewilder.
ma(u)gre, in spite of.
meddelyng, sexual intercourse.
memorye, memorial, something worthy to be remembered.
meten, to measure.
meynt, mixed.
mirrour, exemplar.
morwen(ing), morning.
mo(s)ten, must.
mynen, to burrow.

nad, (ne+had) had not.
narrow, lacking sympathy.
ne, (*conj.*) nor; (*adv.*) not.
nere, (*compar. adv.*) nearer; (ne+were) were not; could I not be.
nis, (ne+is) is not.
niste, (ne+wiste) knew not.
nolde, (ne+wolde) would not.
noll, head.
not, (ne+wot) know(s) not.
nothing, for nothing, on no account.

o(o)(n), (*num., adj., and n.*) one; (*n.*) one thing; (*adv.*) alone; continually; **euer in oon,** continually.
obak, aback.
occasion, cause.
of, (*prep.*) by; about; for; on account of.
offencioun, offence.
onsperen, to unbar.
oppressen, to overpower.
or, (*adv.*) before.
other, othir, (*conj.*) or; (*pron., plur.*) others.
ouerdrawen, to pass over.
ouergoen, to pass away.
ouershaken, to abate.
o(u)thir, owthir, either.
outrage, injury.

pantire, bag-net for birds.
parage, lineage.
parcel, partially.
party, in, to a certain extent.
passand, surpassing.

passen into fate, to die (cf. Lat. concedere in fatum. ? Lydgate only).

passion, violent emotion.

payen, to satisfy.

pecchouris, sinners.

peinen, to trouble.

pepyng, crying.

percaas, perhaps.

performen, to execute artistically.

perre, jewelry.

persen, to penetrate.

pigment-tre, ? the Citrus-tree. Cf. note on 8, 44.

playing-fere, companion.

pleten, to wrangle.

port, bearing; behaviour.

possed, tossed.

posseden, to possess.

potage, thick soup.

pouraille, poor people.

pouste, power.

poyntell, stylus.

pratik, practice.

preisen, to esteem.

prejudice, injury.

pres, crowd.

preve, (n.) proof; experience; ~n, (v.) to succeed.

prikk, at the, on the point of.

pris, excellence.

privete, private knowledge.

processe, poem.

profir, offer.

propynen, to give to drink.

proscrypcyoun, outlawry.

prouoken, to call forth.

purveaunce, providence.

purvey, to provide.

pynch at, ? cavil at.

quaire, book; poem.

quarrel, complaint; reason for complaint.

quemen, to please.

racen, to eliminate; to pierce.

rathest, soonest.

raught, (past part.) reached.

reclinatorie, a covered place provided with a half-seat; couch.

recorden, to remember.

recounford, comfort.

recure, (n.) remedy; ~n, (v.) to recover.

rede, advice; remedy.

regalie, supremacy.

rehersen, to relate.

reioisen, to enjoy.

rekeles, careless.

reken, to care; past tense rought.

remuen, to change.

reneyen, to deny.

rennyng, (adj.) running, variable.

repayre, resorting; (v.) to return.

restauricion, restorative.

retour, return.

re(w)mys, realms.

right, straight; of ~, rightfully.

rithes, rites.

rolles, scrolls.

rosen, rosy.

rother, rudder.

rote, source.

sad, sober.

saluen, to greet.

sapience, the Holy Spirit (Med. Lat. sapientia ; cf. note on 10. 6).

sautis, assaults.

s(c)hene, bright; beautiful.

secrenes, secrecy.

selfe, (adj.) same.

semlyhed, gracefulness.

sermon, talk.

sey, say, (past. t. of v. seien) saw.

shapen, plan, devise; (past plur.) shopen.

sharpe, high-pitched.

shent, harmed.

shrouden, to hide.

signes of, by, by the expression on.

siken, to sigh.

sikernes, security; safety, confidence.

sithe, ofte, often.

sith(en), (adj., conj., prep.) since.

sitting, fitting.

skil, reason, cause.

skyes, clouds.

slawe, (*past part.* of *v.* slaien) slain; *past sing.* **slowe.**
sleghtly, (*adj.*) sly, crafty.
so as, just as; as far as; *so be,* if it be the case that.
soft, (*adv.*) timidly.
solein, solitary.
somwhile, at times.
souffisaunce, means, resources.
sought, examined.
sounden, to heal.
space, opportunity.
spectacle, a pane of glass.
spere, sphere, orbit.
spice, touch, hint.
spillen, to destroy.
splayen, to display; to spread.
spyne, thorn.
starven, to die; to kill.
stert, escape.
stonien, to perplex.
stoundis, season; (*s.*) time, moment.
substaunce, wealth, estate.
suen, to follow.
suffraunce, suffering of pain.
suppowaylen, to be of service to.
supprised, overpowered.
surqued(r)ye, arrogance.
swogh, swoon.

tablementis, cornices, string-courses.
taken kepe, to observe.
tapites, tapestry (fig.).
teen, harm.
tempesten, to vex; to perturb.
that (*rel. pron.*) who, whom; which; that which; (*conj.*) in that, since that.
ther, where; ~ **besyde,** near by.
thinken, (*impers. v.*) to seem; **me thought** (*past. sing.*) it seemed to me.
tho, (*conj.*) then; (*n. plur.*) those.
thought, anxiety.
thurughoute, severely.
tofore, before.
tonne, cask.
transmigracioun, removal into captivity.

treté, (*n.* as *v.*) to enter into marriage negotiations.
trewe (*adj., plur.*) the faithful.
trist, sorrowful.
tristi, secure.
twynen, to weave.

varien, to undergo changes of mind.
vertue, the power of growth exerted by the vegetable soul in the form of sap.
vibrate, gleaming.
vitre, glass.
vncouth, strange.
vnder-pighten, to support.
vndespoosen, to render unfit.
vnfortuned, unfortunate; bestowing misfortune.
vnknowe, unknown; (*n.*) ignorance.
vnkindnes, unnaturalness.
vnwarli, unawares.
voluntee, wish.
vowted, vaulted.

wanhope, despair.
waped, dejected.
warantyse, guarantee.
welbesein, comely.
welk, (*past sing.* of *v.* walken) walked; roamed.
wem, dishonour; ~**less,** spotless.
were, wire.
werre, withoutyn, doubtless.
weymentacioun, lamentation.
wher, whether; ~**so,** wherever; whether; ~**thorgh,** by means of which.
whilome, formerly.
wicke, wicked.
wicket, small gate.
willi, propitious.
wilte, wilt thou.
wissen, to instruct.
wite, (*n.*) blame; -**n,** (*v.*) to blame.
witen, to know; to imagine; (*pres., 1st sing.*) **wot,** (*2nd sing.*) **wost**; (*pres. subj.*) **wete.**
wittes, five, the senses.
wight, creature, person.

wood-wale, the golden oriole.
word, motto.
wreche, vengeance.
wreke, revenged.
wringen, to writhe.
writhing, distortion, error.

yeden, to go.
yeuen, to give.
yold, taken; captured (*fig.*).
yoten, cast.
yrne, iron.
yvour, ivory.

PRINTED IN GREAT BRITAIN
AT THE UNIVERSITY PRESS, OXFORD
BY VIVIAN RIDLER
PRINTER TO THE UNIVERSITY